SNITCH CULTURE

SNITCH CULTURE

. . . how citizens are turned into the eyes and ears of the state

Jim Redden

FERAL HOUSE

I WOULD LIKE TO THANK THE
FOLLOWING PEOPLE, WITHOUT
WHOSE HELP *SNITCH CULTURE*
COULD NOT HAVE BEEN
COMPLETED: FERAL HOUSE
PUBLISHER ADAM PARFREY, FOR
HIS CONFIDENCE AND PATIENCE;
MY PARENTS, FOR NEVER
QUESTIONING MY CAREER
CHOICES; MY BROTHER BILL,
FOR SHARING THE FUN AND
FRUSTRATIONS OF *PDXS* WITH
ME; AND KATHERINE DUNN,
FOR HER FRIENDSHIP, ADVICE
AND UNWAVERING SUPPORT
THROUGH THE DARKEST DAYS.

CONTENTS

THE FINAL CRACKDOWN

The global snitch culture predicted in the first edition of this book is here. The September 11, 2001 attacks on the World Trade Center and Pentagon has produced an international surveillance society that spells the end to personal privacy. The War on Terrorism is in fact the final crackdown on civil rights and liberties, both here and abroad.

Within days of the attacks, law enforcement agencies in 135 counties united to form what the San Francisco Chronicle called a "global civilian front in the war on terrorism"—a worldwide police force that will ultimately collect and scrutinize the financial, medical, employment, and travel records of virtually everyone on the planet.

This war was declared by President George Bush, the son of the former CIA director and President who first announced the dawn of the New World Order. It was ratified by Congress on October 14 with a resolution that authorizes Bush and future Presidents to "use all necessary and appropriate force against nations, organizations, or persons he determines planned, authorized, committed, or aided the terrorist attacks."

General Richard Myers, chairman of the Joint Chiefs of Staff, emphasized the unending nature of this war on October 21. Appearing on ABC's "This Week," he said, "The fact that it could last several years, or many years, maybe many lifetimes would not surprise me."

In addition to the war resolution, the federal government responded to the September 11 attacks with a wave of new laws and policies that undermine the U.S. Constitution. The most important was the USA Patriot Act, passed by Congress a mere 45 days after the attacks. In a blatant attempt to label opponents unpatriotic, the name stands for the convoluted phrase, Uniting and Strengthening America By Providing Appropriate Tools Required to intercept and Obstruct Terrorism.

Few people read the entire bill before it was passed. As U.S. Representative Ron Paul told *Insight* magazine, "It's my understanding the bill wasn't printed before the vote . . . the bill definitely was not available to the members before the vote."

Among other things, the USA Patriot Act creates a new law of "domestic terrorism" that can easily cover peaceful political dissent. It outlaws any crime that endangers human life in order to influence government policy, a definition that includes such traditional acts of civil disobedience as blocking traffic.

More than that, once the government decides that a person has committed "domestic terrorism," law enforcement agencies can wiretap, arrest and prosecute anyone who has provided assistance to that person—even the assistance is so minor as providing lodging.

Other draconian provisions of the act allow: CIA spying on American citizens; covert government "sneak and peek" searches of homes, offices and Internet hard drives; so-called "roving wiretaps" on all phones used by criminal suspects; broad government access to sensitive medical, financial, mental health and educational records; government access to e-mails without a court order; and the creation of a federal DNA database on "all federal offenders convicted of the types of offenses that are likely to be committed by terrorists or any crime of violence."

As the *Washington Post* said on November 4, "The bill effectively tears down the legal fire walls erected 25 years ago during the Watergate era, when the nation was stunned by disclosures about presidential abuse of domestic intelligence gathering against political activists."

But the USA Patriot Act was only the beginning. In the name of fighting terrorism, Bush and U.S. Attorney General John Ashcroft have also discarded legal safeguards designed to protect the rights of American citizens, legal aliens and undocumented workers alike.

New policies adopted after the attacks allow: prison officials to monitor conversations between lawyers and foreigners suspected of terrorism; foreign citizens to be held indefinitely in jail without public notice; and military tribunals to try suspected terrorists in secret without juries before military judges.

By December 1, Ashcroft was openly talking about "relaxing" post-Watergate restrictions against the federal government spying on political and religious organizations in the United States. The proposal followed the questioning of 5,000 recent immigrants from the Middle East who Ashcroft admitted were not even suspected of committing any crimes—a harrowing reminder of the dark days of the McCarthy Era.

In addition to the new laws and policies, government officials began planning a dizzying array of high tech systems to track our every move. The proposals include: routing all Internet traffic through centralized computer servers monitored by the FBI; national ID cards (possibly based on state-issued drivers licenses) with embedded microchips containing all of our financial, medical and educational data; facial recognition cameras in all public places tied into computer databases containing digitalized drivers license photos; retinal-scanning devices built into all computers to verify the identity of everyone who logs onto the Internet; and hidden "key logger" devices that allow the FBI and other law enforcement agencies to record every key stroke on a computer terminal.

History teaches us that these new powers will be abused. Faced with the choice between national security and the Bill of Rights, previous Presidents repeatedly chose to curtail the freedoms of law-abiding citizens.

During John Adam's tenure, war hysteria over a looming conflict with France grew in the late 1790s. Congress reacted by passing the Alien and Sedition Acts, considered one of the most shameful laws in America's history.

The acts providing the government with sweeping powers to fine and imprison anyone found guilty of writing, publishing, uttering or printing anything of "a false, scandalous and malicious" nature against the government.

President Abraham Lincoln went much farther during the Civil War. He suspended the writ of habeas corpus and subjected "all persons discouraging volunteer enlistments" to martial law. A network of provost marshals imprisoned hundreds of antiwar activists and draft resisters, including five newspaper editors, three judges, and a number of doctors, lawyers, journalists and civic leaders.

By one estimate, Lincoln detained 13,535 people during the war, many for extended periods of time even though no evidence was ever presented against them. At one point, Union troops arrested 31 Maryland legislators to prevent them from voting for the state to secede. Later, Ulysses Grant issued his notorious "Jew order" (later rescinded) expelling Jews from all regions under his command. When Chief Justice Roger Taney finally declared Lincoln's suspension of the writ of habeas corpus unconstitutional, he refused to obey the ruling.

World War I brought more government abuses. A week after it was declared, President Woodrow Wilson created the Committee on Public Information to mobilize public opinion. The propaganda committee helped create a war madness that led to ongoing spy scares and witch-hunts. This was followed by the Espionage Act of 1917, the Trading with the Enemy Act of 1917 and the Sabotage and Sedition Act of 1918, all of which further empowered the federal government to crack down on all forms of dissent. In just one case, activist Eugene Debs was imprisoned for a decade for speaking out against the war.

Shortly after Japan attacked Pearl Harbor, President Franklin Roosevelt signed Executive order 9066, authorizing the expulsion of "all persons" of Japanese ancestry from their West Coast homes. Even though 70% were U.S. citizens, more than 110,000 were stripped of their property and shipped off to "relocation centers" were they lived under armed guards until 1946, months after the war with Japan ended. None were ever accused or charged with any crime.

Although all of these episodes are now regarded as national disgraces, they were supported by the establishment media of their days—and the same thing happened following the September 11 attacks. Bush has publicly announced that many aspects of his war on terrorism will never be reported, and the corporate press rolled over. TV network executives publicly agreed to censor their broadcasts. Hollywood quickly signed on to the war effort, promising a new series of "patriotic" movies that will not portray the U.S. government in a negative light. The Ad Council, first created as the government's domestic propaganda arm in World War II, began building public support for the new war.

Abdicating its role as a government watchdog, the establishment media refused to follow up on many nagging questions about whether the attacks could have been prevented. Immediately after the four airliners were hijacked and turned into massive suicide bombs, U.S. intelligence officials claimed they had no advance warnings of the attacks. Their denials were quickly undercut by a series of revelations, however.

Four days after the attacks, the *World Tribune* reported that Ramzi Yusef, the architect of the 1993 bombing of the World Trade Center, was arrested with plans for a coordinated series of commercial airliner hijackings and suicide crashes. Several foreign governments then volunteered that they had warned the CIA that Muslim terrorists were planning something big. Red-faced immigration officials acknowledged that they knew many if not most of the suspected terrorists were in the country. The FBI finally admitted it knew some were taking flight lessons at U.S. schools.

These revelations raise the obvious question, were elements of the U.S. government involved in the attacks? As documented in this book, government agents were behind such previous outrages as the 1963 Birmingham church bombing that killed four African-American girls, the 1979 Greensboro Massacre of civil rights activists by the Ku Klux Klan, the 1993 World Trade Center bombing and the 1995 Oklahoma City federal office building bombing. Although the sheer scale of the September 11 attacks dwarf the other murderous assaults, the basic question—what did the government know, and when did it know it?—still needs to be asked.

But no one in the establishment media followed up on these revelations. Instead, as in the past, the mainstream press became little more than cheerleaders for the war that is reshaping the international political landscape, too.

Bush's call to arms was quickly endorsed by most European nations, Russia, China, Japan and the United Nations. Within days of the attacks, representatives of the law enforcement agencies of 135 nations affiliated with Interpol, the global police network, met in Budapest to work out cooperative agreements. Interpol, which had operated only during businesses hours, switched to a 24-hour-a-day, 7-day-a-week system, opening a new around-the-clock command center. The agency's 29-nation Financial Action Task Force met in Washington DC to further coordinate its efforts.

After hearing directly from Bush, the United Nations adopted a resolution requiring all member nations to cooperate in the war on terrorism—by sharing financial and other data, among other things. Representatives of the 15 nations that make up the European Union also met with Bush to pledge increased intelligence and law enforcement investigation.

Congress also passed a number of new laws to extend the reach of American law enforcement agencies into foreign countries. A recent amendment to the Computer Fraud and Abuse Act allows the Justice Department to go after foreign hackers, even if no computer in the U.S. is attacked. Under the amendment, the federal government can indict and demand the extradition of foreign hackers if their Internet communications pass through any computer in this country.

By late November, nearly 1,500 people had been arrested in 50 countries as a result of these cooperative efforts. They included more than 1,100 foreigners rounded up in the United States alone. Few of those arrested had any apparent links to terrorist organizations. Most were being held for immigration and other small violations—the first victims of the global crackdown that will characterize the rest of the New Millennium.

Although Afghanistan was the first country targeted in the new war, in late November Vice President Dick Cheney warned the 340 or 502 countries could be next—revealing that we are actually in the opening stages of World War III.

As with both previous world wars, it will include domestic and international surveillance operations and the suppression of perceived dissent—supported by the recruitment of more snitches than the world has ever seen.

Jim Redden, 12/01/01

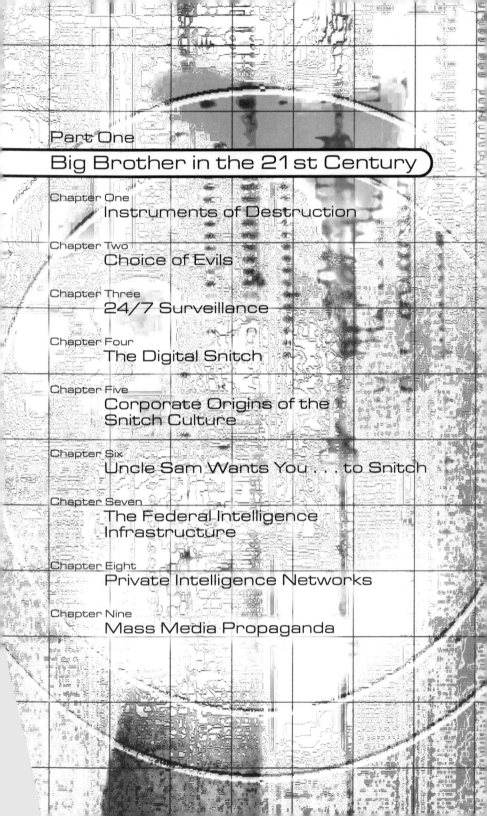

CHAPTER ONE

INSTRUMENTS OF DESTRUCTION

IT WAS A HOT AUGUST NIGHT in 1992 when Don Carlson heard someone trying to beat down his front door. The sound boomed through the front room, magnified by the fact that it was empty. Carlson had recently lost all his furniture to his ex-wife and now the pounding was echoing off the bare floor and walls of his suburban San Diego house. Afraid for his life, he grabbed his pistol and fired two shots at the door. They didn't even go through. Then the pounding got louder and the door started tearing off its hinges. Terrified, Carlson spun around, dropped the gun, and ran out of the room. A bullet tore into his thigh and sent him sprawling across the hallway floor. Staggering into his bedroom, he scooped up a portable phone and started dialing 911 as he fell into a corner. Two more bullets ripped into his back. One splintered and collapsed a lung.

"Don't move or I'll shoot you again," someone yelled. Carlson figured he was dead anyway.

Then a man identified himself as a federal drug agent. He and several other men grabbed Carlson, handcuffed him, and left him bleeding on the floor as they began tearing what was left of his house apart. "Why would they do this to me?" he muttered, barely able to breathe. Carlson was a law-abiding citizen, a computer company executive who had never been in trouble with the law before.

But that hadn't stopped the dozen or so U.S. Drug Enforcement Administration, Customs Service and San Diego police officers who broke in and shot him. They had been told he had 2,500 pounds of cocaine in the house. The tip came from a informant named Ronnie Edmond, an ex-drug dealer who was being paid $2,000 by the federal government to rat on others in the drug trade. But Edmond had lied about Carlson. He was no drug dealer. Edmond had picked the house because he thought it was empty and figured he could come up with another lie when the agents didn't find the cocaine.

There have always been informants, of course, and they have always inspired contempt in the general population. The world's best known snitch is from the Bible: Judas Iscariot, the disciple who betrayed Jesus to the Romans for 30 pieces of silver. The betrayal was so vile that his very name—Judas—is a common insult nearly 2000 years later.

The ancient Romans were bedeviled by "delantors," a class of private citizens who made a living by bringing accusations against others. They are among the earliest recorded examples of snitches, and their work was also shrouded in controversy. According to the *11th Edition of the Encyclopedia Britannica*, the delantors of ancient Rome "were drawn from all classes of society—patricians, knights, freedmen, slaves, philosophers, literary men, and, above all, lawyers." Although the ability to file charges against fellow citizens was not new, it became a way of life when the government began rewarding the informants with a share of the property of the people they turned in. If the accusation led to a conviction for treason, the informant could receive up to a quarter of the person's estate, leading to a dramatic increase in the number of tips against the rich and power-ful. "Pliny and Martial mention instances of enormous fortunes amassed by those who carried on this hateful calling," the encyclopedia adds.

Snitches have historically been treated as villains by the popular culture, going back to the earliest forms of mass entertainment. They played central roles in Greek tragedies, turning on noble leaders for personal gain. Several of Shakespeare's most famous characters are betrayed by their closest friends. A critical figure in Eugene O'Neill's play "The Iceman Cometh" was based on a real-life informant—an anarchist who implicated union organizers in the 1910 bombing of the *Los Angles Times* building. Snitches were used by the government to keep everyone in line in George Orwell's influential novel, *1984*. Director John Ford's classic 1935 movie *The Informer* focused on an Irish Republican Army member who sells his compatriots out for money. The great actor Victor McLaglen portrays the title character as a drunken lout. Justice is done when his disloyalty is discovered and he is beaten to death by his former friends and political allies.

Informants played a central role in the most divisive political debate of the late 20th Century, the Red Scare of the 1950s. U.S. Senator Joseph McCarthy claimed the federal government had been infiltrated by Communists, then chaired a public inquisition which forced close friends to rat on each other. In his influential 1980 book *Naming Names*, Victor Navasky, the founder of *The Nation* magazine, labeled informants "the state's chosen instruments of destruction"—a term which still applies today.[1]

The defining moment of President Bill Clinton's administration, the Monica Lewinsky sex scandal, was sparked by an informant with a tape recorder. Linda Tripp betrayed her close friend and inspired the impeachment proceedings which will forever tarnish Clinton's legacy. The public reaction to Tripp was predictable from the start—she became the villain of the piece, attacked by political columnists, and ridiculed by late night TV talk show hosts. Public opinion polls consistently show that Tripp is far more despised than either the President or his intern.[2]

Even the police are spying on each other. In July 2000, organizations rep-resenting black and Hispanic law enforcement officers complained that the

---

1. Victor S. Navasky, *Naming Names*, New York: The Viking Press, 1980.
2. Conservative political columnist William Safire applauded when Maryland prosecutors first brought wiretapping charge against Linda Tripp. In a December 20, 1999 *New York Times* piece, Safire wrote, "Now, with Maryland's active prosecution of Tripp's taping—a shameful act—being publicized far and wide, future miscreants will no longer be able to profess ignorance that it can be an illegal act."

New York Police Department was monitoring them. The organizations—100 Blacks in Law Enforcement Who Care and the Latino Officer's Association— joined with the American Civil Liberties Union to send a letter to Police Commissioner Howard Safir expressing their concerns. The NYPD had previously acknowledged in court testimony that it had conducted two inquiries into 100 Blacks in Law Enforcement Who Care and its director, Lt. Eric Adams. During the inquiry, Adams was followed and his telephone records were obtained.[3]

There's no single word that describes the incredible variety of snitches at work in America today. Law enforcement agencies rely on informants, confidential sources, and undercover officers. Corporations use testers and undercover operatives posing as employees. Private advocacy organizations glean information from defectors, freelance informants, and professional infiltrators.

Despite this variety, all snitches have one thing in common—access to inside information. This is what separates informants from mere witnesses and crime victims. Witnesses and victims may see crimes being committed. They may help the authorities catch and convict criminals. But they aren't usually familiar with the people they testify against, whereas snitches know the people they rat out. That's how they get the goods on them, and that's why they are so despised—they betray people who trust them.

Either that, or they lie for personal gain.

Is it really worse today? Are snitches more pervasive than during the McCarthy Era or the Vietnam War, when the FBI was infiltrating every left-wing organization in sight? Do Americans have more reasons to fear snitches now than during the Summer of Love, when narcs haunted the emerging counterculture looking for pot smokers to bust?

The answer is clearly yes, as reflected in skyrocketing prison population.

Few criminals are actually caught red-handed. Many, if not most, are arrested and convicted because of tips from associates, friends and family members. According to the Justice Policy Institute, more than 2 million people were imprisoned in federal, state and local jails by February 2000. The number of people under all forms of correctional supervision—jail, prison, probation, or parole—stood at a record 6.3 million.[4]

The greatest increases were for drug offenses, crimes which almost always require snitches to prove. By early 1999, someone in America was being arrested for a drug violation every 20 seconds.[5] From 1980 to 1997, the number of imprisoned drug offenders increased an astounding 1040 percent, swelling more than ten times larger. Almost 25 percent of all prisoners—nearly 460,000 inmates —were serving time on drug charges.

3. "Police Groups Say They Are Focus of Surveillance," *New York Times*, July 30, 2000.
4. "Poor Prescription: The Costs of Imprisoning Drug Offenders in the United States," Justice Policy Institute, July 2000.
5. Timothy Egan, "The War on Crack Retreats, Still Taking Prisoners," *New York Times*, February 28, 1999.

Although most inmates are currently serving time in state prisons or local jails, federal arrests and convictions are increasing at an even faster rate.[6]

This increase is primarily the result of a dramatic growth in federal law enforcement agencies and officers. There were approximately 69,000 federal law enforcement agents in 1993. The total ballooned to 83,000 by 1998, with a large percentage of them working cases involving informants.

"Under our constitutional system, the federal government is supposed to have a very limited crime-fighting role. But for the past 20 years, it seems every session of Congress has escalated the drug war, and that has led to an increase in federal agents, and federal prisons and the federal court system," says Tim Lynch, an analyst with the Cato Institute.[7]

Even former federal prosecutors think the criminal justice system is out of control. Several of them expressed their concerns in an explosive 10-part series published between November 22 and December 13, 1998 by the *Pittsburgh Post-Gazette*. Researched and written by veteran reporters Bill Moushey and Bob Martinson, the stories ran under the title "Win at All Costs: Government Misconduct in the Name of Expedient Justice." It painted a chilling picture of a runaway criminal justice system, where federal agents and U.S. attorneys routinely and intentionally use lying snitches to win indictments and convictions. Remarkably, some of the most outspoken critics in the series were former prosecutors who say such abuses have only become commonplace in the past decade or so.[8]

"I like to think that most prosecutors are honest and most agents are honest, but there are unfortunately enough examples of dishonesty cropping up that is troubling to anybody in this business," Plato Cacheris, a former eight-year federal prosecutor, said.

---

6. "Prison and Jail Inmates at Midyear 1999," U.S. Department of Justice, Bureau of Justice Statistics, April 2000. According to the report prepared by BJS Statistician Allen J. Beck, PhD, at midyear 1999, the nation's prisons and jails held 1,860,520 people. Federal prisons held 117,995 inmates, state prisons held 1,136,582 inmates, and local jails held 605,943 inmates.

7. "Stats Show 'Federalization' of Law Enforcement," Scripps Howard News Service, May 31, 2000. As part of the story, Edward Mallett, a Houston lawyer and the incoming president of the National Association of Criminal Defense Lawyers, said the sheer number of federal law enforcement officials is prompting the government to prosecute relatively minor crimes: "Cases federal prosecutors would have declined a year ago they are prosecuting now. They used to turn down drug prosecutions under five kilos; now they'll prosecute for an ounce and a half. They're looking for work."

8. Bill Moushey and Bob Martinson, "Win at Any Cost," *Pittsburgh Post-Gazette*, November 22, 23, 24, 29 and 30, and December 1, 6, 7, 8 and 13, 1998. In the 10-part series, the *Post-Gazette* documented numerous problems with the criminal justice system. The most serious abuses were committed by federal prosecutors, including the intentional use of lying snitches. Moushey and Martinson broke the problems down into the following areas:

   a. STING OPERATIONS. Federal agents have greater latitude than ever before in sting operations, but when the intended targets aren't caught, agents look to arrest anyone they can, so they can justify the cost of the investigation. It often means entrapping low-level criminals or even people who are innocent.

"You've seen an increase in career prosecutors that you didn't have 15 years ago, people who never practiced in the private sector," said Thomas Dillard, who served 14 years as an assistant U.S. attorney in Knoxville, Tennessee, then four years as U.S. attorney for the Northern District of Florida. "They sit in this lofty tower with a rather skewed vision of the world. They are on a divine mission, and everything that gets in their way is evil. The ends justify the means."

Dillard believes that huge anti-crime budgets are fueling these problems. "The war on crime has gotten to the point that all these [prosecutors'] offices are stuffed to the gills with resources," he said. "They have to justify their existence. They go out and make things crimes that weren't even crimes 10 years ago."

And Bennett Gresham, a former New York State prosecutor who teaches law at Pace University of New York, said the courts no longer provide much protection for the innocent. "The courts used to more consistently monitor both prosecutorial and law enforcement power in general, [but] over the past

---

b. DISCOVERY VIOLATIONS. Prosecutors are supposed to turn over to defense lawyers any information that might help prove defendants innocent, or raise suspicions about witnesses against them. Often they don't, and there's little defendants can do.

c. PERJURY. Federal agents and prosecutors may be quick to act on the words of lying informants or witnesses. And innocent people sometimes pay the price.

d. REWARDS FOR LYING. What's a convicted criminal to do to get out of a long jail term? How about testifying in exchange for a sentence reduction? In 1987, the U.S. Sentencing Commission dramatically reduced the amount of time that was permitted to be cut from a prisoner's sentence for good behavior. Before this change, a prisoner who behaved in prison could reduce his sentence by at least one-third and sometimes by as much as one-half. Under the new rules, a convict may earn only 54 days of good time per year. When added to stiff mandatory sentencing guidelines, the cut in good behavior time has swelled the population of federal prisons and produced another unintended result—a surge in federal prisoners willing to lie against defendants in court. The reason? A witness who helps win a conviction usually gets a sentence reduction at the request of the prosecutor. The testimony often doesn't have to be close to the truth.

e. CROSSING THE LINE. As the government becomes more reliant on criminal informants, more and more agents are getting caught up in the criminal activities of those informants.

f. GRAND JURY ABUSES. Prosecutors have the exclusive right to use this forum to its fullest advantage, but sometimes misrepresent evidence to gain an indictment, a process made easier by the fact that those accused can offer no defense.

g. SENTENCE ENTRAPMENT. In 1987, Congress passed legislation that effectively switched the authority for sentencing a criminal defendant from a judge to a prosecutor. The law establishes sentencing guidelines that must be followed when a defendant is found guilty. The guidelines have fostered a new form of misconduct called "sentencing entrapment," where prosecutors seek to boost the charges against a defendant up front to ensure he will face a maximum sentence. In a drug conspiracy, for example, a person may be found guilty for simply discussing a drug deal. So informants trying to snare a suspect make sure the quantities discussed are huge, to ensure maximum sentences. This gives prosecutors more clout in negotiating a plea bargain.

h. TARGETING DEFENSE ATTORNEYS. Prosecutors are more aggressive in going after defense attorneys, often turning the attorney's own clients into informants against them.

i. LACK OF OVERSIGHT. Federal agents and prosecutors know their misconduct will not be properly investigated by the Department of Justice, so they don't worry about breaking the rules.

10–15 years, the courts have contracted that power to the point of a total nullity," he said. "The courts used to be a buffer between prosecutors and the rights of defendants. They are now simply rubber stamps."

Don Carlson believes some of the agents who stormed his house back in 1992 wanted to kill him to cover up their mistake, but couldn't because so many different jurisdictions were there. "The only thing that saved me was that there were too many agents involved," he told the *Post-Gazette* for its series.

As it was, Carlson spent the next eight weeks in a hospital hooked up to a respirator, then many more months in painful physical therapy trying to regain the use of his body. Although the government admitted he wasn't a drug dealer, they threatened to charge him with attempted murder for the shots he fired in self-defense. Then a federal judge sealed the search warrant for the raid, preventing him from even learning why he had been targeted by the government in the first place.

Carlson retained an attorney who filed a $20 million suit over the botched drug raid in December 1992. The government stalled, failing to even respond to any court papers until ordered to do so by a judge. After years of contentious negotiations, the government finally settled the case for $2.7 million in 1995.

Moushey and Martinson also identified the following new laws and recent court rulings which have increased the chances that innocent people will have their rights violated:

a. THORNBURGH RULE. Former Pennsylvania Governor Dick Thornburgh served as U.S. Attorney General from 1988 to 1991. In 1989, he issued a memo saying that federal prosecutors were not bound by the bar association ethics rules in the states where they served. This allowed prosecutors to engage in conduct—such as contacting criminal suspects without their lawyers being present—that might cause private attorneys to be disbarred. Attorney General Janet Reno made the memo official policy in 1994. Congress tried to end the policy in 1998, but the Justice Department fought the effort.

b. FORFEITURE. Federal forfeiture statutes passed in the 1980s and 1990s were theoretically aimed at getting at the assets of big-time criminals. Prosecutors can use civil laws to seize any property they think is linked to criminal activity, even if the owner of the property is never convicted of a crime. In a series of stories published in 1991, the Pittsburgh Press found that federal agents broadly abuse the laws, and that the homes, cars and cash of ordinary people are most often the targets of forfeiture.

c. EXCLUSIONARY RULE. From 1914 to 1984, the Supreme Court had a simple rule for police who violated the Fourth Amendment of the U.S. Constitution in any search or seizure: Evidence obtained would be excluded from trial. But Congress passed a law in 1984 that provided for an exception to the exclusionary rule: Evidence would be allowed into a trial if officers believed in good faith that they had acted properly in the search or seizure. That has caused defense lawyers and constitutional scholars to lament that there are more good-faith exceptions than there are rules of exclusion.

d. SEARCH WARRANTS. Prior to 1987, police needed clear and convincing evidence that a crime had been committed before a judge would issue a search warrant. But under new laws and court rulings, officers can get a warrant based on the word of an informant who doesn't even have to be named. In 1984, the Supreme Court allowed evidence obtained through a search warrant not supported by probable cause to be used in court, so long as it was "issued by a detached and neutral magistrate." Congress then approved new laws further loosening the restrictions. In his dissent, Justice John Paul Stevens wrote that the ruling meant the courts' destruction of the Fourth Amendment's guarantee against unreasonable searches and seizures was now complete.

Carlson took the money and moved from California to a gated community north of Dallas. He still has trouble breathing and a problem with his leg due to the gunshot wound. His doctor tells him the injuries will almost certainly shorten his life.

Seven years after the raid, Carlson still could not believe he was almost killed because of a lying snitch who had cut a deal with the government. "[Edmonds] was a low-level street dealer, part-time criminal who created this thing to get money out of them," he told the *Post-Gazette*. "He was basically extorting the government."

---

e. ANTI-TERRORISM. The Anti-Terrorism and Effective Death Penalty Act of 1996 allowed the death penalty for certain federal crimes and sharply curtails the rights of defendants in some federal proceedings and appeals. For example, the law allows the government to simply designate any group as a "terrorist organization," and makes it a felony to support even the lawful and humanitarian activities of such organizations. The Act also permits the President, using undisclosed and even illegally obtained evidence, to designate as "terrorists" aliens residing in the United States, and to deport them, even if they have committed no crime.

f. WIRETAPS. The Anti-Terrorism Act of 1996 also expanded the use of roving wiretaps for investigations and allows federal agents to tap any telephone calls of suspects for as long as 48 hours without a court order, including cellular telephones and situations where suspected criminal organizations use call-forwarding to hinder the government's ability to find them.

g. GRAND JURIES. A federal grand jury, which is usually composed of 23 people, hears accusations that a federal prosecutor presents to determine if enough evidence exists to indict a suspect for a crime. Since the defense is not allowed rebuttal, this proceeding gives prosecutors tremendous power. The late U.S. Supreme Court Justice Learned Hand lamented that "a good prosecutor could indict a ham sandwich." While judges overseeing grand juries may hear motions on the conduct of prosecutors in the secret proceeding, such motions are seldom granted, and a recent Supreme Court ruling added to a prosecutor's power: It said that federal courts do not possess broad supervisory powers over grand jury proceedings.

h. PERJURY. In 1935, the Supreme Court ruled in *Mooney vs. Hobhan* that prosecutors may not admit testimony they know to be false. That ruling has been refined and expanded several times, but increasing reliance on the so-called "harmless error" rule of modern law has further diluted it. Under this doctrine, unless a defense lawyer can prove to a judge that perjured testimony would have changed the verdict—even if that perjured testimony was known to prosecutors—a criminal defendant gets no relief.

i. BRADY RULE. A 1963 ruling set the standard for what prosecutors must do to help a defendant. Called "discovery," it requires prosecutors to turn over to defendants any evidence that might help prove them innocent or show the biases and criminal records of witnesses against them. The Supreme Court also has ruled that if a prosecutor improperly withholds discovery material, a conviction should be reversed only if the verdict would have been different had that material been known at the trial. To ensure against discovery violations, some federal prosecutors, as recently as 15 years ago, opened all of their files on a case to the defendant's attorney. Today, prosecutors routinely withhold discovery evidence, but only in extreme cases have verdicts been overturned.

CHAPTER TWO

CHOICE OF EVILS

"IF YOU HAVEN'T DONE ANYTHING WRONG, you don't have anything to be afraid of."

That line has been used for countless years by law enforcement officials to trick people into submitting to warrantless searches and interrogations without their lawyers being present. President Clinton used a variation of it a few days after two disturbed teenagers, Eric Harris and Dylan Klebold, shot up Columbine High School on April 20, 1999. Speaking to a group of students at a Virginia high school, Clinton urged them to report any classmates who exhibit anti-social behavior. "They won't get in trouble if they didn't do anything wrong," he said.

Clinton was wrong. Innocent people are routinely arrested, tried, convicted and sent to jail. Hundreds of convicts have been proven innocent and set free in the last few decades, including close to 90 who were sitting on Death Row waiting to be executed for murders they didn't commit. "With little money available to dig up new evidence and appeals courts usually unwilling to review claims of innocence (they are more likely to entertain possible procedural trial-court errors), it's impossible to know just how many other prisoners are living the ultimate nightmare," *Newsweek* said in its June 2000 Special Report.[1]

Even convicted killers who are not ultimately proven innocent frequently have their convictions overturned on appeal, according to a study conducted by a team of lawyers and criminologists at Columbia University. Led by law professor James S. Liebman, the study reviewed all appeals from 1973, when the U.S. Supreme Court reinstated the death penalty, to 1995. It found that two out of three convictions were overturned on appeal. Seventy-five percent of those who had their sentences set aside were later given lesser sentences after retrials, in plea bargains or by order of a judge.[2]

Many of those released from Death Row in recent years were exonerated by the Innocence Project, a New York-based public interest law firm started by famed criminal defense attorney Barry Scheck. The organization used newly-developed DNA tests to prove they didn't do the crimes of which they were convicted. Several of these former inmates appeared at the National Conference on Wrongful Convictions and the Death Penalty, sponsored by a number of anti-death penalty organizations in early 1999. The conference examined many cases of innocent people who had been wrongly convicted of capital crimes and sentenced to death. In almost every instance, the conviction was

---

1. Jonathan Alter, "The Death Penalty on Trial," *Newsweek*, June 12, 2000.
2. Fox Butterfield, "Most Death Sentences Set Aside," *New York Times*, June 12, 2000.

based on perjured testimony from actual criminals seeking reduced charges or preferential treatment. Some snitches lied to avoid the death penalty for their own killings. In each case, it took many years for the wrongly-convicted defendants to clear their names.

Here are just a few of the cases reviewed at the conference:

- Joseph Green Brown was convicted of murder, rape and robbery in 1974. The main witness against him was an informant named Ronald Floyd. Several months after the trial, Floyd admitted he actually committed the murder and lied to avoid being prosecuted for it. Brown spent 13 years on Death Row before being released.
- Randall Dale Adams was convicted of murdering a police officer in 1977. The key witness against him was a snitch named David Harris, who said he was with Adams at the time of the shooting. In exchange for his testimony, Harris wasn't charged with anything. Adams spent 12 years on Death Row before proving Harris was lying.
- Anthony Silah Brown was convicted and sentenced to death for murdering a deliveryman in 1983. Another man who had been arrested for the crime implicated Brown. The snitch received a reduced sentence in exchange for his testimony. Brown served three years on Death Row before being acquitted of all charges after a retrial at which the witness admitted he had lied.
- Charles Smith was given the death penalty for murder and robbery in 1983. The prosecution called as a witness a man who admitted to having been the getaway driver, who claimed that Smith had committed the murder. Smith spent eight years on Death Row before the snitch admitted cutting a deal with the prosecutor to avoid facing a murder charge. Smith was acquitted at a retrial and released.
- Joseph Burrows was convicted of murder and armed robbery in 1989. Two men who had also been charged with the murder testified against him. Although direct evidence implicated the pair, they avoided the death penalty by naming Burrows as an accomplice. He spent five years on Death Row before a court reversed his conviction and dropped all charges.

As James Peterson, a writer who covered the conference, reported, "The snitch culture is so embedded in our judicial system that there is now an entire industry of convicts who buy information from other criminals or friends on the outside that allows them to rat and cut years from their sentences. And prosecutors go along." [3]

Peterson isn't exaggerating. For two years beginning in 1995, Atlanta attorney Robert Fierer and convicted drug smuggler Kevin Pappas ran an actual business providing inside information to would-be jailhouse snitches. Fierer and Pappas

---

3. James Peterson, "Snitch Culture," *Playboy*, February 2000.

called their business Conviction Consultants, Inc., but defense attorneys on the losing end of the tainted cases had another name for it: "Rent-a-Rat." Some wealthy inmates paid up to $225,000 for the information, memorizing details on pending cases until they could testify under oath like someone who had been involved in the crimes. Then they cut deals with prosecutors, helping win indictments and convictions in exchange for reduced sentences. Finally, in late 1995, a Kentucky inmate tipped off law enforcement officials to the scheme. From October of that year to February 1996, police investigators secretly recorded Fierer, Pappas and others talking about the operation, which they called "jumping on the bus." [4]

The government documented several instances of perjured testimony before indicting Fierer and Pappas. In one case, a convict from Nashville named Bruce Young paid $25,000 to the two men in September 1995. A short time later, Fierer wrote a letter to a prosecutor in Tennessee saying he had an informant who "had some affection for Bruce Young and wanted to help." A few months later, the government recorded Pappas telling Young, "You sat in jail and didn't do anything except pay money to buy freedom."

In another case, the government recorded conversations between Pappas and an inmate named Peter Taylor who was serving a 13-year prison sentence in Miami for smuggling marijuana. Pappas told Taylor to pretend to know another informant, and to testify in support of that informant in an upcoming drug case. Pappas instructed Taylor to tell a prosecutor he and the informant were "life-long friends or something." In February 1996, Fierer told Taylor the bill for the deal—$250,000, with $150,000 for the consulting company, $75,000 for Fierer and $25,000 for expenses.

Federal agents arrested Fierer and Pappas in 1997. Pappas quickly cut a deal with prosecutors, becoming a witness against his former partner. Both men pleaded guilty to obstruction of justice and income tax evasion.

The potential judicial problems caused by snitches has long been recognized. Some of the earliest recorded criticisms surfaced in England, whose courts and common laws formed the basis for this country's criminal justice system. In the 18th Century, English common law scholar and judge Sir Matthew Hale railed against compensating informants for their testimony, reasoning, "If a reward be promised to a person for giving his evidence before he gives it, this, if proved, disables his testimony."

Approximately 100 years later, in his 1863 work *The Constitutional History of England*, Thomas E. May wrote, "The relations between the government and its informers are of extreme delicacy. Not to profit by timely information were a crime; but to retain in government pay and to reward spies and informers, who consort with conspirators as their sworn accomplices and encourage while they betray them in their crimes, is a practice for which no plea can be offered. No government, in deed, can be supposed to have expressly instructed its spies

---

4. Bill Moushey and Bob Martinson, "Win at Any Cost: Selling Lies," *Pittsburgh Post-Gazette*, November 30, 1998.

to instigate the perpetration of crime; but to be unsuspected, every spy must be zealous in the cause which he pretends to have espoused; and his zeal in a criminal enterprise is a direct encouragement of crime. So odious is the character of a spy that his ignominy is shared by his employers, against whom public feeling has never failed to pronounce itself."

More recently, the U.S. Supreme Court expressed its distrust of informants in a 1967 ruling in the case of *Washington vs. Texas*. As the court put it, "Common sense would suggest that [an accused accomplice] often has a greater interest in lying in favor of the prosecution rather than against it, especially if he is still awaiting his own trial or sentencing. To think that criminals will lie to save their fellows but not to obtain favors from the prosecution for themselves is indeed to clothe the criminal class with more nobility than one might expect to find in the public at large."

Writing in *U.S.A. vs. Bernal-Obesco*, federal Circuit Court Judge Stephen Trott explained why snitches should not be automatically believed. "The use of informants to investigate and prosecute persons engaged in clandestine activity is fraught with peril," he wrote. "By definition, criminal informants are cut from untrustworthy cloth and must be managed and carefully watched by the government and the courts to prevent them from falsely accusing the innocent, from manufacturing evidence against those under suspicion of crime, and from lying under oath in the courtroom . . . A prosecutor who does not appreciate the perils of using rewarded criminals as witnesses risks compromising the truth-seeking mission of our criminal justice system."

As University of California law professor Clifford S. Zimmerman put it, "Informant mishandling and misconduct victimizes many innocent people. Examples of the resulting harm include: prosecutions based upon informant perjury; false arrests due to unreliable informants; non-disclosure of informant information by prosecutors in criminal proceedings; informant abuses promoted through rewards; and felonious activity committed with the knowledge and, at times, assent of the police and prosecutors."[5]

University of Oregon law professor Garret Epps is more blunt: "The truth is, everyone has something to hide. For most people, it's not a crime; it may be a health condition that could expose them to discrimination, an unfashionable political allegiance, a deeply held personal religious commitment, a painful family secret or just a juvenile sense of humor. For each of us, there is something we choose not to share with people we do not know well. And when these personal foibles are stripped bare, the people exposed often feel a deep sense of violation and may lose friends, jobs or spouses."[6]

---

5. Clifford S. Zimmerman, "Toward a New Vision of Informants: A History of Abuses and Suggestions for Reform," *Hastings Constitutional Law Quarterly*, Fall 1994.

6. Garrett Epps, "The Prying Eye of Government," *Oregonian*, September 26, 1999. In his piece, Epps, a constitutional law professor at the University of Oregon Law School, said, "No one—and certainly no politician—wants to speak up for the rights of terrorists, drug lords and pedophiles. But unless we take a sober look at current federal initiatives, we will soon find ourselves in an unprecedented web of surveillance."

At the same time, everyone who works in the criminal justice system agrees that it would collapse without informants. "Prosecutions of Charles Manson, the Hillside Strangler, Wall Street insider trading, all were made possible by the use of informants," writes Mark Curriden, a journalist who has reported extensively on informants. Curriden interviewed U.S. Appeals Court Judge Stephen Trott and noted defense lawyer Alan Dershowitz for a story on jail-house snitches for the ABA *Journal*, published by the American Bar Association. They both agree informants are needed to solve serious crimes. "The FBI will tell you that if you don't have informants, you're out of luck when it comes to investigating heavy-duty crime." Trott said. "Informers are very important. They give you leads and tips. They tell you where the guns are buried," Dershowitz agreed.[7]

Perhaps the most valuable snitches to emerge in recent years are the handful of law enforcement officials who have testified about brutality and corruption within their own agencies. Police scandals in New York, Los Angeles, New Orleans and several other American cities have been exposed by a small number of officers willing to break the legendary Code of Silence.

The most serious scandal was unearthed among the Los Angeles Police Department officers who patrolled the city's crime-ridden Rampart area. Specially recruited and trained, the officers were ordered to reduce street crime, especially drug dealing, in the city's minority neighborhoods. As LAPD higher-ups looked the other way, the Rampart officers routinely beat suspects, planted drugs and other evidence on innocent people, and even shot and paralyzed at least one victim.[8]

The scandal broke after LAPD officer Rafael Perez was arrested in August 1998 for stealing eight pounds of cocaine from an evidence room. His first trial ended in a hung jury. Afraid of being convicted in a second trial, Perez turned snitch and asked for leniency, telling investigators about the misconduct among his fellow officers in the Rampart area. The charges became public in September 1999 when he pleaded guilty to four counts of grand theft of cocaine and four counts of possession of cocaine. Perez admitted that in 1996 he and a former partner handcuffed Javier Francisco Ovando, shot him, planted a gun on him, and then lied about the confrontation in court—a short time later, Ovando was released from a prison where he had been serving a 23-year sentence. Ovando was paralyzed in the shooting.

The plea bargain with Perez was finalized on February 24, 2000 when he was sentenced to five years in prison on drug charges. He was granted complete immunity for all his other crimes, including the shooting which paralyzed Ovando. "The atrocities that were committed by me and others were unforgivable acts," he said during the sentencing hearing.

By July 2000, four other LAPD officers had been charged with crimes stemming from the scandal, over 30 officers had been fired, suspended or relieved

7. Mark Curriden, "No Honor Among Thieves," *ABA Journal*, June 1989.
8. "Ex-Officer Who Bared Scandal in Los Angeles Apologizes in Court," *Los Angeles Times*, February 26, 2000.

of duty, and judges had overturned 90 tainted convictions. Several hundred more cases were under review, and the U.S. Department of Justice had launched a formal civil rights investigation into the LAPD.[9]

Eric Turetzky was a rookie with the New York Police Department when he snitched. Turetzky witnessed several other NYPD officers brutalize an immigrant named Abner Louima in a precinct bathroom on August 15, 1997. His testimony was critical for proving that one officer, Justin Volpe, thrust a broken broomstick up Louima's rectum, causing severe internal injuries. Turetzky agonized for more than two days before finally coming forward and agreeing to testify against his co-workers. He spent months under police protection, doing little more than desk work to protect him from retaliation. After he testified in the trial which eventually produced guilty pleas in the case, the *New York Times* wrote, "During some four hours of testimony, Detective Turetzky was forced to publicly confront the central question about himself: is he a selfless hero or a selfish rat?" [10]

As the Perez plea bargain shows, snitches pose numerous ethical and legal issues for law enforcement officials. Many, if not most, informants are criminals themselves. That's why they know so much about various crimes. And the smart ones don't provide the information for nothing. They want something in return—beginning with a free ride for everything they've done wrong in the past. Even if law enforcement officials insist the snitch must spend at least some time in jail, such deals trouble most people.

John Miles Sturgis is a case in point.

After years of mentally and physically abusing his wife, Sturgis shot her to death in their southeast Portland, Oregon home on July 8, 1997. He murdered her shortly after she took out a restraining order against him. The couple's four-year-old daughter ran out of the house screaming, "Daddy's hitting mommy!" Police quickly responded and found Sturgis walking two-and-one-half blocks from his home with two gunshots under his chin, the results of a failed suicide attempt.

Sturgis was a perfect candidate for the death penalty. He had a history of violence and had been convicted of bank robbery earlier in the year. But he turned snitch, cut a deal with prosecutors, avoided an aggravated murder trial and was instead sentenced to 25 years in a federal prison. Shortly after being charged with his wife's killing, Sturgis helped police investigators crack an unsolved bank robbery and killing. On November 14, 1988, a man wearing a rubber devil's mask robbed a bank in Forest Grove, Oregon, shooting and killing 70-year-old Frank Lucero, who had just stopped in to cash a check. Sturgis identified the masked man as a friend named Andrew Sisson. Sturgis told author-ities he drove Sisson to SEA-TAC, the Seattle-Tacoma area airport, after the robbery and murder, and he provided the police with crucial evidence in the case.

9. "Many in Rampart Community Still Back LAPD," *San Francisco Examiner*, July 30, 2000.
10. David Barstow and Kevin Flynn, "Officer Who Broke Code of Silence Defies Labels," *New York Times*, May 15, 1999.

Sturgis was sentenced to 25 years on June 1, 2000. His ex-wife's relatives appeared in court to complain about the plea bargain. Dianna's older sister, Connie McCleary, angrily told Sturgis, "You have the nerve to plea bargain like some rat to save your soul." Outside the courtroom she told reporters, "I'm still mad because my sister didn't get justice. It's like he called the shots. This man needs to be in prison forever."

Deputy Multnomah County District Attorney Greg Moawad told the press he understood her concerns, but had no choice except to cut a deal with Sturgis to solve the other crime. "Sometimes to catch criminals you have to make deals with the devil. While I absolutely understand this family believes they did not get full justice, there's another family out there as well that would not have gotten justice at all." [11]

The truth is, no matter what people say about informants in public, almost everyone is willing to tolerate at least some snitching, depending on the crime. The more serious the crime, the more people are willing to forgive the inform-ant. This is true even in the most emotionally-charged of all betrayals—when children turn on their parents.

Nothing is more offensive to the average citizen than the notion of chil-dren informing the authorities on their parents. Child-snitches are a tool of totalitarian regimes, such as Nazi Germany and the former Soviet Union. Americans generally regard the idea of the state using children to monitor their parents as morally repugnant, even though it happens all the time.

Journalist and commentator James Bovard railed against this practice in his 1999 book, *Freedom in Chains*. Bovard looked at the federally-subsidized Drug Abuse Resistance Education (DARE) program, taught to 25 million American children each year. As Bovard discovered, "The core of DARE consists of police in the classroom as role models and trusted confidants. As a result, some children have concluded from this training that becoming a government informant is the apex of virtue . . . Apparently, the idea that anyone should keep a secret from the proper authorities is inconceivable—as if people have a duty to report to the government everything they hear." [12]

Even the courts are alarmed by this practice. In a 1997 case brought by a Searsport, Maine student, a federal judge found that a DARE officer lied to and threatened an 11-year-old girl in order to force her to incriminate her parents. The judge said the officer's activity was "contemptible and exceeds all notions of fair play and decency" and "strikes at the basic fabric of all parent-child relationships: love, trust and faith." [13]

Such incidents have provoked national ire. In early 1986, after hearing an anti-drug talk at her church, 13-year-old Deana Young decided to turn in her parents. A few days later she marched into a police station in Tustin,

11.   Maxine Bernstein, "Man Who Shot Ex-Wife Gets Plea Bargain for Aiding Police," *Oregonian*, June 2, 2000.

12.   James Bovard, *Freedom in Chains*, St. Martins Press, 1999.

13.   *Ibid.*

California with her parents' stash—a trash bag filled with marijuana, unidentified pills, and $2,800 worth of cocaine. She didn't understand what was going to happen next. The police promptly arrested her mother, a 37-year-old bankruptcy court clerk, and her father, a 49-year-old bartender. And then the police hauled her off to the custody of the Orangewood Children's Home, despite her repeated pleas to be with her parents. The episode sparked a national debate over the nation's drug laws, with former First Lady Nancy Reagan praising her and *The New Republic* evoking the image of 1984 and government "thought control." [14]

Now consider a case that took place 13 years later. In March 1999, three Chicago men were arrested on rape and murder charges after the 10-year-old daughter of one of the suspects recognized her father's picture on a television news report. All three men were accused of raping and strangling a woman named Merceda Ares in her Chicago-area apartment. In addition, the girl's father, Ronald Hinton, was charged with raping and killing a woman named Keary Gagnier in the same area. Hinton's daughter was taken into state care. [15]

No one questioned the young Hinton girl for reporting her father. Instead, the initial news reports quoted several people praising the girl for her actions. All of us understand the difference between recreational drug use and a sex-murder. The trick is to strike the correct balance, to protect innocent citizens from unfounded allegations while allowing the authorities to collect the information necessary to pursue genuine criminals.

In theory, the Constitution and numerous Supreme Court rulings provide those safeguards. Grand juries are supposed to double-check prosecutors, preventing them from bringing flimsy cases based on questionable testimony. Numerous Supreme Court rulings are intended to ensure that trials are fair and open. One of the most significant safeguards is the so-called Brady Rule, adopted by the Supreme Court in 1963. Under this rule, prosecutors must turn over to defendants any evidence which might help prove their innocence or show the biases and criminal records of the witnesses used against them.

But in these days of interlocking computer databases, simply reporting someone to the authorities can destroy their lives. Consider what is happening to black Americans. The crack cocaine scare of the 1980s prompted police agencies across the country to build computer lists of black gang members. The lists quickly expanded to include other, far more dubious categories, including gang associates, gang affiliates and even "gang affected" juveniles. Much of the information put into the computers was unverified gossip picked up during routine patrols. A mere accusation was all it took to open a file. If the police pulled over a car driven by a suspected gang member, all of the passengers became gang associates. If a boastful teenager claimed to be in a gang, that's what the police accepted, with all of his brothers and sisters becoming associates, affiliates or affected by his claimed membership. Nobody

---

14. "The Right Spirit," *The New Republic*, September 8, 1986.
15. Mike Robinson, "Girl's Tip Leads to Murder Arrests," Associated Press, March 15, 1999.

bothered to double-check the allegations; the information just went straight into the computers.

When Denver civil rights leaders got around to looking at their city's list in 1993, they were shocked to discover that it included two out of every three young black males. Similar figures were discovered in other major American cities, too. The Los Angeles County Sheriff's Department currently has more than 200,000 names in their gang database, called GREAT for Gang Reporting, Evaluation, and Tracking.[16]

And these lists have consequences. When the police pull a car over for a traffic violation, they routinely type the license plate number into their onboard computer before approaching the vehicle. When the word "gang" pops up after the owner's name, the stop becomes anything but routine. Guns are drawn, backup is called and the minor stop can quickly escalate into a life-or-death experience for everyone involved.

Once this problem was discovered, criminal defense attorneys and civil rights lawyers tried to force the police to dump, or at least trim their lists back to verifiable levels. This proved to be a difficult if not impossible task. Spencer Neal, an attorney in Portland, Oregon, sued the local police bureau on behalf of two clients whose names were mistakenly placed on its gang list. The police admitted the names should not be there, and promised to purge them. But Neal soon learned that the Portland Police Bureau was not the only agency who had the list. It had been shared with a wide range other law enforcement agencies, most of which copied it directly into their computers. And they weren't bound by the agreement. "There were at least a dozen, including all local law enforcement agencies, the Portland School Police, the Sheriff's Office, the Department of Corrections, the Oregon State Police, parole and probation agencies, you name it," says Neal. "It gets pretty loose out there." [17]

Unfounded child abuse allegations can also cause serious, lingering problems. All states have child welfare agencies which compile and maintain lists of parents suspected of abusing their children. A single phone call from an anonymous source is enough for most states to open a file. Even innocent parents have trouble being cleared of such allegations. If the state can't find any evidence to support the charge, it will simply be declared "unverified." The charge will stay in the computers, which are closed to the public but accessible to all social service and law enforcement agencies.

Michael Divon has struggled unsuccessfully for years to have his name removed from a New York child abuse registry. In 1997, his six-year-old son fell in a school playground sandbox and bruised his face. The accidental fall was witnessed by two teachers. A short time later, as Divon and his son Jonathan were shopping in a grocery store, a woman approached and asked how the child had bruised his face. Although Divon told her about the fall,

---

16. "The GREAT System," Urban Street Gang Enforcement, Bureau of Justice Assistance, U.S. Department of Justice, FY 1999 budget report.

17. Mitzi Waltz, "Dangerous Data," *PDXS*, February 9, 1996.

the woman followed them home, wrote down his license plate number and address, and reported him to the state. A few days later, a state child abuse investigator knocked on their door. Divon explained the fall again, noting that it had been witnessed by the teachers. Although the investigator interviewed the teachers and eventually cleared Divon of abusing his son, it was too late. His name was already on the state's child abuse registry, and Divon couldn't get it off.

"Months after the schoolyard mishap, Jonathan fell again at summer camp and scratched his face," the *New York Times* reported about the case. "His parents demanded a written accident report, which they carried for weeks just in case another stranger approached in another grocery store.

"'I still have it in my wallet,' Michael Divon said. 'You never know.'" [18]

These examples illustrate the harm that can be caused by false or unverified accusations. But there is another problem with the American criminal justice system that is even worse. Police and prosecutors are intentionally ignoring the constitutional and other legal safeguards that are supposed to protect the innocent, and they are routinely getting away with it.

The *Pittsburgh Post-Gazette* series cited in the previous chapter proves that the legal system has been sabotaged from within. Reporters Moushey and Martinson presented dozens of cases where federal prosecutors knowingly used perjured testimony, purposely withheld critical evidence, and blatantly lied in court about their actions to win indictments and convictions, and to prevent appellate courts from overturning unjust verdicts. As the paper said, these examples were just a small percentage of the 1,500 cases reviewed by the reporters. "The *Pittsburgh Post-Gazette*'s two-year investigation found hundreds of cases in which federal agents and prosecutors violated rules and laws to make cases," the paper said. "Some instances went beyond treading across the line of ethical or legal guidelines. These cases involved actions where the abuse of power was cynically calculated to inflict harm well beyond the limits of the law." [19]

Significantly, many of the most severe abuses cited by the paper concerned snitches. The reporters discovered so many examples of lying informants that they concluded, "Perjury has become the coin of the realm in federal law enforcement. People's homes are invaded because of lies. People are arrested because of lies. People go to prison because of lies. People stay in prison because of lies, and, sometimes, bad guys go free because of lies."

Defense attorneys routinely unearth evidence of perjured testimony and other serious abuses committed by prosecutors. They repeatedly forward documentation to the Office of Professional Responsibilities, created in 1975 to investigate complaints lodged against Justice Department attorneys

---

18. David Barstow, "Wrongly Accused Want Names Off List," New York Times News Service, *Oregonian*, April 24, 1999.

19. Moushey and Martinson, "Win at Any Cost: Calculated Abuses," *Pittsburgh Post-Gazette*, December 7, 1998.

"involving violation of any standard imposed by law, applicable rules of professional conduct, or Department policy." But, as the paper discovered, the OPR is simply not doing its job: "The *Post-Gazette* talked to nearly 200 people who had filed complaints with the OPR. Most of them said the agency simply wrote them a letter saying it found no basis for their complaints. A few said OPR told them it was taking action. None of the complainants ever learned what that action was." [20]

The result is that prosecutors know they can use lying snitches to win cases, and that nothing will happen even if they are caught. "Lying has become a significant problem in federal court cases because the rewards to federal law enforcement officers can be so great and the consequences so minimal," the paper said. "Perjurers are seldom punished; neither are law enforcement officials who ignore or accept their lies."

Dale Brown is one of numerous victims of government abuse cited in the series. A living symbol of the American dream, Brown was a former Eagle Scout whose start-up company near the Johnson Space Center outside of Houston did business with NASA. By the late 1980s, Brown was working 18 hours a day, seven days a week on his company, Terraspace Technologies Inc. It attempted to match inventors with new products to the constantly changing demands of the multi-billion dollar-a-year space program.

A man calling himself John Clifford approached Brown in 1992 with a new product that NASA might need. Called a miniature lithotripter, it was an ultrasound device whose technology could be used to improve the medical monitoring of astronauts on space missions. Clifford told Brown that he was prepared to spend lots of money to bring the device to NASA's attention, and he promised to share the potentially hefty profits with him.

As he did with every other client, Brown checked Clifford out with his bank, Dunn & Bradstreet, and with the Better Business Bureau. Everyone told Brown that Clifford was the real deal. "I came to believe this guy was our savior; our knight in shining armor," Brown told the *Post-Gazette*.[21]

But Brown was wrong. Clifford was actually Hal Francis, an FBI agent working a sting called Operation Lightning Strike targeted at NASA managers suspected of taking bribes. The miniature lithotripter wasn't real, either. Legitimate companies had agreed to help the FBI by pretending to manufacture the device.

The FBI spent millions of dollars during this operation, including enormous bills for luxury hotel suites, gourmet meals, deep-sea fishing trips and late night drinking parties at Houston strip clubs. But all this spending had failed to secure a single indictment and the FBI was getting desperate. They needed to

---

20. Moushey and Martinson, "Win at Any Cost: Failing to Police Their Own," *Pittsburgh Post-Gazette*, December 13, 1998.

21. Moushey and Martinson, "Win at Any Cost: The Damage of Lies," *Pittsburgh Post-Gazette*, November 29, 1998.

catch somebody—anybody—doing something illegal. So they set their sights on Brown and a handful of other NASA contractors.

In 1994, two years into the sting, the federal government charged Brown with 21 counts of mail fraud and one count of bribery. The U.S. Justice Department alleged that Brown knew the device didn't exist, and that everything he did to win a NASA contract was a crime. The allegations collapsed during the trial when Brown produced a photograph of the miniature lithotripter, a picture of the prototype he took while visiting the plant which pretended to manufacture it. Francis showed Brown the device to assure him it was real. The FBI agent didn't see Brown take the photo.

All the charges against Brown were dismissed after the jury deadlocked. But the ordeal nearly destroyed him anyway. He lost his business, his savings, his fiancé, his health, and his belief in the government.

And Brown wasn't alone. The other 14 targets of Operation Lightning Strike were also college graduates and white collar workers. Many had families. Only one had previously been the target of a criminal investigation. But, after being set up by the FBI, all but two were coerced into pleading guilty to a variety of minor charges. Federal agents convinced them that fighting the charges in court would only result in long prison sentences, massive fines, and public humiliation. Of the 13 who pleaded guilty, 11 only got probation. One man served a month in prison, and another served two months.

But, like Brown, they all paid heavy emotional and financial tolls. Seven small companies employing 100 people went bankrupt. Three of those arrested had nervous breakdowns. One attempted suicide. Others had health problems ranging from heart attacks to strokes.

As Brown told the *Post-Gazette*, "The government agents intentionally and methodically drove our companies and personal bank accounts into bankruptcy . . . and [have driven] our reputations to ruin."

CHAPTER THREE

24/7 SURVEILLANCE

CHAD HENSLEY IS A YOUNG COMPUTER database technician who used to work at PACCAR, the Seattle-based company which owns the Peterbuilt and Kenworth truck companies. In early July 2000, he was unexpectedly called into a meeting with his manager. Seated across from Hensley in a small conference room, the manager reached into a manila folder, removed some documents, and said, "I have a report from Human Resources that says you've been visiting pornographic websites."

Hensley was startled by the accusation. He knew it was wrong. He knew the company had a policy against employees visiting x-rated sites, and he knew he hadn't violated it.[1]

The manager laid a series of spreadsheets before Hensley, explaining they had been generated by a software program bought from a company called Telemate. As the manager explained it, the software monitors all employee computer use, building a list of the exact URLs they visit and determining whether they are pornographic. According to the documents, Hensley was surfing porn sites.

Hensley stared at the spreadsheets in amazement. They were accurate, but the sites weren't pornographic. One was Gothic.net, an online monthly horror magazine. Another was Feralhouse.com, the website maintained by the company which published this book. In addition to managing databases, Hensley is a freelance writer who writes for *Seconds*, *Juxtapoz*, and *Terrorizer*, a British extreme music magazine. He also writes for a number of websites, including Gothic.net. And he contributed to *Apocalypse Culture II*, a Feral House book. Hensley had merely checked Gothic.net to see if one of his stories had been published. He had also looked at the Feral House site to see when *Apocalypse Culture II* was going to be released.

Taking a deep breath, Hensley began to argue that he hadn't violated company policy, that the sites he visited weren't pornographic. But that didn't seem to matter. The Telemate software said the sites were pornographic, and that was enough.

Telemate is one of several companies marketing such surveillance software. It promotes itself as "the leading provider of Internet usage management solutions," and brags its software can identify 297 categories of Internet sites, with categories ranging from "Pornography" to "Obscene/Tasteless" to "Gambling." The company estimates the total number of pornographic Websites may be as

---

1. Author's interview with Chad Hensley, August 1, 2000.

high as 10 million by the end of 2000. "With greater access to faster network connections at work, the temptation to cruise a porn site during a lunch break or when the boss is not looking increases tremendously," it warns.[2]

Many Fortune 500 companies are apparently alarmed by the thought of such rampant porn site surfing. According to Telemate, its customers include Arthur Andersen, Coca-Cola Bottling, Dayton-Hudson, Georgia-Pacific, International Paper, Parke-Davis Pharmaceutical Research, Sears Roebuck and the U.S. Army.

Hensley's manager took another print-out from the folder. It was a copy of an article titled "NON Sense—An Interview with Boyd Rice," which Hensley had written for Gothic.net's June issue. "But that article is not pornography," he protested. "That website does not contain images of nude people in lewd acts. The website has horror fiction, music reviews, and interviews with writers, musicians, and artists. It is not pornography. My writing is not pornography."

"I know that," the manager conceded. "Your writing is on the fringe. It's in that gray zone."

The manager then took another document from the folder. "The Human Resources manager wants you to sign this." It stated that Hensley had accessed Internet sites categorized as pornography by the company's Internet monitoring system. Future violations would result in further disciplinary action up to and including termination.

"I'm not going to sign this," Hensley said. He was told to meet with the Human Resources manager, who also asked him to sign the document. "I'm not going to sign that document. I was not looking at pornography. I'm a writer. I wrote that article. Neither that article nor the website it was posted on are pornography. My article is not pornography."

"Your article is not the point here," the Human Resources manager responded. "Though your writing is not pornography, that website is." When Hensley asked if she had seen the site, the Human Resources manager said no, that she was relying on Telemate's determination.

The issue stayed unresolved for a few days. Hensley visited Telemate's Website, reading its press releases about the need for employers to protect themselves against employees who surf objectionable sites at work. He thought long and hard about the situation. He saw no other alternative but to resign, forced to quit his job because of a software program written by people he never met.

Ironically, the surveillance systems are set up to collect the maximum information about mainstream members of the consumer culture. The more

2. *Business Wire*, June 22, 2000. According to a Telemate press release, "A recent survey cited that 70 percent of all Internet porn traffic occurs during the 9-to-5 workday. In addition, employees earning $75,000 to $100,000 annually are twice as likely to download pornography at work than those earning less than $35,000." The release quoted Vijay Balakrishan, Senior Vice President of Marketing for Telemate, as saying, "Easy access to faster network connections and the anonymous 'safe' nature of the office is the perfect combination for online porn surfing."

conventional job you have, the more your computer files grow. The more you consume, the more records you create on yourself.

Say you're a typical e-commerce office worker, the targeted demographic of our day. When the alarm goes off, you get up, take a shower, throw on some clothes, head downstairs to brew a few cups of designer coffee, scan the national edition of the *New York Times*, and check the news or sports channels. You might still have some privacy in your bedroom and bathroom, but the rest of your morning routine generates computer records. The newspaper has recorded your subscription, of course. And the cable company is building a file on your channel surfing habits. As the MediaOne Internet webpage reported on April 19, 1999, "Two-way digital cable boxes that save viewing information to a database operated by the cable companies are now replacing analog models. The boxes will be distributed as part of the standard digital cable services that allow viewers to get premium channels and buy pay-per-view movies."[3]

Any phone call you make before leaving the house creates a record at whatever telecommunications company you're using, documenting the number called and the length of long distance conversation in seconds for billing purposes. These records are routinely turned over to law enforcement and regulatory agencies, frequently without a search warrant or other court order.

Let's assume that, as a normal information-economy drone, you go online to check your e-mail before you leave for work. Many more records are created by personal computers and the growing number of companies operating on the World Wide Web. Computers build duplicate files which require special programs to fully delete. The FBI has special units which do nothing but recover "lost" computer files. And logging onto the Internet is essentially the same as opening your front door and letting the world walk through your house. Unless you're prepared to encrypt all your transmissions, install security systems and firewalls, and always communicate through anonymous re-mailers, you have no privacy.[4]

For starters, some operating systems are intentionally designed with traceable serial numbers and other features to allow private corporations to build files on the owners. Windows 98 and other Microsoft programs come with unique identifier numbers which have the potential to tie an individual's name to the number, linking him to both his hardware and the documents he creates. The number, known as a Global Unique Identifier, was discovered and publicized by Robert Smith, president of Phar Lap Software, in early 1999. Smith said they have the potential to create a "digital fingerprint" that could be used to match a document created by a word processing or spreadsheet program to

---

3. Polly Sprenger, "Cable Boxes See What You See," MediaOne, April 19, 1999. For more information, see *Spy TV*, edited by David Burke, Slab-O-Concrete Press, 2000.
4. Even the most advanced encryption programs won't ensure your privacy if the U.S. Department of Justice has its way. As reported by M.J. Zuckerman in the September 30, 1999 issue of *USA Today*, the $80 million Cyberspace Electronic Security Act is designed to help the FBI develop the tools to either crack the toughest encryption programs, or find ways to read the keystroke patterns behind messages ("White House's Internet Security Efforts Draw Controversy").

a particular computer. "Microsoft never asked me if it was okay to send in this number, and they never said it was being sent," says Smith.[5]

Some ISPs, including America Online, have employees which monitor the conversations in their chat rooms. The company, which hosts approximately 180,000 electronic conversations at any given time, has been known to shut down rooms if it doesn't like where the exchanges are headed. In December 1998, AOL tem-porarily suspended a conversation about Ireland in one of more than 12,000 rooms in the "politics" folder. The company also cites subscribers for "offensive" remarks, a term the company defines very broadly. Renee Rosenblum-Lowden of Riegelsville, Pennsylvania, recalls being cited during an abortion debate for advising an opponent, "If you can't stand the heat, get out of the kitchen."[6]

The software you use to surf the Web may also be watching you. A number of downloadable products secretly track and automatically transmit information to private companies. These products have been dubbed "spyware" by privacy advocates. Some of the most commonly used products are those available through RealNetworks RealDownload, Netscape/AOL Smart Download, and NetZip Download Demon utilities.

"Every time you use one of these utilities to download any file from anywhere on the Internet, the complete URL address of the file, along with your computer's individual internet IP address, and a unique ID tag that has been assigned to your machine, is immediately (and secretly) transmitted to the program's publisher," says software developer Steve Gibson of the Gibson Research Corporation. "This allows a database of your entire, personal file download history to be assembled and uniquely associated with your individual computer, for whatever purpose the program's publishers may have today, or tomorrow."[7]

Website operators also use software programs to pull information out of the computers which log onto them. These sites use a myriad of tools—"electronic cookie tags," invisible tracking images and the Web language JavaScript—to identify visitors, collect information from their computers, and track their patterns though the Internet to build profiles of the users.[8]

---

5. John Markoff, "Microsoft to Alter Its Software, Responding to Privacy Concerns," *New York Times*, March 7, 1999.
6. Amy Harmon, "Worries About Big Brother at AOL," *New York Times*, January 31, 1999.
7. "The Anatomy of File Download Spyware," <www.grc.com/newsletter>, August 7, 2000. In his article, Gibson writes, "This unique tagging can have only one purpose: To uniquely identify us and our computer to the program's publisher for the purpose of tracking us, and assembling a profile of our activities. When you consider that each user is uniquely identi-fied, and that every one of their subsequent Internet downloads is then reported back to the download product's publisher along with their unique ID tag and their machine's unique Internet IP address, it is not difficult to wonder why this information is being collected, and to what ends the data is being put."
8. "The details about this collecting get a little hair-raising," *Washington Times* reported on March 10, 2000. "Electronic 'cookie tags'—actually a file affixed to the user's own hard drive—identify visitors at many Websites, then track their patterns through the Internet, accruing elaborate 'inferential' and 'psychographic' data."

Technically speaking, the companies building these profiles aren't supposed to know who you are. The Federal Trade Commission (FTC) has rules against this kind of detailed file building. And many Internet-based companies are supposed to be policing themselves against such practices. But such rules and voluntary agreements are like all other good intentions. They only go so far.

On November 8, 1999, the Internet advertising firm DoubleClick told the FTC that it intended to build a huge database identifying the websurfing habits of individual Internet users. "We are going to take personally identifiable information, link that information to both online information and off-line information, and then use that information," senior vice president Jonathan Shapiro told a commission hearing. "We are going to use that information to target advertising to you." The FTC didn't object at the time.[9]

But then USA Today reported on DoubleClick's plans on January 26, 2000, igniting a firestorm of criticism. As a result of the story, several lawsuits against DoubleClick were filed, and the FTC and two states launched formal investigations. The newspaper wrote a follow-up story on February 25, quoting Seth Godin, author of Permission Marketing, as saying, "They made a giant mistake. They didn't have the guts to ask people's permission. That's cheating."

But Shapiro insisted DoubleClick didn't intend to do anything that isn't already common practice. "We've been telling folks our plans all along," the company CEO told USA Today. "Other folks are doing similar things." Companies with similar programs cited in the article included Engage and VantagePoint.

Six months later, the Associated Press confirmed that other companies were doing the same thing. Reporter D. Ian Hooper discovered that four firms with Internet sites—Toys Я Us, Babies Я Us, Lucy.com and Fusion.com—were collecting and forwarding personal customer information to Coremetrics, an Internet marketing company. "Not only does Coremetrics find out a customer's name and address, it also knows what pages they visit on a site and what goods they buy. It also tracks users between sites that use Coremetrics software," the story said. Two of the retailers, Lucy.com and Fusion.com, were members of TRUSTe, an association on Internet-related companies which had pledged to protect the privacy of their customers.[10]

This constant flow of information is so unregulated that the American Bar Association has concluded there is virtually no privacy on the Internet. On March 8, 2000, the ABA released a report which noted there are few laws to protect the public from such abuses. "In toto, information collectors can

9. Greg Farrell, "Targeted Ads: Consumer Trap or a Net Necessity?," USA Today, February 25, 2000.

10. "Online Retailers Violating Privacy," AP, August 1, 2000.

11. "Facts About Privacy and Cyberspace" is drawn from existing documents, including Congressional reports, industry surveys, legal cases, media reprints and previous American Bar Association studies. Among other findings, the ABA report cites a Federal Trade Commission document which found that 93 percent of the 7,500 "busiest servers on the World Wide Web" regularly collect personal information about their users, while just 44 percent of them post privacy notices.

largely do what they want with most information collected in cyberspace," the legal organization said.[11]

And all that monitoring occurs before you, our typical e-commerce worker, even leave the house.

The monitoring continues during the morning commute, especially in the newest, most technologically-advanced cars. Beginning in 1999, General Motors began installing high-tech "black boxes" in many models which record everything from the car's speed to the driver's braking habits. "Eventually, experts predict that virtually all cars will carry advanced recorders," the *Christian Science Monitor* said.[12]

Many cars already come with navigation systems tied into the network of Global Position Satellites circling the Earth. Advertised as a way of helping lost drivers find their way home, GPS technology can also be used to trace the cars' movements. In mid-May 2000, Denver city officials decided to spend $1.5 million for such a system to keep track of city vehicles. They were responding to news reports that some city employees were goofing off on the job. A spokesman for Mayor Wellington Webb said that, eventually, GPS devices would be installed on more than 2,000 Public Works Department vehicles.

The drive to work may also be tracked by video cameras. Governments are focusing thousands of them on busy highways, major streets and inner city intersections. Designed to allow traffic engineers to monitor driving patterns and congestion, they can also be used to follow specific cars from one location to another. Some cities also use mobile photo radar camera units to snap pictures of speeding cars, capturing the offenders' license plate numbers.

Such trips are now being analyzed by the government's most advanced military computers. Under an experimental program named Project Delphi, all traffic data in Portland, Oregon is being fed into the supercomputers at the Los Alamos National Laboratory, the nation's premiere weapons development facility. The *Oregonian* newspaper described the experiment as an effort to find civilian uses for the lab's programs and hardware. "Software will consider why people do things such as going to soccer practice, shopping for exotic food, going to job interviews or driving to soothe a screaming baby,'" the paper reported.[13]

The U.S. Department of Transportation specifically targeted the Portland area for the project, making local officials an offer they couldn't refuse. The federal government is buying the data from Metro, the regional government, for $1.6 million. "Florida wanted this, and was willing to pay, but the feds wanted us. When they asked what we would pay, we said, 'Nothing,' so we have a 100 percent federal grant, which is unusual these days," Keith Lawton, Metro's director of research and traffic forecasting, told the paper.

---

12. Eric Evarts, "How's My Driving? Just Check Under The Hood," *Christian Science Monitor*, October 10, 1999.

13. Bill Stewart, "Weapons Lab's Computers Will Target Portland Traffic," *Oregonian*, April 3, 2000.

The monitoring only increases at the work site. Many employees are now required to use a personalized computer-chipped card to enter company parking lots or garages, thus creating records of their arrivals. A large number of lots and garages are also equipped with video cameras, creating yet another record of their movements. Such cameras are also installed at many public lots and garages these days. Mass transit commuters are also monitored by video cameras located at transit centers, and even on trains and busses.

Computer cards are also required to enter many office buildings, and even individual elevators, hallways and offices in such buildings. If the cards are used often enough, employees can be tracked on a minute-by-minute basis as they work their way to their cubicles, that nexus of phone and computer lines where they spend the better part of their days. Many bosses routinely spy on workers during their job shifts, listening in on phone calls and monitoring computer use. A 1999 study by the American Management Association study found that the number of bosses electronically monitoring their employees' communications and performance jumped from 35 percent to 45 percent since 1997.[14]

According to *The Wall Street Journal*, more and more employers are "using surveillance software that covertly monitors and records each keystroke an employee makes: every letter, every comma, every revision, every flick of the fingertip, regardless of whether the data is ever saved in a file or transmitted over a corporate computer network. As they harvest those bits and bytes, the new programs, priced at as little as $99, give employers access to workers' unvarnished thoughts—and the potential to use that information for their own ends."[15]

Going online at work creates the same information flows as home computers, plus additional records created by the surveillance programs used by employers. According to *Time* magazine, 27 percent of major U.S. companies admit reading their employees' e-mail messages. And, according to a story in the March 10, 2000 edition of the *San Diego Union-Tribune*, a growing number of companies are tracking their employees' Web surfing habits, too. The newspaper surveyed human resource directors at 224 companies across the country. Nearly 65 percent of their companies had punished workers for "abusing" the Internet. Thirty percent had actually fired employees for their communications or surfing habits.

Homes, public roads and offices aren't the only places where we are constantly monitored. Video cameras are now commonplace at gas stations, fast food stores, restaurants, shopping malls, banks—just about any place where people eat, shop or do business. They are so ubiquitous most people don't even notice them, even though they all have the potential of creating records which can be retrieved days, weeks and even months later.

"Okay, maybe you need this stuff in rough neighborhoods, but what kind of society is it if you're constantly feeling encroached upon?" asks Gary T.

14. Michael J. McCarthy, "You Assumed 'Erase' Wiped Out That Rant Against the Boss? Nope.", *Wall Street Journal*, March 7, 2000.
15. *Ibid.*

Marx, a sociology professor at the University of Colorado who has studied the increasing use of video cameras. "In the past, you needed reasonable suspicion and probable cause. But now surveillance is categorical. Everyone is under suspicion all the time because it's possible to do that." [16]

Credit cards, debit cards and telephone calling cards create even more records. Soon, everything you buy, no matter how inexpensive, might become an electronic file. So-called "smart cards" have already been tested in several American cities. Consumers "charge them up" with money from their checking accounts, then use them for even the smallest purchases. And if you use Automated Teller Machines (ATM), a picture will also be taken of the transaction.

If you have a life, more records will be created of your evening and weekend activities, including where you go, how long you stay there, and, frequently, who you are with. More records are created on business trips, or during the kind of vacations advertised by Disney World and other popular theme parks. The government requires picture identification to board planes. Motels require customers to provide driver's license and credit card numbers to check in, even if they arrive by cab and pay cash. Banks are even requiring thumbprints to cash checks.

But as invasive as this level of surveillance seems, it is nothing compared to the vast amounts of information the government is currently collecting on all Americans. The record-building begins before we are born. All doctors keep extensive files on pregnant women, and some of the information, such as illegal drug use, must be transmitted to social service and law enforcement agencies. Fetuses are being identified as "drug affected," a label which will shape their lives.

Hospitals open numerous files on all babies, processing federal applications on behalf of the parents to ensure their children are registered with the Social Security Administration before they open their eyes. Hospitals are also vaccinating all newborns for Hepatitis B, recording the shots in one of the Immunization Registries currently being built in all 50 states. Within a few years, all these state computer files will be merged into a national database as a result of the National Immunization Program, a project begun in 1993. [17]

Many parents participate in one or more of the many government programs which provide services to children, ranging from home health visits to subsidized meal programs to pre-school classes. All of these programs build files on the families they serve, including personal health and behavioral information.

The public schools build even more extensive files on their students. Although these records are discussed in detail in the chapter titled Brave New Schools,

16. Peter Sleeth, "Watching Your Step," *Oregonian*, February 28, 1999. In his essay, Sleeth noted, "Even when a few, wobbly voices of civil libertarians rise up against a new set of public cameras, no one is talking about the more insidious problem of the growing web of surveillance from private stores to public streets: 'It may be legal, but is anyone questioning whether a society that spies on itself is moral?'"

17. National Immunization Program Immunization Registry Clearinghouse Fact Sheet, Centers for Disease Control and Prevention Website, April 26, 2000.

it is important to note that school officials routinely share these files with other public agencies. Especially since Columbine, schools have set up regular meetings between counsellors and local police officials to share information on students considered to be potential troublemakers.

Any violation of school rules, no matter how small, can plunge students into the juvenile justice system. Many schools in recent years have adopted tough Zero Tolerance policies which treat all infractions as serious crimes. Administrators now call the police to report such common playground behavior as pushing matches and fights, even if no one is injured. Students have been reported to the police for joking about Columbine and similar high-profile incidents.

The police don't always arrest the offending students. Instead, many are sent to a growing number of so-called Juvenile Intake and Assessment Centers across the country. There they are grilled by social workers and mental health counselors about their behavior, both at school and at home. The centers also gather detailed information about their parents and siblings, and all this data is routinely shared with police agencies.

Johnson County, Kansas is typical. A 1997 state law required that all acts of school violence be reported to police. Local elected officials responded by creating and funding a series of centers charged with evaluating whether these students pose a threat to themselves, their classmates or the community at large.[18]

Families are required to bring their disruptive children to these centers, where they are separated from their parents and asked to fill out a lengthy form called a POSIT (Problem Oriented Screening Instrument for Teenagers). The form features 139 personal and potentially incriminating questions, not only about the students, but also about their friends, siblings and parents. They include questions about personal drug use, sexual practices, work habits, and their relationship with other family members. Many of the questions ask the students to admit to committing crimes.[19]

---

18. "Program Aids Young Offenders," *Olathe Daily News*, May 15, 1998. Despite the positive headline, the story included pointed criticism of the program by Lisa Cain, the mother of a 10-year-old boy who was sent through Johnson County Juvenile Intake for shoving another boy who was shouting racial insults at him. "They assumed our family was having problems because my son was involved in a school fight," she said. Johnson County District Attorney Paul Morrison agreed, saying, "Generally, it isn't a positive thing to go through. You're messing around with kids, and it's an emotional thing for parents."

19. The following questions are included on the POSIT forms used by Kansas Juvenile Intake and Assessment System:
   • Do you get into trouble because you use drugs or alcohol at school?
   • Have you ever had sex with someone who shot up drugs?
   • Have any of your best friends dated regularly during the past year?
   • Have you dated regularly during the past year?
   • Do you threaten to hurt people?
   • Do you swear or use dirty language?
   • Have the whites of your eyes ever turned yellow?
   • Have you stolen things?
   • Have you ever been told you are hyperactive?

After completing the form, the child is evaluated by center employees. If the child is determined to pose potential problems, he/she may be sent to a "diversion" program with anger-management classes. Some of these programs require regular urine samples for drug screens, even if the child has never been accused of using drugs. These must be "observed" samples to eliminate the potential for cheating. Children who do not comply with all the terms of the diversion programs can be turned over to the police, who have the power to charge them with a crime based on the original incident. In other words, failure to produce an "observed" urine sample can lead to incarceration in a juvenile detention center.

How many children are currently being referred to such centers? No one knows, because no single agency keeps such figures. But Johnson County officials budgeted for 6,000 "clients" for the year 2000. The county only has around 50,000 school-age children.

But staying out of trouble doesn't stop the government from tracking you. Far from it. In the name of cracking down on deadbeat dads, the federal government is compiling a computerized list of every American who holds a job. The database was authorized under a little-publicized provision of the Welfare Reform Act of 1996. It includes the name, Social Security number, taxpayer identification number and home address of every worker who collects a paycheck—including those who have never been married and don't have children. Although only 16 million single parents are owed child support, the database will eventually contain files on more than 150 million workers.[20]

"As part of a new and aggressive effort to track down parents who owe child support, the federal government has created a vast computerized data-monitoring system," the *Washington Post* said. ". . . Government agencies have long gathered personal information for specific reasons, such as collecting taxes. But never before has the federal government had the legal authority and technological ability to locate so many Americans found to be delinquent parents—or such potential to keep tabs on Americans accused of nothing." [21]

Robert Gellman, an attorney and privacy expert in Washington, DC, told the *Post* that the database is "the Holy Grail of data collection: a central file on every American."

- Do you feel you are addicted to alcohol or drugs?
- Do you feel people are against you?
- Do your friends bring drugs to parties?
- Do you have a hot temper?
- Do you have a constant desire for alcohol or drugs?
- Do you hear things no one else around you hears?
- Do you and your parents or guardians have frequent arguments which involve yelling and screaming?
- Does one of your parents have a steady job?
- Have you ever had sexual intercourse without using a condom?

20. Judith Havemann, "Data Gives Hope for Child Support Collection," Los Angeles Times-Washington Post News Service, *Oregonian*, April 3, 1999.
21. Robert O'Harrow Jr., "Uncle Sam Has All Your Numbers," *Washington Post*, June 27, 1999.

The federal government is also watching people who make large cash deposits or withdrawals at their banks. Under the Bank Secrecy Act, federal authorities routinely monitor bank customers and even flag some of them as potential criminals without their knowledge. First passed in 1974 to fight tax evasion, the act requires bankers to notify the federal government of any transaction over $10,000, and to report any other activity which merely looks suspicious. More than 250,000 "suspicious-activity" reports were filed from mid-1996 to early 1999. They are stored in a gigantic database operated by the U.S. Treasury Department's Financial Crime Enforcement Network (FinCen) in Detroit.

But you don't have to deposit money in your bank to come to the government's attention. Simply transferring it will do the job. On August 18, 1999, the U.S. Treasury Department required electronic money transfer companies such as Western Union to register with FinCen by December 31, 2001. Failure to register is a crime, punishable by fines of $5,000 a day and up to five years in prison. The requirement will apply to an estimated 8,000 businesses nationwide, including such giant corporations as American Express and Travelers Express/MoneyGram, along with independent storefront operations. The businesses—which cash checks, transmit money, and sell and redeem money orders—account for an estimated $200 billion a year in transactions.[22]

Buying a gun will get you on another list. Federal law currently requires everyone buying a handgun or rifle from a licensed dealer to submit to a personal background check conducted by the FBI or local police departments. The law enforcement agencies comb through criminal and mental health records to see if the buyer is legally qualified to have a gun. Although the FBI is supposed to destroy all records generated by its searches, some Second Amendment advocates charge the agency is building a secret, illegal master list of all gun owners.

The same Internet-tracking technologies used by private websites are also being used by the government. According to a June 2000 study by *Wired News*, sites run by dozens of federal agencies send cookies to unsuspecting visitors in violation of FTC rules. The agencies include the U.S. departments of Defense, Energy, and Justice, which oversees the FBI.[23] Two privacy advocates asked Congress to investigate the Office of National Drug Control Policy for using cookies. The groups, the Electronic Information Privacy Center and Junkbusters Corporation, said they violated both White House policy and the Privacy Act of 1974.[24]

---

22. Marcy Gordon, "Money Transmitters Must Now Register," AP, August 18, 1999.
23. "Feds' Hands Caught in Cookie Jar," *Wired News*, June 30, 2000. Other agencies cited in the story by Declan McCullagh were the U.S. Mint, the FDIC, the INS, the U.S. European Command, the Air Force Space Command, a Pentagon records agency, the Army's training command, and four websites at the National Institutes of Health. McCullagh also found that sites maintained by Federal Reserve banks send out cookies, too. "It's typical. Governments think the rules don't apply to them," said Erick Gustafson, director of technology policy at Citizens for a Sound Economy. "They're historically the worst offenders of privacy and the rights of citizens."
24. "Privacy Advocates Seek Inquiry Into Drug Office," *New York Times*, June 23, 2000.

Of course, the government has far more information on anyone ever arrested for a crime, no matter how petty. Law enforcement agencies across the country have access to your arrest and court records, including your mug shots and fingerprints. The largest database is the Regional Information Sharing Systems (RISS), first developed by the U.S. Department of Justice in the 1970s. It connects the computer files stored at six regional centers serving more than 5,300 member law enforcement agencies in 50 states, two Canadian provinces, the District of Columbia, Australia, Guam, the U.S. Virgin Islands, and Puerto Rico.[25]

All six centers are linked through a secure "intranet" which allows confidential information exchanges between member agencies. The centers are also connected to other systems, such as the Southwest Border States Anti-Drug Information System Network, the High Intensity Drug Trafficking Areas database, and various state intelligence systems. Although the databases are supposed to concentrate on drug and organized crime activities, information on political dissidents is also available since they are frequently monitored by the same criminal intelligence divisions.

The RISS centers are funded by the Bureau of Justice Assistance, a division of the Department of Justice. In addition to funding the centers, the bureau sponsors national and regional conferences where law enforcement agencies swap information about tracking suspected drug dealers, gang members, illegal gun sellers, and other criminals assumed to operate on a multi-jurisdictional level.

But RISS is just the start. The federal government funds and coordinates many other crime-related databases, too. The National Crime Information Center 2000 project is designed to link FBI computers with other law enforcement agencies.[26] The Integrated Automated Fingerprint Identification System contains millions of fingerprints from law enforcement agencies across the country. After spending $640 million to upgrade the system, FBI officials announced in August 1999 that local police officers will soon be able to take fingerprints from suspects using electronic pads in their cars and compare them almost immediately with all of the prints already registered in the system. In addition to law enforcement officers, the "digitalized" prints in the system are available to private security firms, day care providers, and others who run extensive background checks on their potential employees.[27]

But perhaps the most disturbing computer system is the National Offender Database, which could soon be collecting DNA samples from everyone. Current federal law requires all 50 states to collect such samples from convicted criminals and send them to the FBI, which maintains the database. Over 1 million samples had been collected by May 2000. Every state takes samples from convicted sex offenders, and most test convicted murderers. About one-third of the states test not only violent offenders, but also burglars. Seven states collect

---

25. Christian Parenti, *Lockdown America: Police and Prisons in the Age of Crisis*, Verso, 1999.
26. Gary Fields, "Upgraded Database to Aid Patrol Officers," *USA Today*, July 12, 1999.
27. Gary Fields, "FBI Digitalizes Fingerprint System Today," *USA Today*, August 10, 1999.

samples from all felons, including those convicted of such white-collar crimes as credit card fraud. Twenty-four states test juveniles.[28]

The project began in the 1980s, when law enforcement agencies first began using DNA evidence to convict criminals. All 50 states started building DNA databases within the next decade. By 1994, the FBI was pulling the state programs into a national DNA computer database. It went online in October 1999.

In August 1999, New York became the first state to begin collecting DNA samples from all convicted felons, with some officials arguing that everyone arrested for a crime should go into the database, too. "We should be collecting it from everybody [arrested]. The only ones who have to worry about DNA testing are the criminals," New York City Police Commissioner Howard Safir told the New York Times.[29] A few months later, the International Association of Chiefs of Police passed a resolution urging Congress to require that DNA samples be taken from every person arrested in connection with a crime.[30]

The DNA database could expand ever further in the coming years. On May 4, 1999, the National Institute of Justice announced police will soon be able to test crime scenes for DNA evidence with a computer-linked microchip device no bigger than a credit card. The device, which is being developed with federal assistance by companies in California and Virginia, will perform tests in seconds that now take weeks to complete. "The possibilities are extraordinary. The technology is amazing," says Albuquerque Police Chief Gerald Galvin.[31] In late July 1999, a federal advisory committee called the National Commission on the Future of DNA Evidence decided that performing tests on everyone arrested for a crime is permitted under the U.S. Constitution.[32]

But even these snitch and surveillance programs pale in comparison to the high-tech Big Brother systems currently under development.

28. "Victims: Use DNA to Nab More Criminals," USA Today, May 9, 2000.
29. "New York Plan Widely Expands the Sampling of Criminals' DNA," New York Times, August 7, 1999.
30. "Police Chiefs Suggest Taking DNA Samples From All Suspects," AP, November 4, 1999.
31. Richard Willing, "Science at the Crime Scene," USA Today, May 4, 1999.
32. Richard Willing, "DNA Tests for All Arrestees Probably Legal," USA Today, July 26, 1999.

CHAPTER FOUR

THE DIGITAL SNITCH

IN THE 1998 ACTION THRILLER *Enemy of the State*, a labor lawyer finds his every move tracked by corrupt officials at the National Security Agency. During the course of the film, star Will Smith is spied on by in-store video surveillance cameras and high-flying satellites. His phone calls are traced and his bank and credit card records are scrutinized. Micro-transmitters are placed in his clothes, forcing Smith to strip to his underwear in a vain attempt to shake his pursuers. His wife almost leaves him and he nearly loses his life before finally prevailing in a typically contrived, big-bang Hollywood ending.

Although the script was weak, the technology which drove the plot is real. And so is the idea that the government is using it against American citizens. In fact, the surveillance systems shown in *Enemy of the State* were outdated when the film was released, and the newest technology is already far beyond anything ever envisioned by such prophetic writers as Aldous Huxley and George Orwell. Some of these systems are so new that existing wiretap and privacy laws don't address them, and new ones are being deployed all the time.[1]

This technology is not the same thing as a snitch. Machines aren't informants, at least not in the traditional sense. But the information collected by these systems can be used the same way. Computers can be programmed to monitor specific individuals, or millions at the same time. They can notify law enforcement agencies of conversations and transactions. The information can trigger investigations, and can be used to build criminal cases and win convictions.

The satellite-based surveillance system in *Enemy of the State* is based on Echelon, the (very real) information vacuum cleaner operated by the NSA. Assembled in bits and pieces over the course of the Cold War, it is capable of collecting and analyzing vast amounts of data, including virtually every electronic communication from anywhere in the world. As the CBS News show *60 Minutes* said on February 27, 1999, "If you made a phone call today or sent an e-mail to a friend, there's a good chance what you said or wrote was captured and screened by the country's largest intelligence agency."

Echelon is not merely a federal government asset, however. Although designed and coordinated by the United States, it is the product of an alliance between five intelligence agencies: the NSA; the Defense Signals Directorate

---

1. The script of *Enemy of the State* acknowledges the rapidly evolving technology. In the film, co-star Gene Hackman plays a former NSA operative who helps Smith evade the agents who are after him, but admits that the NSA's technology has advanced at least one generation since his retirement a short time ago.

(DS) in Australia; the Government Communications Headquarters (GCH) in Britain; the Communications Security Establishment (CSE) in Canada; and the Government Communications Security Bureau (GCSB) in New Zealand. As documented by Nicky Hager in *Secret Power: New Zealand's Role in the International Spy Network*, all these agencies are bound together under the top-secret UKUSA intelligence agreement.[2]

As reported by Hager and other researchers, Echelon is not designed to eavesdrop on a particular individual's e-mail or fax link. Instead, it indiscriminately intercepts massive quantities of communications, using sophisticated computers to identify messages of interest from the vast majority of unwanted ones. Using 120 satellites and a chain of secret interception facilities around the world, Echelon automatically searches through millions of messages looking for ones containing key words or phrases. Every word of every intercepted message is searched in "real time" as they pour into the system's computers.[3]

Although the NSA is not legally allowed to spy on American citizens, Echelon gets around this restriction by pretending the five participating countries are spying on each other. Under the terms of the UKUSA agreement, Britain spies on American citizens and America spies on British citizens, and the two collaborators trade intelligence. The agreement also assigns "spheres of influence" to the participating nations, with Britain watching its former colony of Hong Kong, for example, and the United States monitoring most of Europe.[4]

As part of its surveillance duties, the NSA routinely spies on European businesses and channels information to their American competitors. British journalist Duncan Campbell sparked an international controversy when he levelled this charge in a report titled "Interception Capabilities 2000," which was presented to the Citizens' Rights Committee of the European Union on February 23, 1999. Campbell's report prompted an op-ed in the March 17 issue of the *Wall Street Journal* by retired CIA director James Woolsey, who admitted to the spying, but claimed the only companies targeted were engaged in illegal or unethical behavior. "That's right, my continental friends, we have spied on you because you bribe," Woolsey wrote, referring to two French companies cited by Campbell, Thomson-CSF and Airbus Industrie. Both companies quickly issued statements denying the charges, and the European Parliament (which represents the European Union's 15 members) voted to launch a formal investigation into Echelon the next month, generating a series of news stories which largely confirmed Hager's original research.[5]

---

2. Nicky Hager, *Secret Power: New Zealand's Role in the International Spy Network*, Nelson, NZ: Craig Potton, 1996
3. Nicky Hager, "Exposing the Global Surveillance System," *CovertAction Quarterly*, Winter 1996–1997.
4. *Ibid.*
5. "Britain and U.S. Monitoring All Global Messages," *The Independent*, January 28, 2000. Writing about a new European Parliament report on Echelon, the paper said it discovered the spy system was also monitoring the Internet: "The intelligence services seem so far to have kept pace with the explosion in the quantity of electronic communications through the Internet, something which was thought at one time to pose a significant

The controversy forced the federal government to finally confirm Echelon is real. After denying its existence for more than 50 years, NSA Director Michael V. Hayden appeared before a congressional committee in April 1999. Although Hayden denied his agency was sharing intelligence with American corporations, he was forced to admit what the conspiracy theorists had been saying for years —the NSA is watching you.[6]

The European Parliament investigation has prompted a wave of news stories and special reports about Echelon. Among other things, they charge the Pentagon is deeply involved in the system. For example, the U.S. military maintains fleets of planes which gather electronic data for Echelon, including an entire Navy squadron of P-3 Orion anti-submarine aircraft modified to intercept radio transmissions and transmit the data directly to the NSA. All of this data is then fed into the most advanced computers in the world, maintained at the NSA's headquarters at Fort Meade, Maryland. The entire system is so powerful it can identify targeted individuals making international phone calls by their "voiceprints."[7]

The fuss probably will not force the NSA to curtail its intelligence-gathering operations, however. To the contrary, in early December 1999, *Newsweek* reported the agency was drafting a "memoranda of understanding" to allow it to work with the FBI tracking "terrorists and criminals" in the United States. According to the article, the FBI is so short of technical know-how that it needs the NSA to keep pace with lawbreakers who use digital phones or encode their e-mail transmissions. *Newsweek* said the government justified the NSA's new mission by arguing that the Internet has erased the difference between domestic and international crimes.[8]

"Do we really want the NSA to be spying on U.S. citizens?" Harvey Kushner, chair of the criminal justice department at Long Island University, asked the Reuters news agency after the *Newsweek* story story came out. "Where will it stop? American public opinion over the years has overwhelmingly spoken against covert and clandestine agencies mucking around in domestic affairs."

Despite Echelon's tremendous capabilities, the federal government is not relying solely on it to monitor all electronic communications. In fact, a top priority of the Clinton Administration throughout the 1990s was making it

challenge to the agencies. Much of the globe's Internet capacity is located in the U.S, or passes through it and, the document argues, 'communications from Europe to and from Asia, Oceania, Africa or South America normally travel via the United States.'

"That means that 'a large proportion of international communications on the Internet will by the nature of the system pass through the U.S. and thus be readily accessible to the NSA' and can be sifted relatively easily from their origin and destination. The document points out, however, that the costs and technical difficulties of surveillance are growing."

6. Tom Raum, "NSA Denies Spying on Americans," AP, April 12, 2000.
7. Yves Clarisse, "EU Assembly Set to Launch 'Spy' System Inquiry," *Reuters*, March 27, 2000; "EU: Wider Probe of U.S. Spys," AP, May 7, 2000.
8. "National Security Agency Drafts 'Memoranda of Understanding' to Work with FBI in the U.S.," *Newsweek*, December 13, 1999.

easier for domestic law enforcement officials to eavesdrop on the general public. Arguing that criminals and terrorists were infesting the information superhighway, the government wants to wiretap every phone, computer, and fax machine.

New technologies such as cell phones and the Internet have changed the rules regarding domestic police surveillance programs. The 1968 Crime Patrol and Safe Streets Act requires a court order for all telephone wiretaps. Federal taps must also receive high-level Justice Department approval, and dial-up modems are provided similar protections by the Electronic Communications Privacy Act of 1986. But cell phones and high-speed cable modems cannot be tapped easily and might not be covered by any law—that's why the government insists they be sold with built-in monitoring devices.[9] As University of Oregon constitutional law professor Garret Epps put it, "Until now, the government's ability to intrude has depended on its own efforts. The current set of proposals goes one step further. No new technology can be introduced, the government is arguing, until it has been adopted to maximize ease of surveillance. It is as if the FBI demanded that all letters be mailed in transparent envelopes, or that citizens tape all private conversations and retain the cassettes in case the government later decides it wants to hear them." [10]

Shortly after taking office, President Bill Clinton set about trying to make it easier for the government to monitor the new communication technologies. He appointed an Interagency Working Group to solve the problems in early 1993. It included Vice President Al Gore, Attorney General Janet Reno, Assistant Attorney General Webster Hubbel and White House Counsel Vince Foster. In a report to Clinton, the IWG identified the issue as follows: "Simply stated, the nexus of the long term problem is how can the government sustain its technical ability to accomplish electronic surveillance in an advanced telecommunications environment characterized by great technical diversity and many competing service providers (numbering over 1500, some potentially antagonistic) who have great economic and political leverage . . . The solution to the access problem for future telecommunications requires that the vendor/ manufacturing community translate the government's requirements into a fundamental system design criteria." [11]

In April 1993, the White House announced that the NSA had developed a new microchip known as the Clipper Chip—essentially a wiretap to be built into every new phone, fax and computer. The Clinton Administration claimed the new technology was necessary to prevent anyone from using encryption software to send coded messages between computers that cannot be read by anyone else. "The Clipper Chip proposal would have required every encryption user (that is, every individual or business using a digital telephone system, fax machine, the Internet, etc.) to hand over their decryption keys to the govern-

---

9. "U.S. Hopes to Extend Online Wiretapping," *Washington Post*, July 18, 2000.
10. Garrett Epps, "The Prying Eye of Government," *Oregonian*, September 26, 1999.
11. "Al Gore Bugs America?" *WorldNetDaily*, August 2, 2000

ment, giving it access to both stored data and real-time communications," the American Civil Liberties Union declared.[12]

Although the Clinton Administration eventually gave up on the Clipper Chip, it continued to work to make it easier for law enforcement agencies to monitor the new technologies, beginning with passage of the 1994 Communications Assistance for Law Enforcement Act. In October 1995, the FBI cited the new law to demand that phone companies provide the capability to simultaneously tap one out of every hundred phone calls in the largest American cities, a 1,000-fold increase over previous levels.

The telephone industry fought the new standards for more than four years, but the Federal Communications Commission (FCC) finally sided with the FBI in August 1999, ordering that all new cellular phones include components to allow law enforcement agencies to home in on their exact locations. Because this feature cannot be turned off, new cell phones can now be used to trace their owners' movements on a minute-by-minute basis. FCC Chairman William Kennard declared the rules "will help ensure that law enforcement has the most up-to-date technology to fight crime." [13] The ruling prompted a September 2 editorial in USA Today complaining, "If a crisis is brewing, it isn't that criminals and terrorists will escape. It is that the government's ageless eagerness to pry will supersede the public's right to be free of that prying."

That eagerness apparently knows no bounds. In early 1999, the FBI began approaching Internet Service Providers around the country with a device it wanted to attach directly to their servers: an off-the-shelf PC with a Windows 2000-based software program called Carnivore. It was developed at a special research lab at the agency's headquarters in Quantico, Virginia. After being hooked into an ISP's servers, the computer is kept in a locked cage on the premises and checked by FBI agents on a daily basis.[14]

When some ISPs balked at allowing the FBI to install its computer, the agency occasionally returned with a court order, just like for a conventional wiretap. But Carnivore is anything but an old fashioned bug. Instead of recording communications with a single criminal suspect, it automatically downloads all of the electronic transmissions flowing through the servers, from e-mails to website visits to chat room discussions and more. The FBI claims it then isolates just those transmissions to and from individual suspects, but there is no way to confirm this. Carnivore operates independently of the rest of the ISP communications systems, meaning it cannot be separately monitored.

In late June, the FBI explained the workings of its Carnivore system to a roomful of astonished Internet specialists. Word of the meeting leaked to the Wall Street Journal, which broke the story on July 11. The revelation provoked a public controversy, with U.S. Attorney General Janet Reno saying she wasn't

12. Ibid.
13. David Lawsky, "FCC Wiretap Rules Delight FBI, Disappoint Critics," Reuters, August 27, 1999.
14. "FBI's System to Covertly Search E-mail Raises Privacy, Legal Issues," Wall Street Journal, July 11, 2000.

aware it had ever been used. Privacy advocates immediately denounced the system, charging it violated the rights of all ISP customers by reading both sender and recipient addresses, as well as subject lines of e-mails, to decide whether to make a copy of the entire message. In a letter to the U.S. House subcommittee that deals with Fourth Amendment search-and-seizure issues, the American Civil Liberties Union complained, "Carnivore is roughly equivalent to a wiretap capable of accessing the contents of the conversations of all of the phone company's customers, with the 'assurance' that the FBI will record only conversations of the specified target. This 'trust us, we are the government' approach is the antithesis of the procedures required under our wiretapping laws."[15]

Several ISPs also objected to the FBI's surveillance system. On July 14, Earthlink announced it would refuse future agency requests to install the Carnivore device on its network, saying that the equipment had already caused service disruptions for its customers. The Internet Alliance, an ISP trade group that includes Earthlink and Internet giant America Online, also criticized the far-reaching capabilities of the system.

Even some law-and-order politicians decried the system. Sensing an opportunity to embarrass the White House, conservative Republican House Majority Leader Dick Armey (R-Texas) agreed with the ACLU. In a statement calling on Attorney General Janet Reno and FBI Director Louis Freeh to stop using Carnivore until the Fourth Amendment concerns had been addressed, Armey said, "At a time when there is a lot of talk about concerns for Internet privacy, the Clinton-Gore administration continues to push Big Brother proposals that promote government cybersnooping."

Despite the publicity generated by the *Wall Street Journal* story, it was impossible to know how much information the FBI had already collected with Carnivore, or what had happened to it. Agency officials claimed the system had been used 25 times in drug-trafficking, counter-terrorism, and "infrastructure protection" (anti-hacker) cases. None of them had gone to trial, however, so the FBI had not disclosed detailed information about them.[16]

The federal government's efforts to stage manage the new technology suffered a temporary setback on August 14, 2000. A three-judge panel of the U.S. Court of Appeals for the District of Columbia threw out portions of the FTC's controversial new standards, including one provision requiring that phone carriers provide to law enforcement agents all numbers dialed after the subject of a wiretap order connects a call. Some civil libertarians suggested the ruling might apply to the Carnivore system. But even if it does, the government is already working on the next generation of surveillance systems—and they will be far more invasive than the current ones.

Acting under the guise of fighting terrorism, the NSA is developing a plan for the FBI to monitor virtually all of the nation's computer systems, including

---

15. "FBI Tool Reads E-mail," AP, July 12, 2000.
16. *USA Today* editorialized against Carnivore on July 24, 2000, saying, "The FBI has a long history of violating the privacy of U.S. citizens, often with political motives."

both non-military government computers and those used in the banking, tele-communications and transportation industries. A draft of the plan provided to the *New York Times* by a civil liberties group called for a sophisticated software system to track activities on all the computer networks. It proposed the creation of a Federal Intrusion Detection Network (FidNet). As part of the plan, networks of thousands of software monitoring programs would continuously track computer activities, looking for intrusions and "illegal acts." The system, to be operational by 2003, will have the potential to access computer-to-computer communications, including log-ins and e-mails. [17]

What else does the future hold? Chances are, it's already watching us. After all, the FBI was using Carnivore for more than a year before the *Wall Street Journal* broke the story. How did we reach the point where we can't even trust our machines?

---

17. John Markoff, "Feds Form Plan to Guard Nation's Computers," *New York Times*, July 28, 1999.

CORPORATE ORIGINS OF THE SNITCH CULTURE

To UNDERSTAND HOW THE SNITCH CULTURE has come to permeate modern society, it is important to realize that it arose from the private sector, the businesses we deal with every day. People might go years without ever visiting a government office, but it's hard to go even a few days without dealing with a utility company, service station, grocery store or shopping mall. Corpora-tions developed and deployed the first undercover agents, wanted posters, video cameras and anonymous telephone tip lines. Public law enforcement agencies adopted them only after they had been field tested by private businesses.

And the private sector is still developing the most advanced surveillance systems. Today's most controversial privacy issues revolve around products developed by corporations, including cookies, adbots, spyware, backchannel communications and other Internet monitoring programs. Even the FBI's con-troversial Carnivore system is basically a Microsoft product.[1]

The private sector pioneered such systems because it had to. Effective law enforcement agencies didn't exist when the country was first created. Only the largest cities along the East Coast had anything resembling functioning police departments for many years. Sheriffs were few and far between in the rural parts of the nation, and the frontier was viewed as largely lawless until the early part of the 20th Century. So businesses employed their own security forces, occasionally offering rewards to lure posses and bounty hunters into doing the dirty work for them.

This is the country that Allan Pinkerton found in the 1840s. And more than anyone else, Pinkerton turned informing into an American art form. His life illustrates how the elements of the Snitch Culture first made the transitions from the private to public sectors.[2]

Because of his pioneering work in the field of undercover work, Pinkerton is both revered and reviled today. Conservatives respect him because he created the Secret Service, the forerunner of all federal law enforcement agencies. Liberals despise him because he helped big employers fight off early labor organizers. But more than anything else, Pinkerton is remembered as the country's first private eye. The slogan for his Pinkerton Detective Agency captures the essence of the modern surveillance society—"We Never Sleep."

1. "Reno to Review the FBI's Internet Wiretap System," *Reuters*, July 13, 2000.
2. There are numerous books on the life and times of Allan Pinkerton, including Sigmund Lavone, *Allan Pinkerton: America's First Detective*, New York: Dodd, Meade, 1963, and James A. Mackay, *Allan Pinkerton: The First Private Eye*, New York: J. Wiley and Sons, 1997.

Born in Glasgow, Scotland, in 1819, Pinkerton was a skilled craftsman who agitated against the dominance of the wealthy landowners until the threat of arrest led him to emigrate to Chicago in 1842, where he became a barrel maker. While looking for wood in the forest near his home in June 1846, he ran across a campsite with evidence of a counterfeiting operation. Pinkerton reported his discovery to the sheriff, and the two men returned to stake out the campsite, eventually arresting the gang. For the next few years, Pinkerton supplemented his income by working as a part-time sheriff. A series of highly-publicized cases led him to take up criminal detection as a career, and he quickly assumed the dual jobs of Cook County deputy sheriff and special agent for the U.S. Post Office.

Pinkerton opened his own business, the North Western Police Agency, in 1855 with financial backing from a consortium of seven railroad companies. Charged with stopping employee theft, he came up with the simple but original solution of putting undercover agents on the trains disguised as customers. Breaking a $50,000 robbery from the Adams Express Company helped his business expand on a national basis. In 1861 Pinkerton received country-wide publicity for helping foil a plot to murder President-elect Abraham Lincoln on his journey to Washington, DC. At the beginning of the Civil War, Pinkerton was appointed by General G.B. McClellan to organize the intelligence branch of the Union Army. He planted undercover agents in the Confederate Army and used informants to track its movements. And he organized a security force to protect Lincoln and all future Presidents: the Secret Service.

After the war, Pinkerton started the nation's first detective agency. Operating like an early version of the FBI, he and his investigators ran down a wide range of lawbreakers fleeing from local police jurisdictions. The Pinkerton Detective Agency took part in the long chase after the Jesse James gang, the search for the kidnapped Charlie Ross, and the international round-up of the Bank of England swindlers. Pinkerton is also credited with finding and circulating photos of criminal suspects, the first wanted posters.

As the Industrial Revolution slowly took hold in America, conflicts erupted between large companies and their workers. Big business owners used violence to fight the early labor movement, with security thugs roughing up (and sometimes killing) both organizers and strikers. Some unions struck back, occasionally using sabotage to bring a reluctant employer to the bargaining table. The International Workers of the World was especially willing to break the law to advance its cause. During a labor dispute in 1894, IWW members used a ton and a half of dynamite to blow up the Bunker Hill and Sullivan Company mine in Wadner, Idaho. The company's boarding house and bunkhouse were also burned to the ground.

As part of this ongoing struggle, industrialists began hiring snitches to infiltrate the early labor organizations, identify their leaders, and work with local law enforcement officials to have them arrested on trumped-up charges. Pinkerton got a lot of this work. His firm was hired by some of the large mining and steel companies involved in the most violent labor disputes. The agency's most famous operation took place in the coal mines of northeast Pennsylvania in the 1870s, where the mining company was fighting a secret society established by Irish immigrants called the Molly Maguires.

The Mollies were modeled after an Irish society which used violence to protest the abuses of tyrannical landlords during the Potato Famine of the 1840s. The Irish coal miners in Pennsylvania were also oppressed. The mining companies paid low wages, owned all the available housing, and controlled the local governments and police forces. When the miners went out on strike in 1875, the Irish militants increased their attacks. In retaliation, Franklin Gowen, owner of the Philadelphia and Reading Coal and Iron Company, hired a Pinkerton operative named James McParlan to infiltrate the Mollies. A short time later, the Mollies were blamed for an attack on a mining official which left a pregnant woman dead. Twenty of the organization's members were arrested and charged with the crime. Gowen served as a prosecutor at the trial, and McParlan provided the testimony which resulted in their convictions. Although some biographers now suspect that McParlan was behind the deadly attack, the defendants were eventually executed and the Mollies effectively ceased to exist.

Pinkerton's work against the Molly Maguires set the standard for such undercover operations. As Frank Donner wrote in *The Age of Surveillance*, "In the course of tracking and exposing the Mollies, the Pinkerton Agency developed a *modus operandi* that would become the model for intelligence infiltration of political organizations. Every group was assumed to be led by a tight inner circle of conspirators whose program and tactics were closely held secrets. These insiders were, in theory, surrounded by an outer ring of followers, many of them unaware of the criminal purposes of the leaders. In order to unmask these purposes and apprehend the leaders, it was necessary first to join the outer ring, and then, through craft and daring, to gain access to the leaders. Such penetration had a single aim: the arrest and conviction of the members of the inner group on conspiracy charges." [3]

3. Frank Donner was one of the earliest and most influential writers decrying the growing influence of the national security state. As a civil liberties attorney in the 1940s, he began representing targets of the Red Scare witch hunts, defending people being dragged before Congressional committees and pressured to accuse their friends and associates of being Communists. Donner was named director of the American Civil Liberties Union Project on Political Surveillance in 1971, a time when law enforcement agencies were routinely spying on a broad range of peace and civil rights activists. He collected information on the government's various monitoring programs and advised activists in an attempt to stop such snooping.

Ten years later, Donner pulled everything he learned into the first major book to present a comprehensive overview of the government's domestic intelligence-gathering network, *The Age of Surveillance: The Aims & Methods of America's Political Intelligence System* (New York: Alfred Knopf, 1980). Incorporating his own research, documents unearthed by various lawsuits against the FBI and state and local police agencies, as well as information supplied to him by inside sources, the book presented a central message which is at the heart of today's intelligence-gathering operations—surveillance is a form of governance, with most people targeted for their constitutionally-protected

By the time Pinkerton died in 1894, union-busting had made the transition from private sector cause to public policy. State militias were repeatedly called out to defend the corporations and break the unions, frequently with massive military force. During a dispute with the Carnegie Steel Company, armed members of the Amalgamated Association of Iron and Steel Workers seized the town of Homestead, Pennsylvania in 1892. Government troops launched an assault to recapture the town. Nationwide labor violence broke out in 1894 in response to the Pullman strike by the American Railway Union against the 24 railroad companies represented by the General Managers Association. The confrontations began in Chicago when workers hauled scab engineers and conductors off their trains and assaulted them. Over $1 million worth of property was destroyed in Chicago alone. The strike ended when the government intervened on the side of the railroads, crushing the strikers. By the early 1900s, the early federal intelligence agencies were staging preemptive strikes to round up "subversives," deporting large numbers of foreigners suspected of being anarchists or socialists.[4]

The Pinkerton Detective Agency did not go out of business when the government took over the fight against labor. To the contrary, it is now part of the largest private security company in the world. On March 31, 1999, Pinkerton Inc. became a wholly-owned subsidiary of Securitas AB, based in Stockholm, Sweden. Prior to the acquisition, Securitas had focused exclusively on security officer services, alarm services, central monitoring and cash-in-transit for banks and retail stores around the world. The new company has annual revenues of $3.5 billion and 114,000 employees in more than 32 countries throughout North and South America, Europe and Asia. At the time of the merger, Pinkerton officials said it would allow them to "build the kind of global security network that our clients need."

How did the agency founded by Allan Pinkerton in 1850 become so large after the union-busting work dried up? By going back to basics and concentrating on its original mission, helping private employers crack down on dishonest, disruptive and unproductive workers. One of its most popular services relies exclusively on snitches, a telephone tip line program called AlertLine.

Tip lines are one of the most common of all private sector informant programs. Employees are encouraged to call a toll-free phone number to report supervisors and other workers for breaking the law or company rules. The calls can be anonymous, or employees can give their names if the company is offering a reward for such information. The AlertLine Response Center is staffed 24-hours a day, seven days a week by trained "communications specialists" who take the tips, pass them on to the clients, and enter them into

political beliefs. As Donner saw it, "The selection of targets for surveillance, operations such as informer infiltration and wiretapping, and file storage practices reflect what may be called the politics of deferred reckoning, the need to know all about the enemy in preparation for a life or death showdown . . ."

4. *Ibid.*

Pinkerton's computerized database, where they can be analyzed for trends and compiled into statistical reports.[5]

Telephone tip lines have also been embraced by the government. Some police departments use them to solicit tips on criminal suspects, offering rewards of $1,000 or more for useful information. Regulatory agencies ask the public to report a broad range of offenders, from bad long haul truck drivers to corporate polluters. There are always new threats for the public to report.

But many employees dislike snitch lines. "They create an environment of mistrust," says Barbara Toffler, an industry consultant. The fundamental problem is that they are based on anonymous accusations, "which deny people what the legal system allows them: the ability to stand face-to-face with their accusers," she says.[6] Some employees also fear that a hotline operator may not really keep a confidence. After all, they work for the company.

Public agencies frequently contract with private companies to set up and run their surveillance systems, too. A good example is the "red light photo enforcement" program. The Federal Highway Administration created this program in the 1990s by declaring drivers who run red lights to be a major national problem. No one even questioned whether this was an appropriate issue of the federal government to pursue after the FHA issued a report which claimed that "red light runners" cause 1.8 million accidents and kill 7,800 people a year. To solve this crisis, the agency recommended that cities install automatic cameras at busy intersections to photograph such violators. As a result, police in 21 states were either using or studying such systems by July 2000.

The most widely-used automatic camera system was developed by Lockheed Martin, a major defense contractor. It uses a 60-pound Dutch-made Gatsos camera triggered by underground sensors. The 35-millimeter camera takes photos which clearly show the license plate numbers of the offending vehicles, along with the faces of the drivers. The numbers are checked against state motor vehicle records, with citations for hundreds of dollars mailed to the registered owners within about a week of the picture being taken.

Los Angeles was one of the first cities to contract with Lockheed Martin for the program. Cameras monitor over 50 intersections and railroad crossings in downtown L.A., West Hollywood, Beverly Hills, Oxnard, and in unincorporated areas of Los Angeles County. They cranked out 17,500 citations between January 1 and July 6, 2000. The actual number of pictures taken was much higher, however. Between one-half and two-thirds of the violators aren't pursued because their cars don't have front license plates, or because either the plates or drivers' faces are obscured.

Because this technology is relatively new, the number of cameras deployed around the country will dramatically increase in the coming years as more and

---

5. Author's interview with Heather Newman, program manager, Pinkerton Services Group, February 28, 2000.
6. Andrew W. Singer, "1-800-SNITCH," *Across the Board*, September 1995.

more police departments sign contracts with Lockheed Martin and other companies which operate them. "I suspect there will be a continued movement toward cities adding new cameras and other cities launching programs of their own," says Lockheed spokesman Terry Lynam. "I think it's safe to say we've only barely scratched the surface." [7]

Corporations are also compiling massive computer databases containing personal information on virtually everyone in the country. They are almost completely unregulated, and are routinely bought and sold among private businesses. Some of these databases are compiled by direct marketing companies, some by credit report companies, some by companies which collect the information simply to sell it to other companies. The Acxiom Corp. has files on over 130 million Americans. [8]

Banks are a major source of this information, receiving between 20 and 25 percent of the revenue it eventually generates, according to Julie Williams, chief counsel to the U.S. Comptroller of the Currency, which regulates the nation's banks. "Some banks have generated millions of dollars in revenue by providing third parties with information on millions of customers, including names and addresses, Social Security numbers, and credit card numbers," she says. [9]

A good example is U.S. Bankcorp, which got $4 million plus commissions for selling customer information to MemberWorks, a telemarketer of discount membership programs. The information included birth dates and "behavior scores," which indicate whether customers pay their bills on time. Some U.S. Bankcorp customers complained they were billed for MemberWorks services they never authorized. One 90-year-old woman was billed for a discount computer program, even though she didn't have a computer.

Banks are also major database customers. Over 85,000 banks subscribe to Check System, a privately owned company with a computer file on practically everyone who has ever bounced a check. Banks use such information when deciding whether to accept new customers. [10]

These databases have many other uses, too, including debt collection, a growing problem for the private sector. According to the Federal Reserve, Americans amassed $1.3 trillion in outstanding debt by early 1999, up 7 percent from the previous year. Software programs with names such as Sting, Optimizer and Determinator search the private databases to help find elusive debtors. The computers' "artificial intelligence" programs assess the chances that individual debtors will pay, and match them with appropriate collection agencies.

"Modern debt collectors look back with some nostalgia at the days when they worked from 4"× 6" index cards in shoeboxes," the *New York Times*

7. "It's a High-Impact Drama," *Los Angeles Times Magazine*, July 30, 2000.
8. Jack Whitsett, "Acxiom is Watching YOU, But it Says Privacy is Paramount," *Arkansas Times*, August 11, 2000.
9. Christine Dugas, "Banks Sell Your Secrets," *USA Today*, October 21, 1999.
10. "All Things Considered," National Public Radio, August 10, 2000.

reported. "Now computers dig through proprietary databases, find and dial numbers, determine when debtors are most likely to be home, improve the efficiency of telephone collection centers, calculate how risky a holder of a credit card or mortgage is and generate letters and scripts for phone callers. With some of these applications running, you can't hide." [11]

And a private company has come up with a system for using military satellites to track convicted criminals. Advanced Business Sciences, Inc. of Omaha developed ComTrak, a monitoring system using 24 Defense Department satellites orbiting 12,500 miles above the Earth to follow the exact movements of anyone wearing its electronic wrist bracelet and three-pound tracking unit. By early 1999, 100 convicts in nine states were being monitored by the system at a cost of $12.95 a day each. Company CEO Jack Lamb says growth potential is phenomenal, noting there are nearly 4 million people under some form of state supervision in the country. [12]

Private businesses are also starting to push "biometrics," the use of machines to identify people by their unique physical characteristics. The sci-fi staple is now part of everyday commerce, including iris scanning, fingerprints, voice prints, hand geometry, face geometry, and signature authentication.

Bank United, the largest financial institution in Texas, is the first company to use biometrics to identify its customers. The bank has built a centralized iris database which customers can use to access ATM machines. A camera mounted in the cash machine examines the iris, then checks its characteristics against earlier scans stored in Bank United's computers. Once the match is made, customers are free to get their cash.

Just a few years ago, biometrics was limited to the small number of government agencies and security firms that distrusted drivers licenses and had enough money to buy something else. But the technology is moving so rapidly that these systems are now becoming affordable to any business which needs—or simply wants—such ways to identify customers.

Although different systems rely on different body characteristics, they all work the same way. A camera or sensor digitalizes and encrypts a person's physical trait, creating a bar code-like file which is stored in a computer. The result is almost foolproof, since biometric programs are written to focus on traits which never change and cannot be copied or covered-up. For example, one finger-print recognition program uses nine separate measurements. IriScan, the company that developed the technology United Bank uses, measures 266 different characteristics of a person's iris, a membrane that never changes and can't be altered by glasses or colored contact lenses. IriScan brags its system is "better than DNA" because it can even distinguish between identical twins. [13]

---

11. Tina Kelley, "When Collection Software Runs, Debtors Can't Hide," *New York Times*, May 6, 1999.

12. Gary Fields, "Satellite 'Big Brother' Eyes Parolees," *USA Today*, April 8, 1999.

13. Guy Gugliotta, "Bar Codes for the Body Make It to the Market, Biometrics May Alter Consumer Landscape," *Washington Post*, June 21, 1999.

As these examples illustrate, the future of the Snitch Culture will be largely shaped by the private sector. Tomorrow's snitch programs and surveillance devices are currently being developed by corporations. Perhaps the most potentially invasive is a microchip which can be planted under the skin and tracked by the Global Positioning Satellites (GPS) circling the Earth.

On December 15, 1999, a private company called Applied Digital Solutions, Inc. announced that it had acquired the patent rights to a miniature digital transceiver which it dubbed Digital Angel. The system's power supply is unique. When implanted within a body, the device is powered electromechanically through the movement of muscles, and it can be activated either by the recipient or by the monitoring facility.

The company began seeking joint venture partners to develop and market the chip in May 2000. Pitching its product, the company said, "We expect to produce a prototype of the device by the end of 2000. We believe Digital Angel technology, in all of its applications, has a multi-billion dollar marketing potential. The Digital Angel transceiver can be implanted just under the skin or hidden inconspicuously on or within valuable personal belongings and priceless works of art. While a number of other tracking and monitoring technologies have been patented and marketed in the past, they are all unsuitable for the widespread tracking, recovery and identification of people due to a variety of limitations, including unwieldy size, maintenance requirements, insufficient or inconvenient power-supply and activation difficulties. For the first time in the history of location and monitoring technology, Digital Angel overcomes these limitations." [14]

Theoretically, if everyone is chipped at birth, Echelon will be able to track our movements from cradle to grave—or, given an external power source for the Digital Angel, even longer.

---

14. "Applied Digital Solutions Acquires Rights to World's First Digital Device Implantable in Humans—With Applications in E-business to Business Security, Health Care and Criminal Justice," *Business Wire*, December 15, 1999. In its release, *Business Wire* printed the following patent for the Digital Angel: "UNITED STATES PATENT 5,629,678 GARGANO, ET. AL., MAY 13, 1997: Personal tracking and recovery system Abstract: Apparatus for tracking and recovering humans utilizes an implantable transceiver incorporating a power supply and actuation system allowing the unit to remain implanted and functional for years without maintenance . . . The device is small enough to be implanted in a child, facilitating use as a safeguard against kidnapping, and has a transmission range which also makes it suitable for wilderness sporting activities. A novel biological monitoring feature allows the device to be used to facilitate prompt medical dispatch in the event of heart attack or similar medical emergency. A novel sensation-feedback feature allows the implantee to control and actuate the device with certainty."

CHAPTER SIX

UNCLE SAM WANTS YOU . . . TO SNITCH

DESPITE THE LONG INVOLVEMENT of the private sector in the Snitch Culture, government agencies can recruit many more informants and deploy far more sophisticated surveillance systems than even the largest corporations. The United States government has coercive powers and financial resources which far exceed those of the private sector, including the threat of imprisonment and death, and virtually unlimited money for rewards and the development of new technologies. Politicians from both parties have deliberately marshalled these powers and resources over the years until the government is now served by a steady stream of rats, snoops, and tattletales, with all their tips stored and catalogued for easy retrieval.

There have always been snitches in this country, of course. Some of the earliest ones sparked the infamous Salem Witch Trials of 1692 and 1693. When a group of young girls claimed to have been bewitched by a number of old widows, panic gripped the entire Massachusetts community. The number of accusers and accusations grew until the Puritan leaders tried, convicted and executed 14 women and six men, all on the basis of false stories and forced confessions.

As discussed in the previous chapter, federal, state and local governments first began developing intelligence-gathering programs to help big business owners fight off labor organizers in the late 19th Century. Significantly, the first nationwide surveillance efforts were tied to a war—World War I, when the federal government went after draft dodgers and peace activists. An estimated 50,000 political dissidents were identified and rounded up in so-called "slacker raids" throughout the war.

The government has been linking snitch programs to war ever since, even when the wars are actually domestic law enforcement campaigns, such as the War on Crime, the War on Drugs, and the War on Terrorism. Tying an unpopular activity to a popular cause is good propaganda, and one of the most effective tools for recruiting new informants and justifying more surveillance programs. The most common pitch appeals to the basic decency of the American people, convincing them that snitching is the right thing to do. This is the Civics 101 approach, arguing that good citizens have an obligation to report wrongdoers to the authorities. This message is repeatedly hammered home through public education campaigns, including the never-ending barrage of simpleminded anti-drug ads developed by the Partnership for a Drug Free America.

Sometimes the government requires people to snitch, whether they like it or not. Supported by media-fueled public hysteria over a generation of "crack babies," the federal government now requires doctors to report pregnant women who test positive for drugs to the police. Although this violates the confidential relationship which is supposed to exist between doctors and their patients, it serves the larger interests of the state.

But the government recruits most of its snitches the old-fashioned way, with bribes and threats.

Paying for incriminating information is a time-honored tradition. Law enforcement agencies have shelled out billions of dollars over the years for tips. Wanted posters have long offered rewards for information leading to the arrest and conviction of criminal suspects. But the sheer number of government agencies paying for dirt would surprise most people. They include virtually every agency with any law enforcement or regulatory authority, including the Bureau of Alcohol, Tobacco and Firearms, the Internal Revenue Service, the U.S. Customs Service, the U.S. Fish and Wildlife Service, the Secret Service, the Immigration and Naturalization Service, and many more.

The rewards vary tremendously, depending on the agency involved and the type of information sought. For example, the U.S. Customs Service once paid Fred Mendoza, a former Columbian emerald dealer, nearly $2 million for his help in Operation Casablanca, the department's largest money-laundering investigation. The payment to Mendoza included more than $1.7 million in commissions.[1]

Some of the most heavily-rewarded snitches in American history provided crucial testimony when the federal government was preparing its racketeering case against former Panamanian President Manuel Noriega. According to a May 1996 article in the *Pittsburgh Post-Gazette*, at least 20 members of drug cartels around the world received drastically reduced prison sentences—and were allowed to keep their drug money. One was Max Mermelstein, a Miami dealer who testified that Noriega had taken payoffs from the Medellin cartel in exchange for allowing smugglers to use his country as a refueling and transfer station for drug shipments. Despite admitting to smuggling 56 tons of cocaine worth $1.25 billion into this country, Mermelstein was released after serving only two years in a special protected witness unit and allowed to keep whatever drug money he had left.

Another important witness was Floyd Carlton Canceres, a former Panamanian military official and Noriega's pilot who admitted smuggling 1,000 kilograms of cocaine worth $25 million into this country. He faced life plus 145 years in prison until he agreed to help federal prosecutors. After he testified against his former boss, Canceres was released after only two years in protective custody. The government paid $211,681 for Canceres' living expenses, including the purchase of a car. The government also paid to move more than 20 members of his family from Panama to the United States, including a baby sitter.[2]

1. Tim Golden, "Informant's History Clouds Biggest Drug-Money Case," *New York Times,* April 29, 1999.
2. T.J. English, "The Wiseguy Next Door," *Playboy,* April 1991.

The federal government is also offering large rewards for information in terrorism cases. For example, Emad Salem, the main witness in the World Trade Center bombing trial, was paid more than $1 million for his help in that and several other cases. The FBI is offering $5 million for information leading to the arrest and conviction of Osama bin Laden, the exiled Saudi millionaire accused of financing an international terrorism network. He is suspected of masterminding the August 7, 1998 bombings of the U.S. embassies in Dar es Salaam, Tanzania, and Nairobi, Kenya.[3]

The biggest rewards are offered by the U.S. State Department as part of its Counter-Terrorism Rewards Program. Established by the 1984 Act to Combat International Terrorism, the program will pay up to $7 million for "information preventing acts of international terrorism against United States persons or property, or leading to the arrest or conviction of terrorist criminals responsible for such acts."

The State Department promotes the reward program and solicits tips with an ongoing public awareness campaign. Advertisements in English, Arabic, Spanish, French, German, and Russian have appeared in publications as diverse as the *New York Times*, *Al Hayat*, *Paris Match*, *Die Welt* and *Pravda*. Public service announcements featuring actors Charlton Heston, Charles Bronson and Charlie Sheen have been widely distributed. In his spot, Heston says, "Real life heroes are ordinary people who do extraordinary things for their fellow man—like warning of acts of political violence that could endanger innocent lives!"[4]

Such rewards are not always paid with tax dollars. The federal government has long allowed informants to keep a percentage of the money and property they helped recover under so-called asset forfeiture laws. But Congress greatly expanded the use of asset forfeiture programs in the Comprehensive Crime Control Act of 1984, which cleared the way for the police agencies themselves to keep the money and property of all accused criminals, especially suspected drug dealers. The agencies can bank most or all of the cash, then sell the remaining property and keep that money, too.

 As a result of this law, a mere accusation—even a false one—can cost you everything you own, even if you are innocent. "Hearsay evidence is all that is required: A mere rumor or scrap of gossip can justify government seizure of a person's most valuable belongings," says journalist James Bovard. "If the citizen wants his property back, he must sue the government and prove in court that his property is 'innocent'; the government has no burden of proof. The citizen also must post a bond equal to 10 percent of the property's value (to cover the government's costs in defending itself against his lawsuit) and file a notice within 20 days of the seizure. (Law enforcement agencies sometimes fail to formally notify the citizen of the seizure until after the deadline for such filings.)

---

3. Jack Kelly, "Afghanistan Refuses to Turn in Bin Laden," *USA Today*, November 12, 1999.
4. Press release, Counter-Terrorism Rewards Program, Bureau of Diplomatic Security, United States Department of State.

Legal costs for suing the government to recover one's property can easily exceed $5,000. Thus, if the government seizes only a small wad of cash or an old car, the citizen cannot possibly break even by suing to recover his property. Even if he wins in court and recovers his property, there is no provision for reimbursement of his attorney costs. A federal appeals court complained in 1992, 'We continue to be enormously troubled by the government's increasing and virtually unchecked use of the civil forfeiture statutes and the disregard for due process that is buried in those statutes.'" [5]

The amount of money generated under asset forfeiture laws is fantastic. The federal government reports raking in around $1 billion a year, but the actual take is probably double that. As of June 2000, the Justice Department had not published an annual forfeiture report since 1996, even though federal law requires them to produce one each year. A few spot audits have found current federal estimates to be around 50 percent low. (For more information, see Case Study Five: The Asset Forfeiture Money Machine.)

These reward figures don't even include the thousands of state and local agencies which dole out cash to solve crimes in their jurisdictions. The success of the expanded federal asset forfeiture laws has prompted most states to enact similar programs in recent years, generating millions of additional dollars for snitches. In addition, a number of private, non-profit agencies also help raise reward funds for state and local police. The largest is Crime Stoppers International, founded in 1976 by a detective in Albuquerque, New Mexico. The organization currently has roughly 1,000 chapters chartered around the world, all of which operate through boards of directors consisting primarily of local business owners.

All CSI-chartered boards raise money for reward funds in their areas. The police identify a number of unsolved crimes, then send out press releases saying that CSI is offering rewards of up to $1,000 for tips that result in an arrest. The local media usually cooperates with the program, publicizing the crimes and the rewards. Tips are called into a special phone line, where informants are given a code number to protect their identities. If someone is arrested and the informant calls back with the correct code number, the police arrange to give him the reward in the presence of a local CSI board member.

CSI has also approved chapters at various high schools around the country that operate under the name Scholastic Crime Stoppers. These programs offer rewards to students who snitch on fellow students. The largest rewards are paid for information about students who commit crimes, both on and off campus. Rewards are also paid for information about students who break school rules. A high school principal in Salem, Oregon estimates he's paid out $3,000 for tips between 1995 and 1999. "Some kids and parents say, you're running the place like a jail. But most kids know they are safe," says Rey Mayoral, principal of McKay High School. [6]

5. James Bovard, *Freedom in Chains*, St. Martins Press, 1999.
6. Steve Carter, "Safety: Behavior Once Seen as a Joke No Longer Funny," *Oregonian*, April 25, 1999.

While it is impossible to accurately estimate the amount of rewards being paid out by every agency, the figure clearly runs into the billions of dollars, and the number is increasing every year. Total federal spending on informants quadrupled to $97 million between 1985 and 1993.[7] From 1987 and 1995, the DEA's informant rewards increased from $20 million to $31.7 million, while the U.S. Customs Service more than doubled what it spent on informants during the same period: from $8.1 to $16.5 million. A senior Justice Department official estimated that thousands of people were working as full-time informants in the country by 1995.[8]

But snitches who are offered money for their information are the lucky ones. Many informants today are all but forced into testifying to escape lengthy prison sentences themselves. Although such plea bargains have always been part of the American criminal justice system, Congress and most state legislatures have passed a number of laws over the past few decades to increase the pressure on suspects to rat out their friends and associates.

One of the biggest hammers is the federal Racketeering Influenced and Corrupt Organizations law, commonly known as RICO. Under this law, everyone involved in a criminal conspiracy can be charged with the most serious crime committed by any other member of the conspiracy. According to Harvard Law Professor Alan Dershowitz, RICO almost forces suspects to cooperate with prosecutors. "RICO is such an atomic bomb that people threatened with the RICO statute have no choice but to cooperate," Dershowitz says. "I've seen it in my own clients. I've had clients come and say to me, foolishly of course, 'What does the government want me to say? Just write out the script; I'll say it. Who's the government interested in? I'll tell them.' Once people become cooperators, they become cooperators with a vengeance. I've seen my clients try to make up stories." [9]

Even more pressure can be applied on reluctant informants by the mandatory minimum sentencing laws enacted by Congress and the states over the past two decades, in reaction to the popular perception that liberal judges were letting dangerous criminals go with mere slaps on the wrists. Under these laws, judges have no choice but to impose lengthy sentences on anyone convicted of crimes ranging from simple assault to drug possession to armed robbery and murder. Congress specifically targeted crack cocaine in the Comprehensive Crime Control Act of 1986, mandating sentences of 20 years to life for possessing even a small quantity of the drug, and now thousands of people are currently serving such lengthy sentences. The only way to receive a lesser sentence under these laws is to provide "substantial assistance" to help the government arrest other criminal suspects—in other words, to fink.

One of the men who helped write the law now says it was "the greatest tragedy of my professional life." Eric E. Sterling was counsel to the U.S. House

---

7. Adam Langer, "Thanks for a Nation of Snitches," *Mother Jones*, May 1995.

8. Peter Katell, "The Trouble With Informants," *Newsweek*, January 30, 1995.

9. Mark Curriden, "No Honor Among Thieves," *ABA Journal*, June 1989.

Committee on the Judiciary from 1979 to 1989. By 1999, he had left his congressional job and become president of the Criminal Justice Policy Foundation, a Washington, DC-based think tank.

Sterling discussed his regrets in a 1999 documentary on informants produced by the Public Broadcasting System called *Snitch*. The production, which included additional information on the PBS Internet website, featured an interview where Sterling talked about the harm caused by minimum mandatory sentences. "There [have] been . . . literally thousands of instances of injustice where minor co-conspirators in cases, the lowest level participants, have been given the sentences that Congress intended for the highest kingpins. Families are wrecked, children are orphaned, the taxpayers are paying a fortune for excessive punishment. You know there's nothing conservative about punishing people too much. That's an excess. And it's just a waste. It is such a waste of human life. It's awful."

Sterling said he was shocked to realize that people are being convicted under these laws without any physical evidence. "There don't have to be drugs. All there have to be are witnesses who say, 'I saw the drugs,' or, 'He said there were drugs.' That's what you need." [10]

The result has been a rush to snitch.

"There used to be a considerable amount of pressure not to inform," says John Irwin, a San Francisco State University Sociology professor who studies informants. "The stigma of being an informant was very damaging and even life-threatening. But over the years, that has slowly diminished.

"There are new ethics like 'It's a dog-eat-dog world' and 'Every person for himself,'" he adds. "Basically, there is no honor among thieves." [11]

Of course, these recruitment techniques are not limited to specific crimes. RICO laws aren't only employed against the Mafia. Plea bargains aren't only struck in drug cases. Cash rewards aren't limited to tips on terrorism. Police and prosecutors are free to use all these tricks in every case. And as the number of agencies increases, the number of snitches at work in the country continues to grow.

---

10. Eric Sterling's interview is included on an Internet website maintained by the *Frontline* show on snitches <http://www.pbs.org/wgbh/pages/frontline/shows/snitch/>.

11. Mark Curriden, "No Honor Among Thieves," *ABA Journal*, June 1989.

CHAPTER SEVEN
THE FEDERAL INTELLIGENCE INFRASTRUCTURE

THERE IS NO WAR ON CRIME. There is no War on Drugs. There is no War on Terrorism. There is no War on Youth Violence. There is only the ongoing effort by the federal government to collect as much information on as many people as possible. Domestic law enforcement initiatives are merely excuses to increase the amount of spying on the American people.

Sometimes the government has legitimate reasons for its intelligence-gathering operations, such as preventing sabotage during World War I and II. Sometimes the reasons are bogus, such as the now-discredited fear of a generation of brain-damaged "crack babies." Sometimes the surveillance programs are driven by a handful of strong personalities, such as anti-Communist witch hunter J. Edgar Hoover. Sometimes the programs are in response to a genuine outcry, such as the public reaction to Columbine.

As documented in *The Age of Surveillance*, the government traditionally uses the potential threat posed by a small number of people as an excuse to track large segments of the population.[1] A good example is the internment of Japanese-Americans after Pearl Harbor. Another is the limited number of violent anti-Vietnam War protesters who were repeatedly cited to justify spying on the entire peace movement. More recently, the relative handful of anarchists who break windows are being used to rationalize government surveillance of the entire anti-corporate globalization movement.

Informants have played critical roles in all these efforts, frequently providing incomplete, misleading, and outright false information on law-abiding citizens to a broad range of police agencies. The American people have occasionally been repulsed by the spectacle of the government forcing friends to betray each other in public. But the Snitch Culture continues to grow, with no end in sight.

By the end of the 20th Century, the excuses for expanding the surveillance society had fallen into a predictable pattern. Three primary threats were repeatedly cited as reasons for increasing the spying: organized crime, drugs and terrorism. Although the categories stay the same, the specific dangers change with the seasons. In recent years, the American Mafia has given way to the Russian Mafia, crack cocaine has been upstaged by Ecstasy, and Far Right militias have been replaced by left-wing anarchists.

---

1. Frank Donner, *The Age of Surveillance: The Aims & Methods of America's Political Intelligence System*, New York: Alfred Knopf, 1980.

When did the federal government first begin viewing the American people as a threat? Immediately after winning the Revolutionary War, when returning Continental Army soldiers balked at paying the high taxes imposed by the states to pay off the cost of defeating the British.[2] Especially hard hit were the farmers in rural Massachusetts, who already owed money to merchants—money the merchants were also demanding. The Massachusetts Legislature, dominated by the merchants, refused to help the citizens who had fought so hard to create the new country. Instead, state courts began handing down a growing number of foreclosures. Mobs of poor farmers began rioting. Tax collectors were routinely threatened and attacked.

The violence escalated into a full-scale uprising in 1786. Led by Daniel Shay, a highly-regarded Revolutionary War captain, hundreds of farmers and others took up arms and shut down the courts in Springfield. The rebellion was eventually crushed by the new state government, but only after a series of battles throughout rural Massachusetts.

Shortly after the end of "Shay's Rebellion," farmers in western Pennsylvania resorted to violence to protest taxes on liquor. The taxes required distillers to pay the government for every gallon of liquor they sold. Many farmers responded by attacking both federal revenue officers and distillers who voluntarily paid the tax.

The uprising took on the proportions of an organized revolt in 1791—the so-called "Whiskey Rebellion." At least one unfortunate tax inspector was taken out of his house, tarred and feathered, and tied to a tree. The federal government eventually ordered the governors of four states to call up 13,000 militia members to suppress the uprising. Many Revolutionary War veterans refused, however, and when conscription was put into effect, riots broke out. A substantial army was eventually put into the field, and the rebellion was crushed.

Congress sought to discourage further uprising by enacting the Alien and Sedition Acts in 1798. Passed under the guise of fighting French "subversion," they essentially made it illegal to criticize the government. At least 25 people were arrested under these laws, with 15 indicted and 10 convicted. But it took many years for the federal government to mount the first serious national surveillance programs. Under the concept of "federalism" embodied in the U.S. Constitution, the national government initially thought its powers were limited to regulating interstate commerce, with all other law enforcement powers reserved to the states. That's why President Abraham Lincoln retained private detective Allan Pinkerton to provide intelligence about the South during the Civil War. No federal employees had any such field experience.

The United States government did not even begin investigating violations of federal laws until the early 1870s, and even then the U.S. Department of Justice had to hire private investigators to do the work. It would take another 30 years before the Secret Service gained enough expertise to run its own investigations.

2. Jim Redden, "A Brief History of Terrorism in America," *PDXS*, August 9, 1996.

Theodore Roosevelt was the first President who believed the federal govern-ment could—and should—play a large national law enforcement role. In 1908, he and Attorney General Charles Bonaparte created the forerunner of the FBI. Ten former Secret Service employees and a number of Department of Justice investigators became Special Agents of the Department of Justice. In March 1909, Attorney General George Wickersham, Bonaparte's successor, named the force the Bureau of Investigation (BOI).

When the BOI was first established, there were few federal laws with criminal penalties. As a result, the agency was limited to investigating violations of banking, naturalization and land fraud statutes. The first major expansion in the Bureau's jurisdiction came in June 1910, when Congress passed the Mann Act. Also called the "White Slave Act," the law made it a crime to transport women over state lines for immoral purposes. The Mann Act allowed the federal government to investigate criminals who eluded state and local authorities, but who had not violated any other federal laws.

The BOI continued to grow over the next few decades, with field offices controlled by a Special Agent in Charge opening in major cities across the country. However, Prohibition proved the federal government was not up to the challenge of fighting serious criminal organizations. In December 1917, responding to the national temperance movement, Congress passed the Webb Resolution prohibiting the manufacture and sale of alcohol. When the 36th state ratified the resolution in January 1919, it became the 18th Amendment to the Con-stitution. Congress passed the Volstad Act to enforce Prohibition in October 1919 over President Wilson's veto.

The result was a law enforcement fiasco. Large segments of the public still wanted booze, and well-organized gangs stepped forward to fill the demand. Liquor was manufactured by moonshiners and other illegal distillers, or hauled in from other countries, such as Canada, where it was legal. Speakeasys popped up everywhere, serviced by mobs running truckloads of alcohol from state to state. Responsibility for fighting the new crime syndicates was scattered between several different federal agencies, including the BOI, Department of the Treasury, and the IRS. Despite the popular image of Elliot Ness and his crew of Treasury Department Untouchables mowing down mobsters with their tommy guns, the government lost almost all the battles and finally the war. Prohibition was repealed in 1933.

This defeat did not cause the federal government to pull back, however. In fact, the earliest components of the national surveillance system were already coming together. The Great Depression which began with the stock market crash of 1929 brought poverty to millions of Americans—and created a new generation of desperate criminals. Armed robberies skyrocketed, with banks being primary targets. To combat the crime wave, President Franklin D. Roosevelt persuaded Congress to expand federal jurisdiction into crimes traditionally fought by state and local governments. In 1932, Congress passed a federal kidnapping statute. Then in May and June 1934, with gangsters such as Bonnie and Clyde escaping punishment by running from state to state, it greatly expanded the federal government's jurisdiction. In 1935, Congress changed the name of the Bureau of Investigation to the Federal Bureau of Investigation. By 1936, many of the country's most notorious gangsters were either in jail or dead. Informants played key roles in helping the FBI track them down.

Much of this is directly attributable to one man, a young George Washington University Law School graduate who first came to work for the U.S. Department of Justice's alien registration division in 1917. By 1924, he had been appointed to head the BOI. His name was J. Edgar Hoover.

Hoover is best remembered for his fanatical obsession with Communists. But the investigative techniques he pioneered at the FBI are more important to the growth of the Snitch Culture than the exact people and organizations he targeted. More than anything else, Hoover understood the value of using the American people as informants. In remarks prepared for the Attorney General in 1925, he wrote, "The Agents of the Bureau of Investigation have been impressed with the fact that the real problem of law enforcement is in trying to obtain the cooperation and sympathy of the public and that they cannot hope to get such cooperation until they themselves merit the respect of the public." [3]

As FBI director, Hoover would not allow his agents to personally infiltrate suspected Communist organizations. He was afraid the subversives would "turn" the agents and use them to gather information on the bureau. So Hoover recruited state and local cops as undercover operatives, establishing a critical working relationship between the FBI and the police which still exists today.

Another federal official who understood the importance of working with the police was Harry Anslinger, the nation's first Drug Czar. After being appointed to head the newly-created Federal Bureau of Narcotics in 1930, Anslinger embarked on a public relations campaign to outlaw marijuana, a weed which grew freely throughout Mexico and the Southwestern states. Although the federal government did not have the power to make marijuana illegal, Anslinger came up with a clever idea. He accomplished the same thing by persuading the legislatures in all 50 states to enact the federally-written Uniform Narcotic Act in the late 1930s.[4]

---

3. This quote and much of the other material in this chapter is taken from the 1976 *Final Report of the Special Committee to Study Government Operations With Respect to Intelligence Activities of the United States Senate*, one of the most complete sources on the history of federal domestic surveillance. Chaired by U.S. Senator Frank Church, the committee was appointed after news reports on the FBI's Counter-Intelligence Program were published. The Church Committee investigated far more than the COINTELPRO operations, however, releasing a three-volume report in the Summer of 1976 which documented the origins and growth of an even broader range of surveillance programs. Officially designated Report No. 94-755, it is available from The Superintendent of Documents, U.S. Government Printing Office, Washington, DC 20402.

4. The film *Grass* by director Ron Mann (Unapix, 2000) documents the remarkable career of Harry Anslinger. Like J. Edgar Hoover, Anslinger's single-minded obsession with marijuana shaped this nation's early anti-drug laws, laying the groundwork for the

But the government campaigns against subversives and marijuana would soon give way to a far more serious menace, the growing military power of Nazi Germany. As Adolph Hitler began mobilizing his forces to conquer Europe in 1934, President Franklin Roosevelt asked the FBI to investigate "the Nazi movement in the country." The agency responded by trying to identify any "anti-racial" and "anti-American" activities which had any "possible connection with official representatives of the German government in the United States," with the German-American Bund political party in California coming under special scrutiny. It also gathered information on the Christian Front and the Christian Mobilizers (followers of conservative Father Charles Coughlin), the American Destiny Party, the American Nationalist Party, and the protectionist America First movement.

Two years later, in August 1936, Roosevelt asked Hoover for a more systematic collection of information about "subversive activities in the United States, particularly Fascism and Communism." According to an internal FBI memo from Hoover, by 1938 the FBI was looking for subversive influences in the following fields: the maritime industry; the steel industry; the coal industry; the clothing, garment and fur industries; the automobile industry; the newspaper field; educa-tional institutions; organized labor organizations; Negroes; youth groups; govern-ment affairs; and the armed forces.

When World War II broke out in Europe in 1939, the New York City Police Department formed a special sabotage squad of 50 detectives to root out potential Axis terrorists. President Franklin Roosevelt responded by issuing an Executive Order making sabotage a matter of federal concern. Although President Wilson issued a similar directive in World War I, Roosevelt officially ordered all state and local law enforcement agencies to provide such information to the FBI, formalizing the early stages of the national surveillance network.[5]

Many of the investigations concerned people who were merely exercising their First Amendment rights. Supporting the Bill of Rights was even suspect. One 1941 FBI report focused on a New York group called the League for Fair Play, noting, "the organization was formed in 1937, apparently by two Ministers and a businessman for the purpose of furthering fair play, tolerance, adherence to the Constitution, democracy, liberty, justice, understanding and good will among all creeds, races and classes of the United States."

With the specter of war on the horizon, the FBI turned to its favorite weapon —snitches. The agency created the Plant Informant Program in 1940 to gather information on potential saboteurs in defense facilities. Working with a list of defense plants provided by the Army and Navy, the FBI recruited 23,746 confidential sources in 3,879 facilities by 1942. The FBI also created the American Legion Contact Program in 1940. Approved by the U.S. Attorney General and the national office of the American Legion, the program used local Legion posts to investigate and report incidents of suspected espionage and subversive activity.

---

government's costly War on Drugs. As noted in the film, the government spent $220 million fighting marijuana between 1937 and 1947. The total had grown to nearly $215 billion between 1980 and 1999.

5. Church Committee Report, U.S. Government Printing Office, 1976.

The FBI also recruited informants at colleges and universities, including students, teachers and school officials. These snitches were instructed to look for subversive professors and student organizations which opposed government policies, including involvement in the war.

One of the most important developments in the growth of the Snitch Culture occurred when Congress passed the National Security Act of 1947, creating the Central Intelligence Agency and the National Security Council. President Harry Truman authorized the NSC to create the National Security Agency to run the government's most advanced intelligence-gathering operations. Hoover quickly recruited the NSC for a renewed anti-Communist witch hunt, using the agency's cryptanalysts to crack an alleged Soviet nuclear spy ring. The NSC-generated evidence helped Hoover convince the Justice Depart-ment to indict Julius and Ethel Rosenberg on treason charges. Their arrests helped fuel the Red Scare that would dominate domestic politics for most of the 1950s. The hysteria did not subside until well after thousands of innocent people were ruined. (See Case Study One: McCarthyism, for more details.)

Another significant development in the creation of the Snitch Culture occurred in 1957, when the federal government was forced to admit the exis-tence of La Cosa Nostra, the American Mafia. Although Hoover had long denied the existence of such organized crime families, all that changed in 1957 when the New York State Police received a tip that many of the top mob leaders were planning to meet in their state. Working together, the police and FBI infiltrated the gathering, generating the proof that the Mafia was real.

But the federal government did not formally take on the mob until President John F. Kennedy appointed his brother Robert as U.S. Attorney General in 1961. The next year, convicted mob hitman Joseph Valachi testified before Congress about his life in the Mafia. Congress seized upon the revelation to pass new anti-racketeering and gambling laws. It also funded the Witness Protection Program, which has been used to help recruit thousands of snitches over the years.[6]

President Kennedy didn't live long enough to contribute much to the Snitch Culture, but his successor, Lyndon Johnson, more than made up for that. Along with Pinkerton and Hoover, Johnson is one of the major architects of the modern surveillance society. Although frequently praised for pushing the first federal civil rights laws through Congress, Johnson also created programs which violated the rights of millions of Americans of all races. Within the first few years of his administration, he created the basic structure of today's domestic surveillance systems.

One important decision was the creation of a single agency to enforce federal drug laws. When Johnson first took office in 1963, the Treasury Depart-ment and the Food and Drug Administration were both charged with cracking down on illegal narcotics. Johnson consolidated these responsibilities in the new Bureau of Narcotics and Dangerous Drugs (BNDD), placing it directly

6. T.J. English, "The Wiseguy Next Door," *Playboy*, April 1991.

under U.S. Attorney General Ramsay Clark. The BNDD eventually became today's U.S. Drug Enforcement Administration, and it paved the way for the cabinet-level Office of National Drug Control Policy.

Another important decision was the formation of the Law Enforcement Assistance Administration, the federal agency which has provided billions of dollars worth of high-tech computers, paramilitary equipment, and financial assistance to state and local law enforcement agencies over the last three decades. This funding allowed the federal government to shape and direct the activities of local police agencies across the country. Much of the money has gone to create the Regional Information Sharing Systems (RISS) computer network. Every President since Johnson has followed his lead and increased the federal funding of state and local police departments.[7]

The RISS computer network was originally sold to the public as helping law enforcement agencies collect, store and swap data on criminals. But in fact, the system is also used to monitor political dissidents, including many who have never broken the law. As *CovertAction Quarterly* reported, "Officially, RISS projects concentrate on drug and organized crime activities, but since Criminal Intelligence units are used in many jurisdictions to surveil political suspects as well, their personnel also have access to information that RISS systems store. RISS documents and regulations make clear that its databases are used to exchange data about politically-motivated crimes."[8]

But Johnson's most significant contribution to the surveillance society came as a direct result of his first crisis, the series of urban riots which erupted in major American cities in 1965 and 1966. The inner city turmoil caught law enforcement agencies by surprise, raising the specter of a violent African-American uprising. Johnson responded in 1967 by authorizing a massive domestic intelligence operation called the Ghetto Informant Program. It assumed the urban riots of the previous summers were started by a small handful of militants and outside agitators. The FBI planned to identify these troublemakers by planting informants throughout inner city neighborhoods.[9]

The alleged outside-agitator conspiracy is spelled out in a September 1967 memo from U.S. Attorney General Ramsey Clark to Hoover calling for a full investigation into the potential for further disturbances: "There persists . . . a widespread belief that there is more organized activity in the riots than we presently know about. We must recognize, I believe, that this is a relatively new area of investigation and intelligence reporting for the FBI and the Department of Justice. We have not heretofore had to deal with the possibility of an organized pattern of violence, constituting a violation of federal law, by a group of persons who make the urban ghetto their base of operation and whose activities may not have been regularly monitored by existing intelligence sources . . ."[10]

---

7. Christian Parenti, *Lockdown America: Police and Prisons in the Age of Crisis*, Verso, 1999.
8. Mitzi Waltz, "Policing Activism: Think Global, Spy Local," *CovertAction Quarterly*, Summer 1997.
9. Church Committee Report, U.S. Government Printing Office, 1976.
10. *Ibid.*

In announcing the program to FBI field offices, Hoover stated "it is imperative and essential that the Bureau learn of any indications of advance planning or organized conspiracy on the part of individuals or organizations in connection with riots and civil disturbances." Many of the snitches recruited into the program were barbers, grocers and other other small business owners designated as "listening posts" by the FBI. According to government figures, the number of informants rose throughout the course of the program from 4,067 in 1969 to 7,402 in 1972.

Once again, much of the grunt work was done by state and local police departments. In the wake of the riots, Justice Department officials became alarmed that the police were caught unprepared. A report complained there was also no "useful intelligence or knowledge about ghettos, about black communities in the big cities." Johnson responded by creating the President's Commission on Law Enforcement and Administration of Justice, which urged state and local officials to make advance plans for "a true riot situation." In a report titled "The Challenge of Crime in a Free Society," the commission explained this means the police should establish "procedures for the acquisition and channeling of intelligence" for the use of "those who need it."

This message was reiterated during the winter of 1967–1968 by the Justice Department and the National Advisory Commission on Civil Disorders, which directed local police to establish "intelligence units" to gather and disseminate information on "potential" civil disorders. These units would use "undercover police personnel and informants" and draw on "community leaders, agencies and organizations in the ghetto." The Commission also urged that these local intelligence units be linked to "a national center and clearinghouse" in the Justice Department. By 1969, Hoover was instructing FBI field offices that one way to obtain intelligence on "situations having a potential for violence" was to develop "in-depth liaison with local law enforcement agencies."

The Ghetto Informant Program provided the FBI with reams of information on civil rights leaders, anti-poverty programs, and the reading habits of the nation's inner city residents. A 1972 memo from the Philadelphia Field Office to FBI special agents listed the following assignment as suitable for ghetto informants: "Visit Afro-American-type bookstores for the purpose of determining if militant extremist literature is available therein and, if so, to identify the owners, operators and clientele of such stores."

Although the Ghetto Informant Program ended in 1972, it cleared the way for Johnson to authorize a series of similar operations as the peace and civil rights movements grew throughout the 1960s. Some of these operations had been started by the FBI under previous Presidents, but Johnson expanded them and approved new ones to track the full range of political dissidents, including peace activists, black militants, and white supremacists. These are the infamous Counter-Intelligence Programs, commonly called COINTELPRO. Government operatives not only spied on political activists under these operations, they frequently set them up on criminal charges, and even killed them.

(For more details, see Case Study Two: COINTELPRO Abuses.)

President Richard Nixon continued expanding the COINTELPRO operations after taking office in 1968. Congress supported these programs, arguing that the country was under attack from left-wing revolutionaries.

Once again, state and local police did much of the COINTELPRO leg work. Police departments across the country sent out infiltrators and opened files on suspected radicals, including local chapters of such legal organizations as the ACLU, the National Lawyers Guild, and the NAACP. Police intelligence units infiltrated student, peace and civil rights organizations, funneling much of the information gathered by these snitches to the FBI. In some cities, local police departments also worked with private organizations to track and harass alleged subversives. The Chicago police fed the names of liberal activists to an ultra-conservative group called the Legion of Justice, which tracked them down and beat them up. The Detroit police used a private organization called Operation Breakthrough for a similar purpose. In Houston, the police colluded with the Secret Army Organization.[11]

Much of the information collected during these years was wrong. A state grand jury in Illinois issued a report in 1975 criticizing the Security Section of the Chicago Police Department. The report described the section's "close working relationship" with federal agencies, including the FBI and Army intelligence. It found the police produced "inherently inaccurate and distortive data" which contaminated the federal intelligence. For example, one Chicago police officer told the grand jury that he listed "any person" who attended two "public meetings" of a group as a "member." This conclusion was forwarded "as a fact" to the FBI. Subsequently, any potential employer or law enforcement agency seeking "background information" on that person from the FBI would be told that the individual was "a member" of the group under investigation.

As the grand jury report put it, "Since federal agencies accepted data from the Security Section without questioning the procedures followed or methods used to gain information, the federal government cannot escape responsibility for the harm done to untold numbers of innocent persons."[12]

Nixon also announced a War on Crime which served as another premise for increasing federal assistance. Much of the money went to train local police to recruit more drug snitches and conduct bigger drug raids. Under the Nixon Administration, possession of a single ounce of marijuana could, and did, result in 50-year prison sentences. Nixon also divided the nation into a number of administrative regions to help dole out the cash and goodies, cementing the relationship between Washington, DC and the states begun by Johnson. This funding structure is still in place today.

Ironically, Nixon was finally brought down by snitches. A blown political intelligence-gathering operation led to Watergate. After successfully stonewalling

11. Chip Berlet, "Hunt for Red Menace: How the FBI, and Right-wing Spies, Use Paranoid Nativist Conspiracy Theories to Sustain an Authoritarian Domestic Counter-subversion," Political Research Associates, May 1, 1987 (revised October 4, 1991).
12. Church Committee Report, U.S. Government Printing Office, 1976.

Congress for months, Nixon was forced to resign when White House lawyer John Dean and other federal employees turned on him before the joint Congressional Watergate Committee. The scandal prompted Congress to pass the Privacy Act of 1974, an attempt to stop the FBI from spying on Americans because of their political beliefs. The next year, the U.S. Senate created a special committee to look into the COINTELPRO operations. Although this investigation did not receive nearly as much press coverage as the Watergate hearings, it prompted the Department of Justice to issue new guidelines further restricting the FBI's surveillance operations.

Fallout from Watergate also forced state and local cops to curtail their political spying. Many state legislatures passed laws prohibiting the police from monitoring people because of their political beliefs. Some large cities passed similar ordinances. Liberal activists used them to shut down various police Red Squads. For example, the Southern California chapter of the ACLU filed a number of lawsuits against the Los Angeles Police Department over illegal political surveillance in the early 1980s. In 1984, it won a $1.8 million settlement from the city on behalf of 144 mostly left-wing political organizations. The San Francisco Police Department was caught spying on nearly 100 liberal groups in the weeks and months leading up to the 1984 Democratic National Convention, including the ACLU and the National Lawyers Guild. After several years of controversy, the City Council held a series of public hearings on the scandal in 1989 and 1990, then adopted a set of guidelines designed to prevent such abuses in the future. The council also directed the SFPD to destroy all existing files which did not include allegations of criminal activity.[13]

The local spying never completely stopped, however. Before and during the 1996 Democratic National Convention in Chicago, state and local police departments infiltrated Active Resistance, a "counter-convention" organized by a coalition of left-wing organizations. This happened despite the fact that the Chicago police signed a consent decree in 1981 agreeing to stop spying on political activists who are not engaged in criminal activity, or from using *agent provocateurs* to justify such spying. "There were a half-dozen groups that were interfered with very severely," says Emile Schepers, program director for the Chicago Committee to Defend the Bill of Rights. "They were not only put under illegal surveillance, they had their space invaded by the police without a warrant, they were told that they were seditious, and they had documents, tapes and other items taken by the police."[14]

These reforms did not stop the growth of the Snitch Culture on the federal level, either. To the contrary, the FBI quickly figured ways around the restrictions. Among other things, the agencies began working with a handful of private, politically-oriented advocacy groups which maintained their own intelligence networks. As explained in the following chapter, two of the most

---

13. Mitzi Waltz, "Policing Activism: Think Global, Spy Local," *CovertAction Quarterly*, Summer 1997.
14. *Ibid.*

influential ones in recent years are the Anti-Defamation League and the Southern Poverty Law Center, two non-profit civil rights organizations.

Even the Justice Department guidelines have been gutted over the years. Officially known as "The Attorney General's Guidelines on General Crimes, Racketeering Enterprise and Domestic Security/Terrorism Investigations," they were first loosened by Attorney General William Webster in 1980. At the time, Webster said the new guidelines would allow informants to participate in murders, as long as they don't personally kill anyone.[15] They were loosened again in 1983, and once more in 1989. By early 1995, the Center for National Security Studies was complaining the guidelines were all but meaningless. In an April 26, 1995 memo, the Washington, DC think tank said, "The Bureau can begin investigating when it receives any information of allegation 'whose responsible handling requires some further scrutiny." [16]

But that wasn't good enough for FBI Director Louis Freeh, who expanded them once again in May 1995. Speaking before a U.S. Senate committee, he complained that "for two decades, the FBI has been at an extreme disadvantage with regard to domestic groups which advocate violence." Freeh's solution? "If those guidelines are interpreted broadly and proactively, as opposed to defensively, as has been the case for many, many years, I feel confident . . . we have sufficient authority." [17]

---

15. Clifford S. Zimmerman, "Toward a New Vision of Informants: A History of Abuses and Suggestions for Reform," *Hastings Constitutional Law Quarterly*, Fall 1994.

16. In his book *EcoTerror* (Merril Press, 1997), Ron Arnold includes a good summary of the limited standards the FBI must meet before investigating political dissidents:

    1. USE OF VIOLENCE. The suspected group must simply endorse "activities that involve force or violence." Under the guidelines, the violence does not have to actually occur, but it is necessary that the suspected group endorse activities that involve force or violence.

    2. POLITICAL MOTIVATION. The 1983 Guidelines combined criminal enterprises and terrorism in the same set of directives. Thus, a criminal investigation may be started before a political motive is discovered. If a political motivation is found, investigators proceed under the guidelines' Domestic Security/Terrorism subsection rather than their Racketeering subsection. This makes a big difference in the investigation. Terrorism investigations may remain open even if a group "has not engaged in recent acts of violence, nor is there any immediate threat of harm—yet the composition, goals and prior history of the group suggests the need for continuing federal interest."

    3. FOCUS ON GROUPS. Terrorism investigations are "concerned with the investigation of entire enterprises, rather than individual participants." A terrorism investigation may not be initiated unless "circumstances indicate that two or more persons are engaged in an enterprise for the purpose of furthering political or social goals . . . that involve force or violence and a violation of the criminal laws of the United States." In practice, the FBI concentrates on organizers and leaders—the "brains." Destroying the organization that spawns violence is more effective than merely convicting terrorists that happen to get caught committing a crime. The idea is to "decapitate" the leadership of terrorist organizations for "early interdiction of unlawful violent activity."

17. William Safire, "Beware of 'Proactive,'" *New York Times*, May 8, 1995.

Freeh loosened the guidelines as part of a federal initiative against the so-called Patriot Movement, the most dramatic increase in federally-driven surveillance programs since the early 1960s. The government crackdown was largely the result of two botched law enforcement raids, the 1992 siege at Ruby Ridge and the 1993 showdown in Waco. The outlines of these incidents are well known to most Americans, far more familiar to us now than the details of such seminal Cold War events as the Alger Hiss case.

The Bureau of Alcohol, Tobacco and Firearms tried to coerce former Green Beret Randy Weaver into being a snitch in 1991. When that failed, U.S. Marshals began surveilling the Weaver family at their rural Idaho home. A marshall and Weaver's son Samuel were both shot and killed during an unexpected encounter in the woods. The next day, Weaver's wife Vicki was killed by an FBI sniper. Weaver and family friend Kevin Harris were eventually acquitted of all charges arising out of the nine-day siege, and the government paid millions of dollars to settle a civil wrongful death case.

Then, on February 23, 1993, the BATF created another crisis during a disastrous raid on the Branch Davidians' church and living quarters. Leader David Koresh and his followers fought off the agents, leading to a 51-day standoff with the FBI which ended in flames and death on April 19. Although President Bill Clinton blamed Koresh and the Davidians for the tragedy, millions of Americans saw it the other way.

Exactly two years later, a bomb destroyed the Oklahoma City federal office building, killing over 160 government employees and civilians. Although federal prosecutors argued that only two men—Timothy McVeigh and Terry Nichols—were responsible for the bombing, Clinton exploited the tragedy to claim that the nation was facing a violent uprising by a dangerous coalition of militias, white supremacists, neo-Nazis and doomsday prophets. He convinced Congress to pass the Anti-Terrorism and Effective Death Penalty Act of 1996, the first of a series of new laws and spending measures which nearly doubled federal spending on counterterrorism to $11 billion-a-year by late 1999. Much of the money went to the FBI, whose anti-terrorism budget jumped from $78 to $609 million a year, with the number of agents assigned to counter-terrorism activities increasing from 550 to nearly 1,400.

Some of the money went to create 27 Joint Terrorism Task Forces around the country, consisting of representatives from the FBI, the INS, the Customs Service, and state and local police. They are based in major cities, many of which had specific ordinances against political surveillance. A few were under court order not to spy on political activists.

But questions about the legality of these task forces only surfaced in San Francisco, where the city had entered into a legal agreement which required a waiver from the Police Commissioner to gather and share information on political dissidents. When local activists learned such a waiver was under consideration in January 1997, they lobbied Mayor Willie Brown against it. Brown agreed, saying he would "not go along with or support any attempt to circumvent San Francisco's policy on surveillance." The FBI formed the task force anyway. Similar questions did not even surface in the other cities. Even the Chicago and New York police joined the task forces, despite lengthy histories of abuses much like those in San Francisco.[18]

The Anti-Terrorism Act dramatically increased the number of politically-oriented domestic surveillance operations. The FBI was working on approximately 100 domestic terrorism investigations before the bombing. The number jumped to 900 just two years later. Law enforcement agencies filed charges against suspected militia members in 36 major cases in 22 states between March and December 1996 alone.[19]

Some of the money also went to establish a new organization to help track dissidents, the State/Local Anti-Terrorism Training (SLATT) program. Funding came from a $2 million line item appropriation in the 1996 Anti-Terrorism Act. The money was routed through the Justice Department's Bureau of Justice Affairs, the same division which funds the RISS computer databases around the country. It went to the Institute for Intergovernmental Research, a non-profit corporation formed in 1978. Headquartered in Tallahassee, Florida, the IIR helps the federal government create and run law enforcement programs, including RISS, the National White Collar Crime Center, and the National Youth Gang Center.[20]

Although the FBI defines the term "terrorism" to include all politically-motivated threats and violence, SLATT was clearly created to provide law enforcement officials only with information on the Far Right. The grant application refers to "individuals adhering to 'patriot' extremist or other domestic terrorist philosophies." It describes "extremists" as those who "identify with one or more of the following philosophies: anti-tax, anti-federal government, anti-state government, anti-authority, anti-world alliances, pro-racial purity, pro-white supremacy, anti-Semitic, and a fear of loss of Constitutional rights . . . with an equal fear of a one world order."

SLATT 's training sessions are conducted by the FBI's National Security Division Training Unit. Sessions are offered each month across the nation. Between 1997 and 1999, SLATT trained more than 10,000 law enforcement personnel in 90 workshops that ranged from four hours to three days in length.

Remarkably, despite all the money spent in reaction to the Oklahoma City bombing, the Clinton Administration was ultimately proven wrong about the threat posed by the neo-Patriot movement. In late 1999, the FBI released a report titled Project Megiddo which predicted widespread domestic terrorist attacks at the dawn of the New Millennium. Nothing in the report came true. (See Case Study Seven: The Project Megiddo Fiasco, for more information.)

---

18. Mitzi Waltz, "Policing Activism: Think Global, Spy Local," *CovertAction Quarterly*, Summer 1997.

19. *U.S. News & World Report*, December 29, 1997.

20. Author's interviews with SLATT Research Director Mark Pitcavage, May 12 and June 5, 2000; author's interview with Institute for Intergovernmental Relations Senior Research Associate Bruce Buckley, June 1, 2000; Joseph Farrah, "Reno's $2 Million 'Private Spy,'" *WorldNetDaily*, January 27, 2000.

This embarrassing public fiasco did not cause the federal government to rethink its domestic political surveillance operations. Far from it. By the time Project Megiddo was proven wrong, the government had shifted its focus to yet another "terrorist threat," the anti-corporate globalization movement which came together to protest the World Trade Organization in Seattle in late 1999. Within months, the same array of agencies and programs which had been monitoring the neo-Patriots was focusing on the new coalition of labor, environmental and human rights activists. Seizing on the handful of self-proclaimed anarchists who vandalized businesses in downtown Seattle, political and law enforcement leaders set about labeling the entire movement as "violent" to justify using COINTELPRO-style tactics against it.

By the time the coalition came to Philadelphia to protest the Republican National Convention which ended in late July 2000, it was being infiltrated and tracked by the Pentagon, FBI, the Secret Service, and a range of state and local police agencies. Leaders were being identified, and information on them was being entered into the RISS computer system. When the convention ended, Philadelphia Police Commissioner John F. Timoney declared the movement an illegal conspiracy, and called on the federal government to conduct a full investigation into its leaders, followers and methods.[21] (See Chapter Fifteen: Infiltrating the Anarchists, for more details.)

Ironically, Timoney's pronouncement brought the Snitch Culture full circle. At the beginning of the 20th Century, law enforcement was siding with big business owners against anarchists—the same situation which prevailed at the dawn of the New Millennium.

---

21. David Morgan, "Police Chief Wants Feds to Investigate Protest Movement," *Reuters*, August 3, 2000.

CHAPTER EIGHT

PRIVATE INTELLIGENCE NETWORKS

ONE OF THE MOST IMPORTANT developments in the growth of the Snitch Culture is the large and growing role played by media-savvy, politically-oriented advocacy groups. Primarily private, non-profit corporations, these organizations support the government's efforts to collect more and more information on the American people. They publish dubious reports identifying new threats for the government to pursue, testify in support of increased surveillance operations at legislative hearings, and frequently help craft the final versions of the new programs produced by their lobbying. Over the past few decades, some of the most prominent advocacy organizations have included the American Cancer Society, which has worked to outlaw smoking in public buildings; Mothers Against Drunk Driving, which has convinced state legislatures to pass tougher laws against drinking and driving; and Handgun Control, Inc., which argues for tougher gun control measures.

But the most influential advocacy groups are those which operate their own snitch programs. As strange as it may sound, an untold number of non-profit organizations are currently spying on law-abiding American citizens, building files on people and organizations because of their political beliefs, and sharing much of the information they generate with police agencies. A surprising number of these organizations are considered liberal, including Planned Parenthood, which tracks anti-abortion protesters, and two of the nation's best known civil rights organizations, the Anti-Defamation League and the Southern Poverty Law Center.

Law enforcement agencies have long recognized the value of such private intelligence networks. Many of these groups have been encouraged, if not actually created, by public officials looking to get around laws against political surveillance. Police agencies have swapped confidential information with such organizations on an informal basis for many years.[1]

Some of the country's earliest private intelligence networks focused on the twin evils of pornography and alcohol. The Society for the Prevention of Vice, founded by Anthony Comstock in the 1870s, tried to regulate the artistic and literary taste of Americans for more than 18 years. As noted by Joseph Burke in his 1988 book *The Tyranny of Malice: Exploring the Dark Side of Character*

---

1. Chip Berlet, "Hunt for Red Menace: How the FBI, and Right-wing Spies, Use Paranoid Nativist Conspiracy Theories to Sustain an Authoritarian Domestic Counter-subversion," Political Research Associates, May 1, 1987 (revised October 4, 1991); Frank Donner, *The Age of Surveillance: The Aims & Methods of America's Political Intelligence System*, New York: Alfred Knopf, 1980.

and Culture, Comstock "advocated the use of informants, spies, entrapment and mail tampering to ferret out evildoers." Congress passed the Comstock Act in 1873, outlawing the transmission of obscene material through the U.S. mail. Among other things, it was used to block the dissemination of birth control information. By 1927, Comstock claimed he and his informants had "convicted persons enough to fill a passenger train of sixty-one coaches, sixty coaches containing sixty passengers each, and the sixty-first coach almost full."

An early temperance organization, the Anti-Saloon League, also used informants. Founded to monitor alcohol use in the communities where it organized, the League spied on its political opponents, digging up dirt to smear their characters and reputations. "The backbone of the movement was the local Protestant Church," Robert Goldberg wrote in his 1981 book, *Grassroots Resistance: Social Movements in the Twentieth Century*. "The ASL sought to establish a league organization in every congregation . . . By 1915 almost four thousand congregations participated in such activities."

One of the first government-supported private intelligence networks emerged during World War I, when the Justice Department's Bureau of Investigation, the predecessor to the FBI, formed a volunteer auxiliary force known as the American Protective League. The organization worked closely with J. Edgar Hoover after he was hired by the Justice Department's alien registration section. Hoover used the information provided by the APL to help round up more than 50,000 suspected pacifists and draft evaders during the infamous "slacker raids" of 1918.

Such private groups continued to function after the war, focusing on anarchists, socialists, communists, labor organizers and other left-wing activists. These early networks included the APL, the National Civic Federation, and other "superpatriot" organizations dedicated to fighting "subversives." Among other things, they identified some of the 10,000 alleged radicals who were rounded up during the controversial Palmer Raids of 1919. "Government agents on all levels worked with corporate officials, labor spies, super-patriots, amateur detectives, and assorted vigilantes in infiltration, provocation, raids and the dissemination of propaganda," says Donner.[2]

Like the law enforcement agencies they worked with, many of these organizations began building card files on suspected subversives with information gleaned from newspaper accounts, secured by citizen-informants, and passed on by police agencies. For all intents and purposes, these files were privately-owned "enemies lists," proving the existence of vast conspiracies to overthrow the government and justifying the early stages of the national surveillance system.

The most extensive file collection was assembled throughout the 1920s by a Chicago anti-labor spymaster named Harry A. Jung. Originally employed by a trade organization called National Clay Products Industries, Jung formed a network of informants called the American Vigilant Intelligence Foundation (AVIF). He sold his files to bankers, industrialists and other wealthy individuals, and used the information to name alleged subversives in his publication, *The Vigilant*.

2. *Ibid*, Donner.

Recognizing the value of privately-owned databases, the American military helped compile at least one large collection in the 1930s. After former military intelligence chief Major General Ralph H. Van Deman retired from the U.S. Army in 1929, he established an information collection and processing facility in San Diego with the support of the Army, which paid for two civilian assistants, filing cabinets and office supplies. Van Deman ran an undercover network which not only infiltrated the Communist Party, but also penetrated a range of other liberal groups, including religious, civil rights and labor organizations. His files included photographs of many suspected subversives, along with dossiers on politicians, actors, writers and such progressive educators as Pearl Buck and Linus Pauling. By the time Van Deman died in 1952, he had collected over 200,000 files, many of which had been used by private employers to screen potential workers.

File-building continued to be a favorite activity of anti-subversives after World War II. In 1947, three former FBI agents formed a group called American Business Consultants which offered employee clearance services to the East Coast entertainment industry. It published a newsletter called *Counterattack* and produced a manual titled *Red Channels: Reports of Communist Influence in Radio and Television*. In 1948, the American Chamber of Commerce published a report called *Program for Community Anti-Communist Action* which included instructions on how to build and maintain an intelligence file collection.[3]

The McCarthy era saw a boom in private anti-Communist spy networks. One of the largest was the conservative Church League of America, originally created to counter such liberal religious movements as the National Council of Churches. Headed by former Air Force intelligence officer Edgar C. Bundy, the CLA began with a file collection compiled by a far-right activist named George Washington Robnett. Another person who contributed to them was CLA research director Joseph B. Matthews, a former clergyman who once charged that Shirley Temple "unwittingly serviced the purpose of the Communist Party." By the late 1960s, Bundy's organization claimed a file collection of more than 7 million index cards, promoted as "the most reliable, comprehensive and complete, second only to those of the FBI." Information from the files was published in an affiliated publication, the *National Lawmen's Digest*. After it disbanded, the CLA donated its database to the Reverend Jerry Falwell's Liberty University.

Another large, privately-owned card file belonged to the American Security Council, founded in Chicago in 1955 by ex-FBI agents as the Mid-West Library. Funded by major corporations, it was originally conceived as a resource for employers who wanted to check the background of potential employees. It gathered information from a wide range of sources, including buying the entire card collection compiled by the AVIF. The ASC soon amassed an archive in excess of over 6,400,000 entries. The organization eventually evolved into a Congressional lobbying arm for the military-industrial complex.

---

3. *Ibid*, Berlet.

Such organizations helped the FBI and local law enforcement agencies track the peace and civil rights movements throughout the turbulent 1960s and 1970s. A conservative operative named John Rees specialized in infiltrating anti-war organizations. Rees frequently dressed up as a priest to attend both social gatherings and planning meetings. He reported his information both to the FBI and the John Birch Society.[4]

Many of these conservative intelligence networks collapsed after the Vietnam War ended. A few of the more committed snoops continued their work, however, including Rees, who founded a group called Western Goals Foundation with Congressman John McDonald, a former leader of the John Birch Society. The organization published several books on Communism, and it produced a newsletter for law-enforcement agencies called *Information Digest* for more than 20 years. Western Goals finally went out of business after being sued by the American Civil Liberties Union. The ACLU caught the organization trying to computerize files on alleged subversives stolen from a disbanded intelligence unit of the Los Angeles Police Department. Some of the group's records eventually went to conservative fundraiser Carl Russell "Spiz" Channell, who used them to solicit money for Oliver North's Contra supply network.

Another well-connected conservative who collected information on suspected subversives is retired Major General John Singlaub, another key player in the Iran-Contra Scandal. In December 1987, a Singlaub organization called the U.S. Council for World Freedom ran a full-page fundraising advertisement in *Soldier of Fortune* magazine which implied it was operating a domestic spy network. In the ad, Singlaub bragged, "My sources are in place in Afghanistan, Mozambique, Angola, Nicaragua, Southeast Asia . . . and . . . within the communist-front groups working in America to destroy our Constitution." Contacted by *The Nation* magazine, council executive director Joyce Downey declined to identify which groups the general had infiltrated, adding, "But we do have a lot of people who are in position to help us."

It isn't only conservatives who spy on their fellow citizens, however. So do organizations which might otherwise be considered liberal, including some which describe themselves as civil rights watchdogs. The organizations range from small, regional operations such as the Seattle-based Northwest Coalition for Human Dignity to large, national organizations with undercover agents in every major American city. By the 1990s, the two most influential private intelligence networks in the country were the Anti-Defamation League, a well-established Jewish advocacy group, and the Southern Poverty Law Center, which began as a small law firm representing blacks and other minorities in suits against government agencies.

Despite their liberal origins, the ADL and SPLC both admit "monitoring" political activists and religious dissidents. Although both groups claim they

---

4. Author's interview with 1960s anti-war activist Stewart Albert, who repeatedly saw John Rees dressed as a priest at numerous events and planning meetings before discovering he was working for law enforcement agencies and the John Birch Society.

are only spying on dangerous extremists, they collect information on law-abiding citizens, including libertarian and left-wing activists. They also swap information with police agencies, publishing much of what they learn in newsletters, booklets and special reports distributed to the news media.

Publicly, the ADL and SPLC describe their missions as fighting the Far Right, which they characterize as ranging from conservative tax protesters to violent neo-Nazis. Among other things, both groups release annual surveys which claim to track the number of active "hate groups" in the country. In 1997, for example, the SPLC published a report listing 474 "Active Hate Groups in the United States." The single largest block was 127 Ku Klux Klan chapters, followed by 100 neo-Nazi organizations. The report did not give complete addresses for any of the groups, however, making it impossible to confirm the figures.[5]

The newsletters and booklets published by the two organizations are replete with inside information which could only come from snitches. The publications frequently include detailed accounts of secret meetings between various "extremists," complete with exact quotes. Sometimes they even include photographs taken at these gatherings. It is impossible to tell from the publications whether these accounts and pictures are provided by informants working for the organizations, or from law enforcement agencies who are sharing the results of their undercover investigations.

Even some liberals are concerned about the close ties between these organizations and the government. "If you claim to be a broad-based human-rights group, you should not have a backdoor relationship with the police," says Chip Berlet of the Boston-based Political Research Associates.[6]

Berlet's concerns are based in part on a spy scandal which severely tarnished the ADL.

The Anti-Defamation League was formed in 1913 in response to religious persecution in Europe and anti-Semitic sentiments in America. Headquartered directly across from the United Nations building in New York City, the ADL operates over 30 regional and satellite offices around the country. The ADL is

5. Laird Wilcox is an independent expert on extremist groups in America. He has compiled exhaustive guides on both right- and left-wing organizations in the country for many years, and has consistently found fewer Far Right organizations than either the Anti-Defamation League or Southern Poverty Law Center. Wilcox has also self-published a critical examination of private advocacy groups titled *The Watchdogs: A Closer Look at Anti-Racist 'Watchdog' Groups*. It is available from Editorial Research Service, P.O. Box 2047, Olathe, KS 66051. In the foreword, Wilcox writes, "Indeed, there is an anti-racist industry in the United States which has attracted bullying, moralizing fanatics, whose identity and livelihoods depend upon growth and expansion of their particular kind of victimization. In certain respects the anti-racist movement has become a massive extortion racket, as lawyers have used every nuance of civil rights and equal-opportunity laws to extract massive judgements for objectively lesser offenses, and anti-racist street fanatics have attacked and vilified individuals for their values, opinions and beliefs. This is not what the civil rights movement was originally about."

6. Joseph Shapiro, "Hitting Before Hate Strikes," *U.S. News & World Report*, September 6, 1999.

so widely respected that many politicians, including President Bill Clinton, have addressed its annual conventions.

At the same time, the ADL has always spied on people and groups it considers hostile to Jews. "To anyone who knows the ADL and its work, the fact that the organization has files on various groups is no surprise. The group was founded early in this century to keep tabs on known and potential anti-Semites and hatemongers wherever and whoever they may be," Thomas Elias, a columnist with the Southern California Focus newspaper syndicate, wrote in April 1993.

The ADL frequently uses paid informants to gather such information. Some are *agent provocateurs*, joining and leading the very organizations they oppose. One was James Mitchell Rosenberg, who regularly attended and spoke at Ku Klux Klan rallies in Michigan in the 1980s. He became so active in the Klan that another civil rights organization, People Against Racist Terror, complained about his activities. "James Mitchell Rosenberg, a paid operative for the ADL, was involved in numerous white supremacist groups including the KKK, and his activity crossed the line from collecting information, which is vital and necessary in dealing with violence-prone racists, to acting as an initiator of racist organizing and proponent of racist violence," the group noted.[7]

Federal law enforcement agencies informally swapped intelligence with the ADL for many years. Then, seeking to get around the post-Watergate restrictions on political surveillance, President Ronald Reagan authorized the FBI to enter into formal information-sharing agreements with the ADL and similar organizations.[8] The internal FBI memo authorizing the arrangement with the ADL in 1985 says, "The ADL has undertaken to monitor and report the activities of domestic terrorist groups, including the Ku Klux Klan. It was established that each FBI Office contact each Regional Office [of the ADL] to establish a liaison and line of communications to promptly receive any allegations of civil-rights violations. Each receiving office should contact the Regional ADL Director listed in your Division and establish this liaison."[9]

But the full extent of the ADL's spy network was not known until 1993, when one of its paid informants, an art dealer named Roy Bullock, was caught keeping computer files on a broad range of political activists, including AIDS protesters, black militants, and peace groups. Bullock not only spied on these groups, he obtained confidential information on them from law enforcement agencies including the FBI and the San Francisco Police Department. One of his most important sources was an SFPD intelligence officer named Thomas

---

7. "ADL Complicit in Police Spying," *Turning The Tide*, May–June 1993.
8. "The New FBI," *CovertAction Quarterly*, Winter 1989. According to the article by Frank Morales, Executive Order 12333 formally "permitted the FBI, among other things, to contract with private groups for intelligence gathering and to conceal the existence of such contracts in warrantless break-ins under certain circumstances (which remain classified); and to accept any material if received in the course of a counter-terrorism or counterintelligence investigation regardless of how that material was received."
9. Federal Bureau of Investigation memo, "Anti-Defamation League of B'nai B'rith (ADL) Information Concerning Civil Rights Violations," February 4, 1985.

Gerard, who illegally provided Bullock with data on thousands of people. Even worse, Bullock and Gerard eventually went into business together, selling some of the information they dug up on anti-apartheid protesters to the racist govern-ment of South Africa, which had a practice of killing its opponents.

As news of the scandal broke, reporters learned that the ADL maintained a vast national spy network employing a number of full-time undercover operatives in major cities across the country. The San Francisco District Attorney released a list of thousands of individuals and organizations being monitored by the ADL. As the liberal *Village Voice* noted, "In fact, the ADL has become a clearinghouse for law enforcement agencies. In the '70s and '80s, as many police intelligence units that gathered political information on citizens were shut down under court order because they violated constitutional guarantees to privacy and freedom of speech and assembly, their files were often bequeathed to the ADL. The ADL, in turn, would often lend the files back to the original donor or broker them to another intelligence agency. 'It's like sending your money to the Bahamas,' says [a] San Francisco law enforcement source. 'It's a way for police agencies to avoid violating their own rules.'" [10] (See Case Study Six: The ADL Spy Scandal, for more information.)

Although the ADL eventually promised to curtail its surveillance activities as a result of the scandal, it is unclear how far the organization has cut back. It continued to publish detailed reports on alleged extremists, expanding them to include the Patriot movement in the mid-1990s. A few years later, Neil Herman, head of the FBI's counter-terrorism division, went to work as director of the ADL's "fact-finding" division.

The organization has also spent a great deal of time monitoring the Internet for "hate sites" in recent years. In 1996, it published *The Web of Hate: Extremists Exploit the Internet*, a slick 60-page report charging that the Internet had become a recruiting tool for both traditional and new-style hate groups. Lavishly illustrated with downloads from sites run by such neo-Nazi groups as White Aryan Resist-ance (WAR) and the Aryan Nations, the report paints the Internet as a serious threat to all decent Americans: "As computers become less expensive, simpler to use and consequently more common in American homes, bigots of all kinds are rushing to use the power of modern technology to spread their propaganda."

The ADL also began marketing "blocking software" to prevent Internet users from accessing prohibited sites. Called HateFilter, it runs on Cyber Patrol, a software package developed and sold by Mattel. HateFilter is designed to block access to an ever-increasing list of websites deemed bigoted or extremist by the organization. According to an ADL press release, "The League will compile a special list of hate sites to be embedded in the Cyber Patrol software. Internet users with ADL's Cyber Patrol who attempt to access hate sites will be directed to ADL's own website, <www.adl.org>, with educational content devoted to informing people about prejudice and hate."

---

10. "The Anti-Defamation League is Spying on You," *The Village Voice*, May 11, 1993.

The Southern Poverty Law Center was founded by an Alabama lawyer named Morris Dees. The son of poor farmhands, he started a publishing company to help finance his college education. The company, which published both children's books and cookbooks, was far more successful than the young student had ever imagined it would be. He sold it to the Times Mirror Company in 1969, making him a wealthy man.[11]

As a young lawyer in Alabama, Dees represented minorities in a number of significant civil rights cases, including a 1969 suit which forced the YMCA to open its doors to minorities. In 1970 Dees went to work raising money for Democratic presidential nominee George McGovern. He developed what many call the most effective direct-mail fundraising campaign in American politics, pulling in approximately $24 million for the liberal candidate. When he left the McGovern campaign, Dees took the 7,000-name mailing list with him, using it to raise money and establish the SPLC in 1971.

Founded as a non-profit law firm, the SPLC has expanded over the years to become one of the nation's largest private intelligence-gathering organizations. By June 2000, the organization had over $120 million in reserves, making it among the wealthiest non-profits in the country. Based in Montgomery, Alabama, the SPLC began gathering information on the Ku Klux Klan in the 1980s, when Dees sued an Alabama Klan chapter for killing a young African-American named Michael Donald. By late 1999, the SPLC had purchased and installed a massive state-of-the-art computer system to keep track of all the people it was monitoring. In a November 1 fundraising letter, SPLC President Joseph J. Levin boasted that the computer held over 100,000 entries, including nearly 20,000 photographs, compiled over the previous 19 years. Much of the information in the computer system came from informants, both paid and voluntary.[12]

One of the organization's most significant snitches was Dave Mazzella, a Californian who became enthralled with the Third Reich at an early age. Shortly after turning 14, Mazzella heard a radio talk show about contemporary neo-Nazis. Fascinated, he dropped out of school, shaved his head, and became a skinhead in the WAR, an avowedly racist organization run by veteran white supremacist Tom Metzger and his son John. Mazzella appeared with the Metzgers on numerous talk shows, including *Oprah* and *The Sally Jesse Raphael Show*.[13]

By 1988, Mazzella had run up a lengthy criminal record, including several assault charges. After serving a short jail sentence in California, he moved to Portland, Oregon and hooked up with a group of racist skinheads called East Side White Pride. Mazzella claims that he taught the group to fight minorities by leading them on attacks against up to 50 blacks and Hispanics the first night he reached town. He also put one of the group's members—Ken Mieske—on the phone with Tom Metzger shortly after arriving in Portland.

11. Richard E. Meyer, "The Long Crusade," *Los Angeles Times Magazine*, December 3, 1989.
12. Joseph Shapiro, "Hitting Before Hate Strikes," *U.S. News & World Report*, September 6, 1999.
13. Many of the details on Dave Mazzella's role in the civil wrongful-death suit against Tom and John Metzger come from the author's coverage of the trial for *Willamette Week*.

In the early morning hours of November 13, 1988, Mazzella, Mieske and a number of other skinheads were partying in an apartment in southeast Portland. When the party ended, Mazzella went off by himself, while Mieske left with two other skins, Kyle Brewster and Steve Strasser. Within a few minutes, the young racists got into a fight with three Ethiopian immigrants who happened to be in the area. Mieske killed one of them—Mulegeta Seraw— with a baseball bat.

Based on statements from the two surviving Ethiopians and other witnesses, police began asking local skinheads about the killing. On November 16, they picked Mazzella up for questioning. According to the official police transcript, he immediately turned into a snitch, volunteering that the Metzgers had sent him to Portland, and naming all three skinheads involved in the fight without hesitation. Mieske, Brewster and Strasser were arrested and charged with murder. Threatened with federal prosecution, they pleaded guilty in exchange for lengthy state prison sentences.

Mazzella bounced between Oregon and California for the next year. Then, claiming to have renounced racism, he contacted the Anti-Defamation League and volunteered to implicate the Metzgers in the killing. The ADL put Mazzella in touch with the SPLC, which filed a wrongful death lawsuit against the Metzgers on behalf of Seraw's family.

Mazzella was scheduled to be the star witness in the case. He moved to his mother's house in southern Oregon and waited for the trial to begin. While he waited, Mazzella began acting like a racist activist again, starting a new organization called Southern Oregon Skinheads. Mazzella and the other SOS members got involved in several fights, and then started planning a much more serious crime—firebombing an interracial dance club in Medford, Oregon.

Before the attack could be carried out, Mazzella was arrested and jailed on several skinhead-related assault charges. While in jail, he wrote the Medford skins and urged them to go into the illegal drug business with a black inmate who was about to be released. Alarmed by the proposal, the SOS members cut off contact with their former leader. They thought he was trying to set them up.

Mazzella was bailed out in time to testify against the Metzgers. In a nationally-publicized trial, he claimed that the Metzgers sent him to Portland as an authorized agent for their organization, WAR. Under questioning from Dees, Mazzella testified about the years he spent with the Metzgers. He said they wanted him to provoke a racial assault, just like the one where Mulegeta Seraw was killed, to generate publicity for their twisted cause.

Mazzella's testimony was damning. But he also perjured himself on the witness stand, raising questions about his overall truthfulness. Mazzella repeatedly swore he had not engaged in any racist activists since first going to the ADL and offering to testify against the Metzgers. Given his role with the Medford skinheads, this was a lie. But the jury held the Metzgers legally liable for Seraw's death anyway, fining them over $12 million.

After the trial Mazzella and his girlfriend, Ruth Moran, lived in a number of cities, including Atlanta and New Orleans. Eventually the couple settled in Billings, Montana, where they married and had a child. During this time, Mazzella told friends and associates the couple was being supported by an SPLC "witness protection program." This should not be confused with the Federal Witness Protection Program, which shields witnesses in major felony cases. On July 9, 1993, Mazzella told two researchers working on a book on racism that the SPLC was essentially paying him to keep quiet about the trial until the Metzgers had finished appealing the verdict against them. "They didn't really want me to talk to anybody while the appeal was going on," Mazzella said. "They didn't want to give the Metzgers any ammunition. They didn't want me to say anything that might not have been mentioned in the trial . . . They kept me sheltered until the appeals were final, so that the Metzgers would not have anything to get back in court with. Not that I lied, or anything like that."[14]

The Metzger case helped make the SPLC one of the most visible private intelligence networks in the nation. Over the next decade, the organization expanded its surveillance targets to include the various elements of the Patriot movement. In early 2000, the SPLC also began reporting on the growing anti-corporate globalization movement, claiming the left-wing activists were tools of the Far Right.

Much of the SPLC's information comes from snitches, both paid and unpaid. As *U.S. News & World Report* reported about the organization's intelligence-gathering operation, "The work can be drudgery. Fourteen researchers with the SPLC's 'Intelligence Project' spend long hours in front of computers, cross-filing data from press reports, hate-group literature, and websites, as well as from informers who volunteer or sell information about fellow neo-Nazis, Klansmen and militia members. Cops call with tips, too. 'What's garbage today is gold years later,' says Joe Roy, director of the Intelligence Project. 'The trick is to catalog it, retrieve it, and connect the dots.'"[15]

Another significant private intelligence organization was the Cult Awareness Network (CAN), created in 1979 to monitor unconventional religions. CAN had its roots in the counterculture movement of the late 1960s and early 1970s, a time when many young Americans turned their backs on traditional religions and political parties, embracing new belief systems. They included unconventional religions such as the Church of Scientology, the International Society for Krishna Consciousness (Hare Krishnas), the Unification Church and the Way International; alternative political parties such as the New Alliance Party and various groups started by failed Presidential candidate Lyndon LaRouche, including the U.S. Labor Party; and the California-based "human potential movement" organizations such as Erhard Seminars Training (est), Lifespring and Synanon.

14. Jim Redden, "Dave Mazzella, Saint or Sinner?," *PDXS*, February 27, 1995.
15. *U.S. News & World Report*, December 29, 1997.

Many parents were alarmed when their children joined these odd organizations. Some called law enforcement agencies to complain that their children had been kidnapped and brainwashed by unscrupulous charlatans. When the police couldn't turn up any evidence that a crime had been committed, some of these parents turned to their elected officials for help. This was especially true in California, which has always had more than its share of alternative religions and political movements.

Fielding a lot of these early calls was Theodore (Ted) Patrick, Jr., who served as a community relations representative in Southern California for Governor Ronald Reagan in 1971. At that time, Patrick began hearing from parents whose children had joined a group called the Children of God. Founded by David "Moses" Berg, it was one of the first and largest of the "Jesus Freak" organizations which swept the country in the early 1970s. After his daughter dropped out of school and moved to a church ranch, retired Navy lieutenant William Rambur launched a personal campaign to warn other parents about the group he considered a cult. In 1972, Rambur and Patrick formed the Parents' Committee to Free Our Children from the Children of God, which was later shortened to Free the Children of God, commonly called FREECOG.[16]

Several other anti-cult organizations also started in the early 1970s. In Los Angeles, a group of parents organized to oppose both the Children of God and the Tony and Susan Alamo Christian Foundation. Volunteer Parents of America was led by a man named Bob Chalenor, who wrote a booklet for parents whose children had joined alleged cults. Titled *Do's and Don'ts for Parents*, it recommended that parents engage in such classic informant practices as keeping records on their children and filing written complaints with public authorities. "DO record all names, addresses, phone numbers of persons known to be associated in any way with your children's activities," the booklet advised. "DO file a written complaint with your County Supervisor and other public officials."

The anti-cult movement first began receiving national media attention in 1973. In January, a young woman named Kathy Crampton joined a group called the Love Family in Seattle. Alarmed, her parents, Curt and Henrietta Crampton, contacted Ted Patrick, who introduced them to Volunteer Parents of America. The Cramptons hired Patrick to kidnap their daughter from the group and "change her mind" about it, a process Patrick called "deprogramming." He invited CBS News to document his efforts, which failed to convince Kathy to leave the group. The CBS report aired in August under the title, "Deprogramming: the Clash Between Religion and Civil Rights." Although the Cramptons thought it cast them as the villains, the report prompted people all across the country to call and write them, telling stories of their relatives, mostly children, running off to join strange groups. They used the contacts to build a national

---

16. Ted Patrick with Tom Dulak, *Let Our Children Go*, New York: Thomas Congdon Books, E.O. Dutton & Co., Inc., 1976.

mailing list for the VPA, a list which would grow larger and larger over the years.

Similar groups began appearing over the course of the next few years, including Citizens Engaged in Reunited Families, the Association of Individual Freedom, and the Positive Action Center. Representatives from many of these organizations met in Denver 1974 to form a national umbrella organization. Called the Citizens Freedom Foundation, it was headed by Rambur and based in San Diego. By the next year, the CFF had apparently broadened its agenda. In a July 1975 newsletter, it declared one of its tasks to be "revealing" the existence of "fraudulent, criminal and/or subversive groups in government, religion, education and business."

All of these groups gained credibility when over 800 followers of religious leader Jim Jones died in a jungle commune in Jonestown, Guyana on November 18, 1978. Lurid stories about commune members committing mass suicide by drinking poisoned Kool-Aid dominated the news media for weeks. Three days after the story broke, Patrick called a news conference in Miami to say that 50 million Americans—nearly a quarter of the population—were "cult followers." He based his claim on information he had gathered over the years as a self-made cult expert, much of it gathered during his deprogramming sessions.

Around this time, the CFF retained a Texas consulting firm to conduct a feasibility study on the creation of a full-time, well-funded, national anti-cult organization. The firm issued a report titled *Strategic Plan for Dealing with Destructive Cults in North America*. It laid out an ambitious blueprint for such a group— including proposals for snitching on alleged cults. One of its recommendations called for the creation of a "data repository" on fringe religious and political groups. The report also recommended that the organization "educate" public officials, law enforcement agencies, and the courts about cults. And it suggested that the group serve as police informants, calling for it to "expose criminal practices of cults."[17]

This report was used to create the non-profit Cult Awareness Network in 1979. Based in Chicago, CAN promoted itself as a national clearinghouse, publishing newsletters tracking "cult activities" around the country. Before too long, CAN became the nation's leading authority on cults, and soon began exchanging information with law enforcement agencies. CAN's executive director, Cynthia Kisser, was invited to address police conferences on cults. Government officials also addressed CAN conferences.

CAN eventually opened intelligence files on nearly 1,500 organizations it classified as cults. By 1996, CAN was tracking organizations ranging from obscure Christian sects to such well-known groups as the Church of Scientology, the Nation of Islam and the Unification Church of the Reverend Sun Myung Moon. The files also included nearly every Far Right group monitored by the FBI in the 1990s, including the Aryan Nations, the Freemen, the National Alliance,

---

17. The brief history of anti-cult organizations was taken from "A History of the Citizens Freedom Foundation" by Henrietta Crampton, published in a CFF pamphlet titled "Who We Are . . . and What We Do: A Handbook for Newcomers," date unknown.

the White Aryan Resistance, the Church of the Creator, the Ku Klux Klan and the Covenant, the Sword and the Arm of the Lord.

Much of the information in the files came from self-proclaimed "deprogrammers," such as Patrick. Like him, they were usually hired by distraught parents to kidnap their children, hold them at isolated locations for days at a time, and try to talk them out of their new-found beliefs. Some deprogrammers used coercion, physical force and even sex to accomplish their goals.

By the time CAN was created, this practice had already become controversial. Though few deprogrammers were ever arrested or convicted, it was denounced by the National Council of Churches. In a 1974 resolution, the Council called deprogramming "criminal," saying that it "violates not only the letter and spirit of state and federal laws but the world standard of the Universal Declaration of Human Rights." At the same time, the resolution concedes, "Grand juries have refused to indict and petit juries have refused to convict persons charged with such acts, apparently because [they] are done at the behest of parents or other relatives and ostensibly for the good of the victim."

As a result of this controversy, CAN did not offer deprogramming services directly. But the organization's employees frequently sent distraught parents to deprogrammers across the country. In October 1994, CAN staff member Marty Butz admitted making 500 such referrals since 1989.

By the late 1980s, CAN was influencing the way law enforcement agencies looked at unconventional religions and political movements. The FBI formally embraced the organization's concept of cults when it launched an investigation into the New Alliance Party, a fringe left-wing political party based primarily in inner city minority communities. Founded in 1979, NAP ran candidates for federal, state and local offices. In 1988, the party's Presidential candidate, Dr. Lenora Fulani, became the first woman and the first African-American Presidential candidate in U.S. history to be on the ballot in 40 states. The FBI began investi-gating NAP that same year, labeling the group a "political/cult organization."

The investigation, based on a tip by a Phoenix, Arizona "informant of unknown reliability," included at least 24 FBI field offices and the national headquarters, all of which opened files on the party. The FBI contacted numerous state and local law enforcement agencies during the investigation, warning them that NAP members—who at the time were actively engaged in the 1988 presidential campaign—should be considered "armed and dangerous." The FBI eventually concluded the organization had not broken any laws. NAP sued the FBI for harassment in 1993, charging that the use of the term "cult" to justify the investigations violated the First, Fourth and Fifth Amendments of the U.S. Constitution. The suit noted the term does "not appear in any federal statute or regulation or in the Federal Rules of Evidence as a predicate for declaring a person legally incompetent, depriving a person of parental rights, or subjecting a person to psychological warfare and the use of deadly force by federal law enforcement authorities."

The Cult Awareness Network also played a critical role in the 1993 Branch Davidian siege, perhaps the greatest fiasco in U.S. law enforcement history. A self-proclaimed cult expert named Rick Ross first heard of the Davidians in 1988. Although not a member of CAN's board of directors, Ross had attended many of the group's annual meetings, and had received a number of deprogramming referrals from the staff.[18] Ross researched the Davidians for several years before being retained to kidnap and deprogram a member named David Block. The actual deprogramming sessions took place at the home of Priscilla Coates, head of CAN's Southern California chapter, in 1992. After renouncing his beliefs, Block told Ross and Coates that Davidian leader David Koresh was sexually molesting his followers' young daughters, and that the group was stockpiling firearms, including illegal machine guns, at their church complex.

Ross went to the Bureau of Alcohol, Tobacco and Firearms with the stories. They decided to raid the church complex, arrest Koresh, and seize the group's guns. The BATF consulted with Ross while planning its raid in late 1992. Ross also talked with reporters at the local Waco newspaper, the *Tribune-Herald*, passing on the inflammatory stories he had heard from Block. The paper decided to publish a series centering on the allegations, with the first story scheduled for February 27, 1993. It quoted Ross as describing the Davidians as "a very dangerous group" with a high potential for violence. The BATF arranged to raid the Davidians' complex the next day. But, tipped to the raid in advance, the Davidians fought off the BATF agents, provoking a tense a 51-day standoff with federal authorities. Ross consulted with FBI officials throughout the siege.[19]

Ross and CAN officials also helped shape the public image of the Davidians during the siege, presenting their theories on doomsday cults to a baffled public through the corporate media. Ross was hired as an expert consultant by KDFW, the CBS affiliate in Dallas. CAN President Patricia Ryan told the *Houston Chronicle* that the government should use any means, including "lethal force," to arrest Koresh. A Houston CAN official was quoted as saying, "They [the Branch Davidians] are never going to come out. They [the FBI] are going to have to go in and get them. I don't expect this to end well."

As predicted, the confrontation ended in flames and death on April 19, 1993. Several months after that, Nancy T. Ammerman, a religious scholar at Princeton University, faulted the FBI for relying on information provided by Ross and CAN. She explained why such snitches are poor sources of information in a September 3 report presented to the Justice and Treasury departments:

---

18. Cynthia Kisser, executive director of CAN, said this of Ross: "He is very knowledgeable about cults. His name is among the half dozen best deprogrammers in the country."
19. Letter from Rick Ross to Attorney General Janet Reno, October 25, 1993. After outlining his extensive contacts with BATF and Treasury agents, Ross concludes by saying, "One thing is sure, David Koresh was an absolute authoritarian cult leader who exercised total control over his followers/victims. In the final analysis, he decided to end the conflict."

"In their attempt to build a case against the Branch Davidians, BATF did interview persons who were former members of the group and at least one person who had 'deprogrammed' a group member. Mr. Rick Ross, who often works in conjunction with the Cult Awareness Network (CAN), has been quoted as saying that he was 'consulted' by the BATF. My suspicion is that he was merely one among many the BATF interviewed in its background checks on the group and on Koresh. However, it is unclear how information gained from him was evaluated. The Network and Mr. Ross have a direct ideological (and financial) interest in arousing suspicion and antagonism against what they call 'cults.' These same persons seem to have been major sources for the series of stories run by the Waco newspaper beginning February 27. It seems clear that people within the 'anti-cult' community had targeted the Branch Davidians for attention.

"Although these people often call themselves 'cult experts,' they are certainly not recognized as such by the academic community. The activities of CAN are seen by the National Council of Churches (among others) as a danger to religious liberty, and deprogramming tactics have been increasingly found to fall outside the law. At the very least, Mr. Ross and any ex-members he was associated with should have been seen as questionable sources of information. Having no access to information from the larger social science community, however, BATF had no way to put in perspective what they may have heard form angry ex-members and eager deprogrammers."

CAN never admitted it did anything wrong. However, another Ross deprogramming led to the organization's demise. In December 1990, a woman named Katherine Tonkin called the Seattle CAN office worried that her three teenage sons had joined a cult, the Life Tabernacle Church, a small United Pentecostalist congregation in Bellevue, Washington. A CAN volunteer listened to Tonkin's story and then referred her to Ross. He and two associates flew out to Seattle, kidnapped the three boys, and held them for five days in a secluded house on the Washington coast, forcing them to watch videos on religious cults and trying to get them to denounce their church. Although the boys finally agreed, Tonkin's oldest son, 18-year-old Jason Scott, was just telling Ross what he wanted to hear. When the entire group went out for what was supposed to be a celebratory dinner, Scott bolted from the restaurant and called the police.

Ross was charged with kidnapping, but the jury acquitted him after Katherine Tonkin took responsibility for hiring him and explained she felt her children were in danger. News of the trial caught the attention of the Church of Scientology, however. The controversial organization had clashed with CAN for many years, and it bankrolled a civil suit against both Ross and the organization on Scott's behalf, claiming that CAN and the deprogrammer had conspired to violate his constitutional rights. When the case went to trial in 1994, the jury ruled in favor of Scott, assessing judgments of $1.8 million against CAN and $3.4 million against Ross. When CAN couldn't pay the judgement, the Scientologists were awarded the organization's assets, including its entire file collection stuffed in 150 boxes.

For a complete list of the organizations in the CAN files, see the Snitch Culture page on the Feral House website, <www.feralhouse.com>.

Private intelligence networks such as the ADL, the SPLC and CAN are an important element of the Snitch Culture. But even with their help, the federal government could not have built its national surveillance network without the active support of the establishment media.

CHAPTER NINE

MASS MEDIA PROPAGANDA

THE ESTABLISHMENT MEDIA has enthusiastically embraced every excuse to expand the Snitch Culture. This is to be expected in times of war, when all segments of society pull together to defeat a common enemy. But the corporate media has played the same role in every manufactured domestic crusade as well, including every variation of the War on Drugs.

This support has taken the form of both news coverage and entertainment programming. It has extended from the editorial stances of major newspapers to the neverending stream of public service announcements we see and hear every day. This steady drumbeat in support of the government's every law enforcement initiative is inescapable. It permeates every level of society, replacing reality with a paranoid fantasy world.

This government/media nexus has taken on increasingly sinister overtones in the last few years. For example, in late 1999, the Dutch newspaper *Truow* reported that U.S. Army psychological operations personnel—commonly called "psyops"—were assigned to the Atlanta headquarters of the Cable News Network during the NATO War in Kosovo. The CNN military personnel were members of the Airmobile Fourth Psychological Operations Group, stationed at Fort Bragg, North Carolina. This unit of almost 1,200 soldiers and officers is specifically charged with spreading government propaganda. Their job is to influence media and public opinion in armed conflicts in which American state interests are said to be at stake.[1]

The psyop troops were assigned to CNN through an Army program called "Training With Industry." According to Major Thomas Collins of the U.S. Information Service, the troops at CNN were assigned to help with the "production of news." Asked by reporter Geoff Metcalf of *WorldNetDaily* whether the introduction of military personnel into a civilian news organization was standard operating procedure, one source replied, "I hope so. It's what we do."

The *Truow* exposé was ignored by the establishment press. It was only reported in this country by such alternative sources as the *WorldNetDaily* and *Progressive Review* Internet websites, and by political commentator Alexander Cockburn's newsletter, *CounterPunch*.

But the truth is, the corporate media has always provided propaganda services to the government, slanting its news coverage and creating popular entertainment programs to coincide with the public enemies of the day.

---

1. Geoff Metcalf, "Army 'Psyops' at CNN News Giant Employed Military 'Psychological Operations' Personnel," *WorldNetDaily*, March 3, 2000.

When the government was fighting bootleggers during Prohibition, the press railed against the threat of gangsters and Hollywood produced such films as *Little Caesar*, casting Edward G. Robinson as the neurotic Rico. After Prohibition was repealed and the newly-formed Federal Bureau of Narcotics began going after marijuana, film studios jumped on board, portraying "tea" as the greatest threat facing America's youth. Movie executives even gave FBN Director Harry Anslinger control over all film scripts to make sure they adhered to official policy.[2]

According to researcher Christopher Simpson, the government formalized its relationship with the news and entertainment industry under Franklin Roosevelt during the early stages of the Second World War. In his 1994 Oxford University Press book *The Science of Coercion: Communication Research and Psychological Warfare 1945–1960*, Simpson documents how Roosevelt created the Office of the Coordinator of Information in 1941, putting his close friend, Wall Street lawyer Bill Donovan, in charge. The next year, Roosevelt split the responsibilities of the OCI into "white" and "black" operations. The white (or overt) role was assigned to the Office of War Information, which did such things as suggesting story lines to the producers of comic books, soap operas, movies and other forms of popular entertainment. Some of their guidelines called for Japanese to always be portrayed as treacherous, and for the British to be consistently shown as heroic.

The black operations were assigned to the Office of Strategic Services which became the government's premiere international intelligence-gathering agency, responsible for counter-espionage and other covert political activities abroad. Congress established the Central Intelligence Agency as the successor to the OSS in 1947 at the beginning of the Cold War.

The establishment media cooperated completely with the government during the war, becoming little more than a propaganda arm of the Pentagon. News outlets ignored Allied atrocities such as the firebombing of Dresden, while fabricating stories which made the Germans, Italians and Japanese appear even more barbaric than they actually were. The entertainment industry joined the war effort, too, with Hollywood cranking out a steady diet of films featuring gallant Allied soldiers fighting heartless Nazis and feral Japs. Broadway even produced a series of star-spangled spectacles such as the 1943 hit "Winged Victory," about members of the Air Force who pass their training course and earn their "wings."

Many employees of these agencies would become major media figures after the war. As longtime liberal Washington, DC commentator Sam Smith put it, "After the war, graduates of the Psychological Warfare Division, OSS, and OWI essentially ran the U.S. news media and publishing industries."

Since the end of World War II, the corporate media has marched lockstep behind every manufactured excuse to create and expand the Snitch Culture, beginning with the revived Red Scare of the 1950s. From the McCarthy

2. Ron Mann, *Grass*, Unapix, 2000.

hearings to the Cuban missile crisis to most of the Vietnam War, the news giants worked up countless variations of the Communist Menace story, running from State Department infiltrators to the Domino Theory and beyond. Hollywood joined in with such films as *Big John McClain* (1952), starring John Wayne and James Arness as two-fisted investigators for the House Un-American Activities Committee. TV and radio weighed in with shows and even entire series extolling the virtues of FBI agents infiltrating and exposing Communist front organizations. When anti-war activists challenged the Johnson and Nixon administration, long-haired, drug-addicted "peaceniks" began appearing as villains on *Dragnet, Adam-12* and other police procedurals.

Since the fall of the Soviet Union, only the bad guys have changed. After Nixon declared his War on Crime, young thugs, punks and robbers menaced defenseless inner-city dwellers in *Dirty Harry* (1971), *Death Wish* (1974) and *The Streets of San Francisco,* a popular TV series which ran from 1972 to 1977. When crack cocaine became Public Enemy Number One, murderous black street gangs began replacing the common riff-raff. Fanatic Muslims threatened widespread destruction in the late 1980s and early 1990s, only to be replaced by the homegrown militia menace in such films as Steven Seagal's *The Patriot* (1999) and *Militia* (2000).

One of the most blatant examples of pro-government propaganda was *In the Line of Duty: Ambush in Waco,* a made-for-TV movie about the fatal confrontation with David Koresh and the Branch Davidians. The film was actually shot during the 51-day siege, with actor Timothy Daly portraying Koresh as a Charles Manson-type cult leader driving his brainwashed followers to commit suicide. One scene shows Koresh handing a pistol to an elderly church member, asking if she is prepared to die for him. In another sequence, a young girl, who left the church before the initial government raid, tells a government agent that Koresh had instructed her on the proper way to commit suicide. Forming her right hand into a gun, the girl sticks the "barrel" in her mouth. *Ambush in Waco* was first broadcast on May 23, 1993, just a little more than a month after the fiery holocaust which killed Koresh and more than 80 of his followers, including over a dozen children. After new evidence reignited the controversy in early 1999, the film was rebroadcast numerous times on Court TV.

Cooperation between the federal government and the entertainment media reached new heights in 1998, when the CIA opened the doors of its ultra-secure headquarters to Showtime and Paramount Network Television to film key scenes for their movie, *In the Company of Spies.* The movie, which aired on Showtime on October 24, 1999, concerns a retired CIA operative who returns to duty to prevent North Korea from buying missiles which can carry nuclear warheads to America. Sixty off-duty CIA officials participated as extras. To celebrate the collaboration, CIA Director George Tenet invited the film's stars to a private screening and reception at CIA headquarters. Director Tim Matheson and a host of Washington political luminaries also attended the lavish event. "The CIA's objectives were clear," Roger Towne, the screenwriter who also was the film's executive producer, told the Associated Press. "They hoped to see a human face put on the agency and we had just the story to do it."[3]

Perhaps the best recent example of the insidious relationship between government and media was exposed by *Salon* on January 13, 2000. In a story by reporter Daniel Forbes, the Internet magazine revealed that the federal Office of National Drug Control Policy secretly paid six major TV networks $25 million to weave anti-drug themes into such popular shows as *ER*, *Beverly Hills 90210*, *The Drew Carey Show*, and *7th Heaven*. The payoffs ensured the scripts adhered to the official line of always portraying even recreational drug users as losers and psychopaths. As part of the deal, a 20th Century Fox Television executive specifically commissioned an episode of *Chicago Hope* which revolved around young partygoers who do drugs. They suffer a drug-induced death, a rape, psychosis, a two-car wreck, a broken nose, and a doctor's threat to skip life-saving surgery unless the patient agrees to be drug tested. Even more fantastic, the drugs cause one character to miss a flight on the space shuttle![4]

The secret payoffs were part of a five-year, $1 billion advertising program approved by Congress in 1998. Under the program, networks accepting paid anti-drug ads from the government were required to run an equal number of ads for free, a 2-for-1 deal. But after Congress approved the program, the networks balked at shelling out so much free time. So the ONDCP, which administered the program, came up with a creative compromise—if the networks included tough anti-drug messages in their regular programs, it would waive the requirement for donated time. The networks were then free to sell the ad time which had been committed to the campaign.

The deal was cut under the direction of Barry McCaffrey, commonly called the Drug Czar. As head of the ONDCP, McCaffrey holds a cabinet-level position in the Clinton Administration. He is a retired U.S. Army General who rose to prominence during the Vietnam War, a conflict notorious for its constant use of domestic government propaganda to prevent the American people from understanding what was happening on the ground in Southeast Asia.

Five networks took advantage of the deal in 1998—ABC, CBS, NBC, FOX and WB. A sixth, UPN, jumped on board in 1999. The results were dramatic, if not good drama. According to a White House report, the number of TV shows with anti-drug themes jumped from 32 in March 1998 to 109 in the winter of 1999. According to the *Salon* report, they included *The Wayans Bros.*, *Hang Times*, *Sports Night*, *The Practice*, *Promised Land*, *Trinity*, *Providence*, *Cosby*, *Smart Guy*, *Sabrina the Teenage Witch*, *Boy Meets World*, *General Hospital* and four teen-oriented Saturday-morning live-action shows on NBC.

White House officials tried to dismiss the controversy when the story first broke. Appearing on CNN's *Talk Back Live*, McCaffrey described the covert anti-drug messages as just another public health campaign.

---

3. Robert Burns, "Publicity-Shy CIA Welcomes Hollywood," AP, October 13, 1999.
4. Daniel Forbes, "Prime Time Propaganda," *Salon*, January 13, 2000.

This argument was strongly rejected by Sanho Tree, director of the Drug Policy Project for the Institute for Policy Studies, a liberal Washington, DC-based think tank. "It's terribly offensive to me when McCaffrey says these are basically just another series of public service announcements, like the ones telling you to buckle your seat belts or get your blood pressure checked," he said. "I have to ask, what other departments of public health rely on helicopters, machine guns, prisons, surveillance and all these other things as their primary means of enacting policy? It's a good thing they're not put in charge of issues like depression or anorexia." [5]

Even the corporate press criticized the secret payments when they were first revealed. On January 18, the *New York Times* published an editorial which warned the arrangement raised "the possibility of censorship and state-sponsored propaganda."

But even that mild rebuke was hypocritical, at best. Just two days later, the *Washington Post* reported that the *New York Times* received a $100,000 credit from the ONDCP for printing an anti-drug supplement distributed to public school teachers in the New York area. The supplement was produced as part of the paper's Newspapers in Education program, which provides reprints of news stories to teachers for use in their classrooms. The supplement approved by the drug office included reprints of eight previously-published stories on drug abuse, including one about an experimental treatment for heroin addiction.

In its January 20 story, the *Post* disclosed that the ONDCP had spent over $11 million on advertisements in 250 newspapers—and had granted many of them "credits," just like the TV networks. At least seven papers had their 2-for-1 match requirements reduced by running banner ads on their Internet websites which linked users to an anti-drug site maintained by the drug control office.

Remarkably, despite the controversy stirred up by the *Salon* story, Congress failed to rein in the ONDCP, and McCaffery moved to expand its influence. Testifying before a congressional committee in July 2000, McCaffery said his office plans to bring its propaganda campaign to Hollywood, working closely with writers and directors at major studios to make available to them the body of knowledge of the anti-drug community—in other words, to ensure movies conform to the official line against drugs. "Through continuous dialogue, we believe we can raise awareness about how images of substance abuse in the movies impact audiences, particularly young audiences," he said. [6]

By the end of the 20th Century, mega-mergers were reducing the owners of the mass media to a handful of powerful corporations, international business entities which do business with politicians and bureaucrats every day. The National Broadcasting Corporation (NBC) is owned by General Electric, a major defense contractor. The American Broadcasting Corporation (ABC) is

---

5. Author's interview with Sanho Tree, January 23, 2000.
6. "Aiming to Unlight that Fire,", USA *Today*, July 12, 2000.

part of the same conglomerate that owns Disney, which relies on sweatshops to produce the clothes and other products sold at its theme parks and stores. Their executives all contribute massive amounts of money to the politicians who write and approve international trade laws. The result is an unparalleled level of cooperation between elected officials, corporations and the news organizations which are supposed to be watching them.

Today, a single bizarre incident triggers an avalanche of news bulletins, special reports, live coverage and round-the-clock talk shows. Experts are paraded before anxious viewers to proclaim that the incident is not merely an isolated act, but the beginning of a terrifying new wave of crime or terrorism, depending on the spin. Whatever the threat, government officials always call for more laws, more money to enforce them, and more snitches to point out the bad guys. The press never challenges this premise. Instead, the government is always presented as our saviors, the good guys riding in to save the day.

Columbine provided many examples of this unquestioning support for government intervention. During the summer break which began shortly after the April 1999 killings, police agencies across the country decided to train their SWAT units how to assault the schools in their areas. Mock raids were staged in many states, cheered on by the establishment media. The CBS Evening News reported on one drill, showing dramatic images of heavily-armed, black-clad SWAT members deploying down a school hallway, weapons in hand. "CBS News discovered that a patchwork strategy is starting to evolve and many have one thing in common: the grownups are starting to take control of the schools again, and they're imposing strict grownup controls," the reporter intoned solemnly.

Sam Smith was one of the few commentators to even question the message behind the CBS story. "One reason America has been moving so effortlessly into a post-constitutional, post-democratic era has been the willingness of the mass media to terrorize the public with stories and images of a country out of control," he said. "The work that more primitive societies once did with government ministries and state broadcasting is now done voluntarily, primarily by television networks. Programs glorifying extreme police actions are daily fare, sending the subliminal message that control by cop is a normal form of government and anesthetizing viewers against violence, much as is done with troops to ready them for battle."[7]

Even law-and-order conservatives are beginning to be appalled by the constant stream of cable shows which put federal crime fighters in the limelight on a nightly basis. "The media is always looking for the big crime story, and society in general is looking for someone to one-up its array of crime," says former U.S. attorney Robert Merkle, who served as federal prosecutor for the Middle District of Florida under Ronald Reagan.[8]

7. Sam Smith, *Progressive Review* Internet newsletter, September 21, 1999.
8. Bill Moushey and Bob Martinson, "Win at Any Cost: Out of Control," *Pittsburgh Post-Gazette*, November 22, 1998.

But such complaints have no effect on the corporate media, which offers snitching and constant surveillance as entertainment. The best-known inform-ant show is *America's Most Wanted*, a weekly program on the Fox TV network. It was started in 1988 by John Walsh, whose son, Adam, had been abducted and murdered. The show profiles a handful of criminal suspects each week, telling viewers when rewards are available for their arrest and conviction. Thousands of people have called the AMW hotline over the years, ratting out friends, co-workers and even family members. In late 1999, AMW claimed credit for over 600 arrests and the return of more than 30 missing children. And now the networks are offering *Big Brother*-style shows, training their cameras on average citizens stranded on tropical islands, locked in a house together, or simply going about their lives as though constant surveillance was a normal part of everyone's day—which, in fact, it is.

At the end of the 20th Century, it has become almost impossible to separate the truth from the hype. A prime example was the Clinton Administration's decision to scare Americans about the threat of bio-terrorism. Government experts claimed that foreign and domestic terrorists could kill millions of people with anthrax and other potentially deadly diseases. The pronounce-ments were reported by all major media outlets, including the 24-hour news networks. Cable stations like A&E and the Learning Channel produced documentaries on this new threat. Movies and TV dramas started featuring bio-terrorists.

On Friday, October 1, 1999 the ABC News program *Nightline* began airing a fictional five-part series based upon the idea of a bio-terrorist attack on a city which looks and sounds a lot like Atlanta, Georgia. According to the scripted scenario, terrorists have released anthrax spores on subway tracks during the afternoon rush hour. Like Orson Welles' famous *War of the Worlds* broadcast, the Nightline series presented the fictitious attack as though it were a real story, presenting various experts who "document" the mounting death toll. As the plot progresses, public health officials are unable to stop the spread of the disease and the city quickly degenerates into anarchy. Order is only restored after the federal govern-ment declares martial law.

Concurrently, the *New Yorker* magazine reported that the CIA was investigating a contagious disease outbreak in New York as a possible act of bio-terrorism. And by October 8, the Center for Disease Control had identified 50 cases of the West Nile fever virus. Without quoting anyone at the CIA directly, the magazine described agency analysts as having a "whiff of concern" that it might have been deliberately released in the United States. "We're taking it seriously. We'll see where the data takes us," the magazine quoted "a person at the CDC" as saying.[9]

And why did the CIA ask the CDC to investigate the outbreak? According to the *New Yorker*, an Iraqi defector—a snitch—named Mikhael Ramadan had written a book which said that Iraqi leader Saddam Hussein was planning to

---

9. "CIA Reportedly Probing New York Virus Outbreak," *Reuters*, October 10, 1999.

make a weapon out of a strain of the West Nile virus. In the book, Ramadan described the virus as "capable of destroying 97 percent of all life in an urban environment," just like the anthrax attack featured in the *Nightline* series.

As it turned out, the West Nile outbreak was not a terrorist attack. But by then, who could be sure?

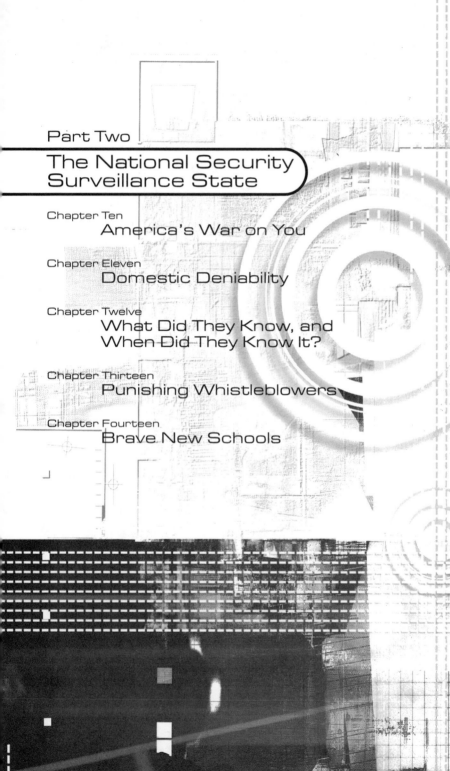

AMERICA'S WAR ON YOU

NOT TOO LONG AGO, A TIP TO THE POLICE might have produced a knock on the door and a visit from the beat officer assigned to your neighborhood. He would tell you what he heard and rely on his instincts and training to tell if you lie to him. But such days are over. Today, a tip from a snitch is more likely to trigger a military-style assault by a Special Weapons and Tactics team armed with automatic machine pistols and dressed in full body armor, helmets and face shields.

The militarization of domestic law enforcement is rooted in the urban riots which shook America's inner cities from 1965 to 1968. Patrol officers armed with six-shooters were unable to stop the looters, arsons and mob beatings. Congress was appalled by the sight, and President Johnson responded by creating the Law Enforcement Assistance Administration, primarily to provide military-style weaponry, communications equipment and special training to police forces across the country. As Christian Parenti noted in his 1999 book *Lockdown America: Police and Prisons in the Age of Crisis*, "Thus Johnson laid the initial groundwork for the tremendous combination of police power, surveillance and incarceration that today so dominates domestic policy."

The amount of military-style equipment available to state and local police increased dramatically when President Nixon announced his War on Crime. The federal assistance allowed the Los Angeles Police Department to create the nation's first SWAT team. Other cities quickly followed suit, financed by an almost unlimited pool of federal dollars and warehouses full of refurbished military equipment.

The federal government has used the so-called War on Drugs to erase the line between the military and civilian law enforcement. In 1981, Congress passed the Military Cooperation with Law Enforcement Officials Act, authorizing the Pentagon to "assist" state and local police departments in enforcing drug laws. Eight years later, in 1989, President George Bush created six regional Joint Task Forces within the Department of Defense to coordinate the military's involvement with domestic anti-drug operations. Both of these agreements violate the Posse Comitatus Act of 1878, which prohibits the military from engaging in domestic law enforcement operations.

The public was repeatedly told throughout the 1980s that police needed more and bigger weapons to battle black drug gangs. Crack dealers wielding fully-automatic Uzis, AK-47s, and other military assault weapons became a standard feature of the evening news and entertainment programs. Hollywood and the TV networks always presented drive-by shootings as involving cars full of young black males with blazing machine guns. In fact, although drug dealers frequently carry semi-automatic pistols, machine guns are tightly regulated and hard to come by. Police rarely run across anyone with a fully automatic assault weapon, regardless of skin color.

Nevertheless, by the early 1990s, police agencies across the country were being supplied with machine guns, sniper rifles, helicopters, and armored personnel carriers. Even patrol officers began carrying 18-shot Glock semi-automatic pistols, combat shotguns and semi-automatic versions of the U.S. Army's AR-15 assault weapons. As Newhouse News Service reporter Jim Nisbitt put it, the new weaponry was intended to "close a perceived firepower gap with heavily armed drug dealers. The public's fear of crime came into play, creating an atmosphere for the approval of tougher tactics."

It might be assumed that President Bill Clinton, lambasted as a "liberal" by conservative Republicans, would stop the domestic arms race. But shortly after Clinton took office, Janet Reno, his new U.S. Attorney General, signalled the administration's plans to increase the military's involvement in day-to-day police efforts. Speaking to representatives of the military-industrial complex in November 1993, Reno compared the War on Crime to the former Cold War. "So let me welcome you to the kind of war our police fight every day. And let me challenge you to turn your skills that served us so well in the Cold War to helping us with the war we're now fighting daily in the streets of our towns and cities across the nation," she said.[1]

Following Reno's speech, the Defense Department and the Department of Justice signed a formal agreement—called a memorandum of understanding—allowing the Pentagon to transfer military technology to state and local law enforcement agencies. Previously, these kinds of direct transfers were only made to friendly foreign governments. Another program, titled "Technology Transfer From Defense: Concealed Weapons Detection," authorized the two departments to enter into a five-year partnership to share such technology as "devices to detect concealed weapons," including unobtrusive scanners to avoid Fourth Amendment limitations against unreasonable searches and seizures.

A September 1999 study by the Cato Institute documented the federally-funded militarization of state and local police forces. Titled "Warrior Cops: The Ominous Growth of Paramilitarism in American Police Departments," the study found, "Over the past 20 years Congress has encouraged the U.S. military to supply intelligence, equipment and training to civilian police. That encouragement has spawned a culture of paramilitarism in American law enforcement."

According to the study, between 1995 and 1997 alone, the Department of Defense gave over one million pieces of military equipment to police forces across the country. The newest items included grenade launchers, armored personnel carriers, M-16 rifles, automatic weapons with laser sights, laser surveillance equipment, wireless electric stun projectiles, pyrotechnic devices such as flash-bang

---

1. Frank Morales, "The Militarization of Police," *CovertAction Quarterly*, Spring/Summer 1999.

and smoke grenades, and kevlar body armor. The study cited a 1997 survey by Peter Kraska and Victor Kappeler at Eastern Kentucky University which found that nearly 90 percent of police departments in towns with populations over 50,000 maintain SWAT teams. And 70 percent of departments in towns under 50,000 do too.

"It's the militarization of Mayberry," says Kraska. "This is unprecedented in American policing, and you have to ask yourself, what are the unintended consequences?"[2]

This equipment has not gone unused. Although SWAT teams were originally sold to the public as necessary to handle hostage and other extraordinary situations, they are now dispatched to serve warrants and conduct drug raids. When Kraska and Kappeler asked police agencies if they used SWAT teams for routine neighborhood patrols, 107 responded yes. Sixty-one percent of those surveyed thought it was a good idea, and 63 said SWAT teams "play an important role in community policing strategies."

Not surprisingly, the proliferation of military-style equipment has led to an increase in police shootings, with innocent civilians occasionally caught in the crosshairs. "The more a police officer thinks of himself as a soldier, the more likely he views the citizen as the enemy," James Fyfe, a criminal justice professor at Temple University and a former New York City policeman, told reporter Nesbitt.

Exact figures of police killings are hard to come by. Although the federal government has been legally required to collect national data on police use of excessive force since 1994, Congress has failed to provide the money for it to do so. But a number of private organizations have conducted their own studies. According to journalist Frank Morales, these show that police killings are up across America. "In 1990, 62 people died at the hands of the police, while in the first nine months of 1998 the number had grown to 205, an increase of more than 230 percent," he wrote.[3]

The following examples were gleaned from mainstream media accounts:

- In October 1996, Larry Harper told his family that life was no longer worth living and he headed out the door of their home with a handgun. Harper, a resident of Albuquerque, New Mexico, had begun using crack again and wanted to kill himself. His family called the police for help. The city's SWAT team responded. Nine officers clad in camouflage and armed with automatic rifles and stun grenades stormed the park where Harper had fled, chasing him through the woods. They eventually found him cowering behind a tree and shot him to death from 43 feet away. He had committed no crime.[4]

2. Kelly Patricia O'Meara, "Deadly Force and Individual Rights," *Insight Magazine*, October 15, 1999.
3. Frank Morales, "The Militarization of Police," *CovertAction Quarterly*, Spring/Summer 1999.
4. Timothy Egan, "Soldiers of the Drug War Remain on Duty," *New York Times*, March 1, 1999.

- In early August 1999, police in Stockton, California, broke into the home of Manuel Ramirez. An informant had fingered Ramirez for drugs. The police shot and killed Ramirez in his own room. No drugs were found.

- Just before midnight on August 9, 1999, the Special Emergency Response Team of the El Monte, California, police department conducted a "dynamic entry" raid at the home of 64-year-old Mario Paz. The police shot the locks off the front and back doors, tossed in a flash-bang grenade, and shot Paz twice in the back, killing him. The police said he was reaching for a gun. His family's lawyer said Paz thought the police were burglars. Although the SERT squad was looking for drugs, none were found.[5]

- Retired 75-year-old black preacher Accelynne Williams died of a heart attack after 13 heavily-armed members of the Boston Police Department broke into his apartment looking for drugs. Responding to an anonymous tip, the police had gotten the address wrong. After the incident, a police spokesman said the cops were looking for "four heavily-armed Jamaican drug dealers."

- As documented in the book *Undoing Drugs*, George and Katrina Stokes were watching TV in their southeast Washington, DC home when the local SWAT team crashed through the doors. George was ordered to the ground at gunpoint, cutting his head. Katrina fell down the stairs. The SWAT team was accompanied by a local TV news crew, who had cameras rolling when the police discovered they had raided the wrong house and ran back to their cars.

- In September 1999, police in Salem, Oregon decided to raid a rural home rented by 31-year-old Thomas Finney, who was suspected of selling drugs. Although a search warrant was originally sought by the bureau's Community Action Team, police commanders decided to send the SWAT team instead after an informant reported that Finney was abusive and had weapons. The team raided Finney's house at 5:30 on the morning of September 22. Awakened by the commotion, Finney was at the door when the police broke in, tripping and falling on the floor as the SWAT team poured into his house. Two officers immediately jumped on him and began pulling his arms behind his back to handcuff them. But during the struggle, one of the officer's fully-automatic 9mm submachine guns went off, shooting Finney in the back and killing him. The local District Attorney investigated the incident and cleared the police, saying the shooting was an accident.[6]

5. Cassandra Stern, "FBI Probes Fatal Drug Raid in California," *Washington Post*, September 6, 1999; Joel Miller, "The Problem with Drug Raids," *WorldNetDaily*, September 15, 1999; Joseph Farah, "The American Police State," *WorldNetDaily*, September 16, 1999.

6. "Salem Police Fatally Shoot Man Suspected of Being Drug Dealer," *Oregonian*, September 23, 1999; Angela Potter, "Officials Offer Three Theories on How a Weapon Fired," *Salem Statesman-Journal*, October 9, 1999.

But it isn't only state and local law enforcement agencies which employ SWAT teams on a routine basis. Federal agencies do as well. The best known unit is the FBI's so-called Hostage Rescue Unit, which includes a special sniper team made up of the agency's best sharpshooters. Other agencies with their own military units include the Customs Service, the DEA, the INS, the State Department, the U.S. Marshals Service and even the Department of Energy.

In recent years, Navy SEALs and Army Rangers have begun training local SWAT units. The U.S. Marshals Service has acted as a liaison between the police departments and military trainers.

But even more cooperation between the Pentagon and domestic law enforcement agencies has occurred under the so-called War on Terrorism. President Clinton signaled what was coming on April 20, 1993, the day after heavily-armed FBI agents used military helicopters and 85-ton tanks to attack the Branch Davidians in their Waco church complex. Speaking to the American people, Clinton said the government was not responsible for "the fact that a bunch of fanatics decided to kill themselves." Then he warned, "There is, unfortunately, a rise in this sort of fanaticism across the world. And we may have to confront it again."

By then, Clinton had already broken the Posse Comitatus Act by authorizing U.S. military involvement in the Branch Davidians siege. As finally confirmed by the government in late 1999, the Pentagon sent high-ranking officers and the Army's Delta Force anti-terrorist operatives to monitor the siege, along with classified surveillance equipment. "The tragedy at Waco by no means is the first or only example of violations of Posse Comitatus, but it does underscore the volatile cocktail that can result from mixing special-operations troops and civilian law enforcement," Kelly Patricia O'Meara wrote in *Insight* magazine. "Separation of civilian and military forces has long been an American tradition, but under the guise of the 'war on drugs' and the 'war on terrorism,' Congress in the last two decades has enacted piecemeal legislation allowing military intervention in civilian law enforcement, which many believe violates the intent, if not the letter, of the law." [7]

As noted by O'Meara, the military has also been conducting massive live-fire training exercises in major American cities for years. Known as Military Operations in Urban Terrain, or MOUT, these exercises have been staged in dozens of cities across the country, including Pittsburgh, Houston, Chicago and Charlotte, North Carolina, where residents "have been awakened in the dead of night by hundreds of military troops rappelling from helicopters hovering at treetop level, firing automatic weapons and exploding flash-bang and smoke grenades."

The military insists these exercises are designed to prepare troops for door-to-door fighting in foreign countries. As Colonel Bill Darley, a spokesman for the Department of Defense, told O'Meara, "[T]hese exercises are not law-enforcement missions. They're secret combat activities for very explicit purposes,

---

7. Kelly Patricia O'Meara, "Deadly Force and Individual Rights," *Insight Magazine*, October 15, 1999.

such as scenarios involving recovery of a weapon of mass destruction, incidents of terrorism and hostage rescue. The activities would be approximating the same situation as in a foreign country. We conduct these large-scale exercises in the Southern states as make-believe foreign countries. Charlotte, North Carolina, for example, could be Paris, Munich or any other built-up urban area outside the United States."

But Darley's denials were undercut by two events which occurred just before the *Insight* article was published. On September 20, Congress voted to allow the military to dispatch troops and weapons to state and local police to help them react to threats or acts of domestic terrorism. The authorization was buried inside the Fiscal Year 2000 defense appropriation bill.[8]

Two weeks later, at an October 7 press conference, top military officials and their civilian superiors announced changes in the Pentagon's command structure designed to give the military a supporting role in responding to domestic terrorist attacks or natural disasters. U.S. Defense Secretary William Cohen brushed aside concerns about federal troops operating at home, saying the military must "deal with the threats we are most likely to face. The American people should not be concerned about it. They should welcome it."[9]

The federal government is apparently planning to use terrorism as an excuse to increase the Snitch Culture well into the 21st Century. How bad will it get? Consider what's already happening to foreigners legally living in this country. Under the Effective Death Penalty and Anti-Terrorism Act of 1996, foreigners accused of terrorism are being arrested and locked up without ever being told the evidence against them. Even their lawyers aren't allowed to know who has accused them of terrorist activities, or what they are supposed to have done.

Nearly two dozen resident aliens were arrested and detained by the Immigration and Naturalization Service during the first four years after the law was passed. Almost all of them are of Arab ethnicity or belong to Muslim religions. The cases against them have almost always fallen apart when their lawyers finally succeed in getting them before a judge. But it can take years for the first hearing, as Dr. Mazen Al-Najjar learned.

Al-Najjar was a teacher of Arabic at the University of South Florida. He was living legally in the Tampa area with his wife and three daughters when the government accused him of being a "mid-level" member of a fund-raising group linked to the Islamic Jihad and Hamas terrorist organizations in the Middle East. He was arrested in 1997 and was beginning his fourth year in prison when his sister testified about his plight at a Congressional hearing. "It's like fighting ghosts," she told the House Judiciary Committee on May 30, 2000. "My brother is facing an indefinite sentence without any charges or indictment, trial, conviction or sentence."

---

8. Steven Komarow, "Military Chiefs Set Up Command to Address U.S. Terrorist Threats," *USA Today*, October 8, 1999.
9. *Ibid.*

FBI general counsel Larry Parkinson told the committee that withholding the evidence was necessary "to protect national security." According to Parkinson, disclosing the evidence against Al-Najjar would expose secret intelligence. "We take these matters seriously, and we do not casually resort to the use of classified information," he said.[10]

Within days of the hearing, U.S. District Judge Joan A. Lenard of the Southern District of Florida in Miami ruled that the use of secret evidence to deny bond to Al-Najjar is a violation of his due process rights. The ruling vacated earlier findings of the Board of Immigration Appeals and an immigration judge, holding their reliance on "classified evidence that neither petitioner nor his counsel were able to review compromised the fundamental fairness of petitioner's hearing by denying him notice of the evidence against him and a meaningful opportunity to defend against that evidence."

Judge Lenard ruled that "mere association with a known terrorist organization is not sufficient in and of itself to support a finding of a threat to national security for bond purposes." But she did not completely prohibit the use of secret evidence, holding that the government's interest in national security must simply be balanced with the individual's right to due process.

This loophole allows the government to continue using unnamed snitches and undisclosed information to arrest and hold resident foreigners.[11]

Even career law enforcement officials are appalled by the militarization of traditional police functions. The Clinton Administration gave the world a look at the new face of domestic law enforcement during the highly-publicized custody battle over young Cuban refugee Elian Gonzalez. A crude raft carrying Gonzalez and his mother to America broke up before reaching Florida. The boy saw his mother and several of their friends die, then floated alone for several days in shark-infested waters before being rescued. The INS originally placed Gonzalez with distant relatives in Miami. They were part of the anti-Communist Cuban community, and used the opportunity to denounce Castro and his regime.

When Gonzalez' father came to America to reclaim his son, the Miami family balked at turning him over, and U.S. Attorney General Janet Reno authorized the INS to physically remove him from the home. In the early morning hours of April 22, 2000, a heavily-armed INS SWAT team burst into the house. Dressed in green fatigues and body armor, the immigration agents looked like frontline army soldiers. An AP photographer snuck into the house during the raid, snapping a dramatic series of pictures showing a SWAT member shoving a machine gun in the terrified boy's face.

The raid and pictures provoked a public outcry. One of the most vocal critics was Robert Ressler, the FBI's former top hostage negotiator. Ressler served with the FBI for 20 years and in law enforcement for more than four decades.

---

10. Lance Gay, "Panel Hears Testimony For, Against Secret-Evidence Law," Scripps Howard News Service, May 23, 2000.
11. Sam Smith, "Secret Evidence Ruled Illegal, *Progressive Review*, June 2, 2000.

Shortly after the raid, he told the NewsMax Internet website the raid was "unwarranted," and that Reno should have been fired for authorizing it. "It violated everything that is taught by the FBI in handling situations like this," NewsMax quoted Ressler as saying. "The federal government and Reno went berserk."

Ressler said he would have followed textbook rules for dealing with such situations. "I would have sent just two marshals, wearing suits, with briefcases, and maybe with a social worker to collect the child," he explained. Only if that failed or resistance was met should the government have even considered escalating the confrontation, he added.

Significantly, the Department of Justice defended the use of force by implying they had inside information from a snitch. Justice Department officials told reporters they had reason to believe there were guns in the relatives' house, information which could have only come from an informant. No guns were actually found during the raid, however.

This dramatic escalation of technology and military firepower has fundamentally altered the role of the snitch in American society. Domestic law enforcement initiatives have become shooting wars, complete with military tactics, weapons and goals. And informants have become domestic spies, operating under the premise that the means justifies the end.

CHAPTER ELEVEN

DOMESTIC DENIABILITY

GOVERNMENTS HAVE HISTORICALLY relied on spies for information about the size, strength and movements of their enemies in "hot" wars such as World War II and "cold" wars such as the protracted confrontation between the United States and the former Soviet Union. Because the stakes are so high, spies are expected to do anything and everything necessary to accomplish their missions—including deceit, bribery, blackmail, burglary, assault, framing innocent people, even cold-blooded murder. Spies are also expendable. They are expected to provide the governments they work for with deniability in case they are caught.

Domestic police informants are supposed to be different. The people they investigate are presumed innocent, and the government isn't legally allowed to trick or coerce them into breaking the law. And the informants themselves have rights. The government is expected to uphold the deals it strikes with them, and it is not supposed to expose them to undue risks.

But today, domestic law enforcement authorities are running their informants like military or CIA spies. They are allowed to break the law to accomplish their missions. They frame innocent people on bogus charges. They lie under oath. It's *Mission: Impossible*, with you as the target. Snitches routinely set up friends, associates, family members and even complete strangers. But if they screw up and get caught or killed, the government won't even apologize.

Polls show the majority of the American people have consistently supported all of the federal government's domestic law enforcement initiatives, including Richard Nixon's War on Crime, Ronald Reagan and George Bush's War on Drugs, and Bill Clinton's War on Terrorism. But would the public continue to support these policies if they knew that the informants which fuel them are getting away with murder? Law enforcement authorities frequently cut deals with killers, ignoring their murders or letting them off with ridiculously light sentences in exchange for information.

Perhaps the most famous murderer-turned-snitch is Sammy "The Bull" Gravano, a mob hitman who worked directly under John Gotti, reputedly the last of the powerful Mafia Godfathers. When the feds went after Gotti, Gravano flipped and testified against his former boss, sending him to prison for life and breaking the back of the Gambino Family which controlled businesses worth billions of dollars throughout New York and much of the East Coast in the early 1990s.

Gravano symbolizes the moral problems of working with informants. He admits killing 19 people on his way to the top of Gotti's operation, including a brother-in-law who failed to pay back a loan and a childhood friend who got greedy in a business deal. "Each time I felt nothing. No remorse. Just ice," Gravano says of the killings.[1]

Gravano served less than two years for each murder before entering the federal Witness Protection Program and moving to Arizona, where he started a construction company. But as it turned out, the mob-snitch apparently had not changed his ways. Gravano was arrested in late 1999 and charged with running a large drug operation, providing Ecstasy and other party drugs to the Phoenix rave scene.

Even more embarrassing for the government is its relationship with James Bulger and Stephen Flemmi, two Irish-American mobsters from Boston. They became informants in the 1970s and helped the FBI shut down the New England branch of La Cosa Nostra. Some of their tips were spectacular, including one which allowed the FBI to tape-record an entire initiation ceremony, including a finger-cutting and the oath, "I enter alive into this organization and I will have to get out dead." Bulger and Flemmi eventually gave the FBI enough information to indict and convict 42 Mafia members and associates.

At the time Bulger and Flemmi were recruited as snitches, they were little more than shakedown artists demanding "protection money" from assorted bookmakers, loan sharks and other petty criminals. But after the FBI eliminated all of their competition, the two men became the most powerful organized crime figures in Boston and much of the East Coast.

John Connelly, the FBI agent who recruited and worked the two Boston mobsters, retired in 1990. Five years later, the U.S. Department of Justice indicted Bulger, Flemmi and a number of their associates on racketeering charges. Although Bulger went underground, Flemmi stayed in Boston and was arrested. In 1997, Flemmi threw the legal system into turmoil when his lawyer declared that he was an FBI informant—and that the federal government had authorized him to commit all of the crimes in the indictment.[2]

U.S. District Judge Mark L. Wolf took the claim seriously and presided over a series of pre-trial motions that took up most of 1998. Flemmi and other witnesses, including current and former FBI officials, appeared at the hearings. They testified that law enforcement officials looked the other way while Bulger and Flemmi became major gangsters. The stories included tales of boozy dinners and other social gatherings between FBI agents and criminal informants. An FBI supervisor named John Morris admitted accepting thousands of dollars in cash bribes from the two men, along with cases of wine which he liked so much the mobsters nick-named him "Vino." On top of that, the FBI repeatedly protected the two men from other investigations directed

1. Howard Blum, "The Reluctant Don," *Vanity Fair*, September 1999.
2. "The Hearings Exposed the Cozy Relationship Between Bulger and Flemmi and Their FBI handlers," *Boston Globe*, September 10, 1999.

against them, tipping Bulger and Flemmi off to probes conducted by the DEA and the Massachusetts State Police, among others.

As result of the testimony, a federal grand jury was convened to investigate the allegations of FBI corruption and misconduct raised at the pre-trial hearings. U.S. Attorney Donald Stern brokered a deal with confessed hitman John Martorano, allowing him to serve only eight years in prison in exchange for his testimony "against any current or former member of local, state or federal law enforcement, including, without limitation, any prosecution based upon any illegal or corrupt relationship between that individual and James (Whitey) Bulger and Stephen (The Rifleman) Flemmi."

Martorano has admitted murdering 20 people in Massachusetts, Florida and Oklahoma, some at the direction of Bulger and Flemmi. One of those killed was Roger Wheeler, the millionaire chairman of the Telex Corporation and owner of World Jai Alai. According to the Boston Globe, Martorano asserts that Bulger and Flemmi orchestrated the murder with the knowledge of an unnamed FBI agent. When he announced the plea bargain agreement with Martorano, Stern said, "The only thing more distasteful than signing this agreement was not signing this agreement. If we didn't go forward with this agreement, there would always be the lingering suspicion that part of the reason for not going forward was to protect the FBI."

Then another former gangster who worked under Bulger and Flemmi accused them of even more murders. Kevin Weeks joined their crew when he was a teenager in the 1950s. In July 2000, Weeks stepped forward and charged that the two men killed five people between 1982 and 1985. Weeks admitted serving as "lookout" on one murder, holding two men captive before they were killed by Bulger and his associates, dumping murder weapons, and repeatedly burying bodies. One of the victims was Brian Halloran, a gangster who was gunned down in May 1982, shortly after turning snitch and telling the FBI that Bulger and Flemmi were behind the Wheeler killing. Halloran apparently didn't realize that the killers had struck their deals first.[3]

In exchange for his cooperation, federal prosecutors agreed to recommend a prison term for Weeks of no more than 15 years, or just three years per murder.

Law enforcement agencies also sacrifice snitches without any remorse. As in times of actual wars, they've let them die and denied any responsibility.

Police agencies are rarely held legally or financially liable when informants are injured or killed during undercover operations. As strange as this may sound, the U.S. Supreme Court has ruled that police have no obligation to protect you, even if they know your life is in danger. This legal principle is

---

3. "Gangster Implicates Bulger in Plea Deal," Boston Globe, July 13, 2000. According to reporter Shelly Murphy, James Bulger and Stephen Flemmi also killed Michael Donahue, a friend of Brian Halloran; Deborah Hussey, the daughter of Flemmi's longtime girlfriend; Arthur Barrett, who disappeared shortly after taking part in the 1980 Memorial Day weekend robbery of $1.5 million in cash and jewelry from Depositors Trust in Medford, Massachusetts; and John McIntyre, who vanished in November 1984 after implicating Bulger in an ill-fated plot to smuggle weapons to the Irish Republican Army.

known as "sovereign immunity," and it means the government has no financial or other responsibility for its actions.[4]

One grisly example is the case of Joshua DeShaney, a Wisconsin child who was nearly beaten to death by his father in 1989. Winnebago County child care officials had been repeatedly told that Joshua's father was abusive, but they did nothing. The beatings continued and Joshua suffered irreparable brain damage. When a lawsuit against the child care agency brought on Joshua's behalf reached the Supreme Court, Chief Justice William H. Rehnquist threw it out. Writing for the court majority, he said that public agencies do not have an "affirmative obligation" to protect citizens, even when a danger is apparent. "A state's failure to protect an individual against private violence" is not a basis for holding an agency liable, he held.

Some lower courts have held police responsible in a few cases involving informants, however. The following exceptions to the liability rule illustrate the dangers facing informants—and the challenges of holding the authorities accountable when something goes wrong.

In November 1992, police went to the Ontario, California home of Sandra Mancha and her, 16-year-old son, Christopher, to investigate a burglary. Christopher told the cops he had seen a familiar car in front of the house. Promised confidentiality by a lab technician, the boy said it belonged to Richard Salazar, a gang member who lived in the neighborhood. But when a detective questioned Salazar a short time later, she told him Christopher had turned him in.

Christopher was dead within 24 hours, shot five times and run over by a car. Salazar was convicted of the murder and sent to prison for life. Sandra Mancha sued the police, stressing that they had not only promised to keep her son's name a secret, but failed to warn him when they didn't. In December 1998, a San Bernardino County jury handed down a $5-million verdict against the city of Ontario.

"This was a person who came forward reluctantly to report a crime and lost his life because of it," Marina R. Dini, a Los Angeles lawyer who represented the family, told the *Los Angeles Times* for its December 2, 1999 story on endangered informants.

On December 4, 1997 a grisly multiple murder shook the well-heeled denizens of Capitol Hill. Three Starbucks employees were found slain in a Washington, DC coffee shop frequented by the likes of Presidential advisor George Stephanopoulos. All had been shot at point-blank range, execution-style. One of the employees had been a White House intern, prompting Monica Lewinsky to tell Linda Tripp that the killings might have been a message for her to shut up about her sexual relationship with Bill Clinton.

Thrashing around for leads, the police received a tip from Eric Butera, a junkie. Butera told police that he had overheard people talking about the murders in a row house where he occasionally purchased drugs. Butera said he had also seen weapons during his visits to the place. Four officers decided to use

---

4. Richard W. Stevens, *Dial 911 and Die*, Mazel Freedom Press, 1999.

Butera as an undercover operative. They arranged for Butera to return to the row house, giving him $80 in marked bills to buy crack cocaine. The police planned to use the purchase as an excuse to search the row house and look for evidence tied to the murders.

With the approval of Lt. Brian McAllister, Detective Anthony Brigidini dropped Butera off near the row house late one night, then drove a block or so away to wait for him. Sgt. Nicholas Breul and Detective Anthony Patterson sat in another car on a nearby street. But Butera was turned away from the crack house. As he walked off, he was jumped from behind, robbed of his "buy" money and beaten to death. Forty minutes passed before a neighbor called 911 and a patrol car discovered the body.

A police internal investigation concluded that the officers handling Butera did nothing wrong. Frustrated, Butera's mother Terry filed a civil wrongful death suit, charging that the police did not adequately protect her son. "They signed Mr. Butera's death warrant when they dropped him off that night," an attorney for the Butera family, told the jury.

During the trial, James Bradley Jr., a former DC police official, said that the plan was haphazardly designed and executed. Testifying as an expert witness for Terry Butera, Bradley noted that patrol officers had gone to the row house the night before, making it extremely unlikely that anyone in the house would then sell drugs to her son. Bradley also pointed out that the homicide investigators failed to alert precinct commanders about their plan or put it in writing, a violation of national standards and DC rules. On top of that, Bradley pointed out that the officers supervising Butera parked so far away from the house that they could not see it.

The jury agreed, ordering the police department and the four officers to pay nearly $100 million in damages to Butera's mother. The jury ordered the District and its officers to pay $70.5 million in compensatory damages and $27.5 million in punitive damages.

"I hope that no other family will have to endure what I've endured," Terry Butera said after the trial. "If that's the case, then this was a victory." [5]

A similar case occurred in January 1998 when 17-year-old Chad McDonald of Yorba Linda, California was arrested for methamphetamine possession by the Brea Police Department. Using the charge as leverage, the police coerced him into making at least one drug buy. Several weeks later, he and his 16-year-old girlfriend visited a ramshackle drug house in Norwalk, California. Three dealers living there suspected McDonald and his girlfriend of being snitches who needed to be taught a lesson. They tied them up and beat them. McDonald was strangled to death, and his battered body was dumped in an alley. His girlfriend was raped and shot in the face, then dumped in a culvert near the San Gabriel Reservoir. She miraculously survived the brutal assault and helped lead the police to the assailants.

---

5. Bill Miller, "Jury Awards $100 Million in Death of Informant," *Washington Post*, October 21, 1999.

Michael Martinez, Florence Noriega and Jose Ibarra were arrested and charged with torturing and murdering McDonald, and with kidnapping, torturing and attempting to murder his girlfriend. Martinez and Ibarra were also charged with raping her. The trial featured compelling testimony from McDonald's girlfriend, whose name was not released. She told about how Martinez, Noriega and Ibarra accused them of being informants. She also testified that Noriega said they should be shot, telling the two male assailants, "She'll take five bullets, so load it up all the way."

A Los Angeles County Superior Court jury convicted the defendants on virtually all charges on October 18, 1999. McDonald's mother Cindy filed civil wrongful death suits against both the Brea and Yorba Linda police departments. The story also caught the attention of the California Legislature, which passed a law requiring police to get permission from a judge before using children between 13 and 17 as informants. Few other states have adopted similar laws.[6]

In times of war, the government furnishes its spies with fake identities, including all the documentation needed to start a new life. The same thing happens under the Witness Protection Program, but as a reward for services rendered. Headquartered in Arlington, Virginia and run by the U.S. Marshals Service, the program works by giving cooperating witnesses new names, phony backgrounds, and relocating them far away from the associates of the defendants they testified against. The amount of government assistance can be substantial. Entire families are relocated in some cases, with everyone, including the children, being given phony names and Social Security numbers.

Some informants continue working for the government after entering the program. They use their new identities to approach criminal enterprises, working their ways into the organizations and ratting them off for reward money. In such cases, the government occasionally helps them get away with new crimes.

In the late 1960s, a Brooklyn-born con artist named Michael Raymond got caught trying to buy two small Midwestern banks with stolen Treasury notes. He was convicted by an Illinois state court and sentenced to four years in prison. But Raymond cut a deal with the federal government. In exchange for testifying before a U.S. Senate subcommittee on the mob, he was placed in the Witness Protection Program.

As part of the deal, Raymond was given a new identity and moved to southern Florida. The government began paying him $1,500 a month, plus $50,000 for "job assistance," a euphemism for more informing. His handlers apparently didn't notice—or didn't care—that some of his acquaintances were disappearing under mysterious circumstances. In one three-year period, three of Raymond's business associates dropped off the face of the earth. One was a wealthy 67-year-old widow whom he was dating. She was last seen getting into a car with him just after emptying out her bank accounts. When the police began investigating her disappearance, Raymond quickly became the

---

6. Richard Marosi, "3 Guilty in Death of Informant," *Los Angeles Times*, October 19, 1999.

top suspect. Another informant said he bragged about killing her, quoting him as saying, "They're never going to find the stone she's under."

But when Florida authorities began looking into the past of the man they knew as Michael Burnett, they were astonished to find he had no personal history whatsoever. All traces of the real Michael Raymond had been expunged by the federal government. Worse, program administrators helped him disappear again just as the murder investigation was getting under way, relocating him to another part of the country and covering his tracks in Florida.

In the following years, Raymond continued to move around the country, living a lavish lifestyle and occasionally making contact with various law enforcement agencies. But his luck ran out while he working as an informant on an FBI sting operation in Chicago. The federal government finally realized that he was a greater threat than the criminals he was helping to catch. Busted on a weapons possession charge in 1987, he was shipped off to prison without being allowed to cut any more deals.

But for 20 years, Raymond/Burnett lived a life worthy of an Ian Fleming novel. He was a superspy in the government's War on Crime.[7]

In Graham Greene's novel *The Spy Who Came in From the Cold*, a longtime undercover operative who can't stomach the work any more decides to call it quits. On rare occasions, domestic law enforcement snitches can't stand what they're asked to do anymore, either. One example is Donald Michael Stewart, who spent most of his adult life working as a government undercover operative before finally denouncing his handlers.

Stewart was a Chicago-area native who moved to Sacramento and began infiltrating motorcycle gangs and drug rings for the local police before going to work for the FBI. As a federal informant, he infiltrated several California neo-Nazi organizations in the mid-1970s, committing well-publicized acts of violence to make them appear more dangerous than they actually were. By November 1974, Stewart had worked his way into the National Socialist White People's Party, a small far-right group based in San Francisco.

Stewart was with a small group of NSWPP members when they staged a demonstration in a park in Sacramento on August 19, 1975. A reporter and photographer for the *Sacramento Bee* newspaper showed up to cover the protest, which consisted of little more than an informal march through the park. The demonstration attracted several counter-protesters, including Sacramento teen-ager Bill Webster. The reporter and photographer walked over to Webster to interview him. Seeing this, Stewart pulled on a pair of worn leather gloves, pushed his way past the journalists, and punched Webster without provocation, knocking him to the ground and setting off a small melee. A photo of Stewart assaulting Webster ran the next day in the Sacramento paper above a story headlined, "Young Heckler Victim as Nazi Group Visits." The article described Stewart as an NSWPP member who refused to identify himself.

---

7. T.J. English, "The Wiseguy Next Door," *Playboy*, April 1991.

A short time later, Stewart was with several members of the American Nazi Party when they attempted to speak on the campus of San Francisco State University. The neo-Nazis attracted a loud group of protesters who shouted them down. After making sure that a newspaper photographer was present, Stewart grabbed a fire extinguisher out of his van and attacked a protester with it. An Associated Press photo shows him swinging the extinguisher at the head of protester who has crumpled onto the ground.

Stewart was still working undercover within the ANP when a filmmaker produced a documentary on the group titled *California Reich*. Stewart is seen briefly in the film sitting in his van, his face hidden from view, identified only as an "illegal gun dealer," creating the impression that the organization was trafficking in illegal weapons.

By the early 1990s, Stewart had grown disillusioned with the agencies he worked for, especially the Bureau of Alcohol, Tobacco and Firearms. He became a critic of these agencies, voicing his concerns during the federal government's August 1992 confrontation with Randy Weaver and his family at Ruby Ridge, Idaho. Stewart visited the scene of the standoff, where he told freelance writer Alan Block that BATF agents routinely entrap people who have committed no previous crimes, and who have no inclination to do so. Stewart also said that the federal government routinely infiltrates "fringe" groups and provokes the most volatile members to commit violent crimes to justify long-term surveillance and law enforcement operations.

"It's all about job security," Stewart said. "If there's no action, nobody makes any money, there's no overtime, no promotions, no awards. A lot of these guys are Vietnam veterans who miss the adrenaline rush of combat and look for ways to get it without any real danger the people they're targeting will shoot back. They like to get people under their power, to hear them beg for mercy and promise to cooperate, to create fear and terror. You can see some of them almost have orgasms when they stick guns in peoples' faces." [8]

---

8. Allan Block, *Ambush at Ruby Ridge: How Government Agents Set Up Randy Weaver and Took His Family Down*, 1995, publisher unknown.

CHAPTER TWELVE

WHAT DID THEY KNOW, AND WHEN DID THEY KNOW IT?

WHEN THE POLICE SAY a tip from a snitch helped solve a crime, one question should always be asked—*when* did the snitch tell the police about the crime, before or after it happened? Although they rarely admit it, law enforcement officials occasionally stand back and let crimes be committed. Sometimes this is necessary to protect their informants, and to build larger cases against the criminals. But sometimes the consequences are so serious that the public should ask whether the law enforcement agencies have another agenda—a secret agenda to inflate their budgets and expand their powers. This is the question which should have been asked in many of the most politically-significant crimes of the past 40 years.

Gary Thomas Rowe had been convicted of impersonating a police officer when the FBI hired him in 1960 to infiltrate the Ku Klux Klan. Federal authorities were just beginning to extend their jurisdiction to include racially-tinged crimes traditionally investigated by state and local governments. Although Rowe was in a position to prevent KKK chapters from continuing to attack African-Americans, he participated in several of the most notorious racial crimes of the Civil Rights Era, including the murder of activist Viola Gregg Liuzzo, the infamous bombing of a black church that killed four little girls, the shooting of a black man, an attack on an elderly African-American couple and the assault on a busload of Freedom Riders in Birmingham, Alabama.

The attack on the Freedom Riders was an especially significant event. Rowe had warned the Birmingham police of the attack before it occurred, and the police told Rowe that they would let the Klan members and their supporters beat the Freedom Riders for 15 minutes before they intervened. Rowe told the FBI about this arrangement, and the federal agents did not interfere, allowing the Freedom Riders to be savagely assaulted. The attack was filmed by a TV news crew and broadcast across the nation, sparking a public demand for increased federal intervention.[1]

Rowe's role as a government informant was not revealed until 1978, when Alabama authorities revealed he had told them that he shot a black man to death, then kept quiet about the killing at the instructions of an FBI agent. On July 10, the *Birmingham Post-Gazette* reported, "Gary Thomas Rowe has

---

1. Clifford S. Zimmerman, "Toward a New Vision of Informants: A History of Abuses and Suggestions for Reform," *Hastings Constitutional Law Quarterly*, Fall 1994.

failed two polygraph lie detector tests in which he denied involvement in the 1963 bombing which killed four black children at the 16th Street Baptist Church in Birmingham, according to records compiled by the Alabama attorney general's office and Birmingham police."

These revelations prompted the *New York Times* to publish an article on July 11, 1978 which stated, "According to sources close to the renewed investigation into racial violence in Alabama in the 1960s, Rowe is now suspected of having acted as an *agent provocateur,* participating in and helping plan the violent activity that the FBI had hired him to monitor." [2]

One of the largest acts of domestic terrorism in U.S. history was the 1993 bombing of the World Trade Center in New York City. Until then, the country seemed free from the sort of attacks which occur frequently in the Middle East and parts of Europe. After the bombing, political leaders and establishment media pundits declared that a new era had begun, an era where Americans had to be willing to give up some of their constitutional rights to protect themselves against terrorism.

As it turned out, the FBI was fully aware of the bomb plot before the attack took place. The scheme was hatched by a small group of fundamentalist Muslims who worshipped at a New York mosque led by Omar Abdel Rahman, a blind sheik who had been exiled from Egypt because of anti-government preachings. The group had been infiltrated by Emad Salem, a former Egyptian army intelligence officer who had moved to America and begun working with the FBI.

The FBI began arresting members of the plot within days of the bombing. At the time, federal officials said the break in the case came when one of the terrorists returned a rented van used to transport the bomb to the center to recover his security deposit. But that story quickly broke down when the *New York Times* revealed that Salem had kept the FBI posted about the bomb plot—and had secretly tape recorded conversations with his FBI handlers.

In a series of stories written in October and November 1993, the *Times* reported Salem volunteered to neutralize the bomb with inert material, but was told to leave it alone because the investigation was under control. The paper also revealed that the FBI even provided Salem with a timer for a bomb. Then, fearing the timer could tie the agency to the plot, the FBI broke into the warehouse where the bomb was being built and stole it. Salem continued working on the bomb after that, prompting the *Chicago Tribune* to run a December 15, 1993 story on his involvement headlined, "FBI Tipster Said He Built NY Bomb."

On the tapes, Salem repeatedly asserts that the FBI has the ability to prevent the bombing. Salem's handlers dissuade him from raising his complaints with higher-ups at the FBI. The plot went forward as planned. When the bombing suspects went to trial, defense attorneys raised Salem's role as an FBI informant. The jury convicted them anyway.

---

2. Church Committee Report, U.S. Government Printing Office, 1976.

Salem was then used to convict Sheik Omar Abdel Rahman and more of his followers on charges of plotting additional bombings. The federal government alleged that, in addition to the World Trade Center, this larger group planned to attack such New York landmarks as the United Nations building, the George Washington Bridge, 26 Federal Plaza, and the Lincoln and Holland tunnels. Although Sheik Rahman's defense attorneys argued that he was not involved in any of these plots, Salem testified that he tried to have Egyptian President Hosni Mubarak killed when he visited New York.

Rahman and the others were found guilty on all charges. Although Rahman was never directly tied to any of the proposed bombings, he was convicted under a Civil War-era conspiracy law which makes it illegal to plot to wage war against the United States government. His conviction was upheld by a three-judge panel of the United States Court of Appeals for the Second Circuit on August 16, 1999. "To plan the waging of war against the United States is manifestly a grievous assault on the American people, meriting extremely serious punishment," the panel wrote. Much of the ruling was based on the testimony of infiltrator Salem, who told the trial court Rahman had instructed him that "he should make up with God" by "turning his rifle barrel to [Egyptian] President Mubarak's chest, and kill him." [3]

Government officials have never admitted that they allowed the World Trade Center to be bombed. Despite the overwhelming evidence to the contrary, they have repeatedly claimed that miscommunications with Salem prevented them from moving in time. This is a laughable defense, given the tapes of Salem's conversations with his FBI contacts. But the government also ignored warnings from one of its own undercover agents in Waco, Texas on February 28, 1993—with far more tragic results.

Most people first heard of the Branch Davidians when four BATF agents were killed during a botched raid on the group's complex. The BATF invited a TV news crew to accompany them on the raid. When Americans sat down to watch the news that evening, they were astonished to see black-clad federal agents crouched behind cars and firing shots at a large wooden structure. The dramatic footage included scenes of several agents climbing ladders to the second floor, breaking a window and clamoring inside, followed by a hail of bullets coming through the walls out of the room, striking the remaining member of the unit and driving him back down the ladder. When the shooting was over, the BATF agents retreated, carrying their dead and wounded down a long gravel driveway and taking up positions around the complex.

Shortly after the botched raid, the government revealed that it had an informant inside the complex. BATF agent Robert Rodriguez infiltrated the Davidians months before the February 28 assault and fed the BATF detailed information about the group, including the strong anti-government views of leader David Koresh, and details about the group's large arsenal of weapons.

---

3. Benjamin Weiser, "Appellate Court Backs Conviction in '93 Terror Plot," *New York Times*, August 17, 1999.

This information, in and of itself, should have convinced the BATF that such a raid would result in heavy causalities. The Davidian complex was a large, rambling structure. Over 100 people lived there at any given time. It was physically impossible for the BATF to surprise every Davidian in every room of the complex. At least a few would have been able to reach weapons, no matter how well the raid was carried out.

But, as it turned out, the BATF lost the element of surprise well before they reached the building. The TV news crew ran into a mailman on the way to the staging area and told him what was about to happen. The mailman was related to one of the Davidians and told Koresh the agents were coming. Koresh called a quick meeting and told his followers that government agents were on the way. Rodriguez, the undercover agent, was at the meeting and quickly excused himself to tell his supervisors what had happened. But they ignored the warnings and ordered the raid to proceed anyway, resulting in the shootout which claimed the lives of four BATF agents and six Davidians.

Why did the BATF officials go ahead with the raid, even though they were aware the Branch Davidians knew they were coming? As revealed by the 1998 documentary film *Waco: The Rules of Engagement*, agency higher-ups were desperate for good publicity following the disastrous confrontation with Randy Weaver and his family in rural Idaho several months earlier. Congress was about to begin holding hearings on the agency's budget. As shown by the film, BATF officials thought that seizing the group's weapons would erase the stain of the Idaho fiasco.

The FBI assumed control of the situation after the botched raid. The Department of Defense was brought in, dispatching Delta Force troops and sophisticated monitoring equipment to the site. The standoff lasted 51 days before federal agents assaulted the complex with military tanks on the morning of April 19, 1993. Over 80 Davidians, including 17 children, died in the resulting fire. The controversy echoes to this day, despite repeated government attempts to cover up its numerous mistakes and illegal actions.

Rodriguez says his superiors tried to blame him for the death of his co-workers. In an interview with SKATE-TV which aired on September 15, 1999, the BATF undercover agent said his supervisors claimed he hadn't adequately warned them that the element of surprise had been lost. "I put a lot of guilt on me. I felt responsible for a very long time for the murder, for the deaths, of these agents," he said.

Rodriguez told the TV station that the allegations were so distressing he tried to kill himself: "I put the gun to my forehead, in my mouth, and I just wanted to so bad, but I couldn't."[4]

According to the U.S. Justice Department, the government's mishandling of the Waco stand-off led directly to the largest single act of domestic terrorism in United States history—the April 19, 1995 bombing of the Alfred E. Murrah federal office building in Oklahoma City. Federal prosecutors claim that

---

4. AP via Sam Smith, *Progressive Review*, September 17, 1999.

former U.S. Army buddies Timothy McVeigh and Terry Nichols blew up the building to avenge the death of the Davidians. But, as with the previous examples, at least one informant had tipped off the government to the plot in advance, raising the question of why it was allowed to proceed.

At the very least, news reports and court records suggest the government and private advocacy groups were tracking McVeigh years before the bombing. He visited Waco during the 51-day siege, talking with other government critics and openly selling anti-New World Order literature and bumper stickers on the hood of a car. As it turns out, the government was watching those who came to show their support for the Davidians. "The FBI kept tabs on 'right-wing' sympathizers who flocked to Waco during the siege, and monitored Internet traffic," the Associated Press reported on October 9, 1999.

Shortly after McVeigh was arrested for the bombing, the Cable News Network reported that he had come to attention of undercover government operatives at a gun show in Arizona. At that time, McVeigh was reportedly making a living buying and selling weapons and anti-government literature at gun shows around the country. The report did not say whether the operatives were BATF agents or paid informants.

Another sign that the government was or should have been aware of McVeigh surfaced on April 21, two days after the Oklahoma City bombing, when the Anti-Defamation League issued a press release tying McVeigh to *The Spotlight*, a populist weekly newspaper with anti-Semitic overtones published by a small, far-right, conspiracy-minded organization based in Washington, DC called the Liberty Lobby. The ADL release, which was picked up by the *Washington Post*, said that McVeigh had purchased a classified advertisement in the August 9, 1993 issue of *The Spotlight* to sell "rocket launchers." According to the ADL, McVeigh purchased the ad under the name T. Tuttle.

The ADL press release was mostly accurate. McVeigh had bought an ad for a flare gun he called a "Law Launcher replica" using the name T. Tuttle. But how did the ADL know about the ad? The ADL either had someone close to McVeigh, or the government was tracking him and sharing the information with the organization.

In the months following the bombing, the government alleged that McVeigh and Nichols were assisted in the bomb plot by one or more "John Does." A drawing of John Doe #2 was released and widely circulated. As time went on, however, the government backed down from this claim, eventually saying that McVeigh and Nichols acted alone. Many independent reporters and researchers still believe that other people were involved in the plot, however.

A freelance journalist named J.D. Cash was the first to report that McVeigh and at least a half-dozen other men planned the bombing at Elohim City, a Christian Identity community in rural Oklahoma. McVeigh had been tied to Elohim City shortly after he was arrested. The phone card mentioned in the ADL press release had been used to call the community two weeks before the bombing.

On February 11, 1997, Cash published a story in the small *McCurtain Daily Gazette* which revealed that a BATF informant named Carol Howe had infiltrated Elohim City before the bombing. Howe had seen McVeigh (whom she knew as Tuttle) and a number of other residents and visitors plotting to blow up the Oklahoma City federal office building in late 1994. Although these allegations were largely ignored by the corporate press, they were later confirmed by internal BATF documents which proved Howe was an informant, that she saw McVeigh and others plotting to blow up the Alfred E. Murrah building, and she notified her superiors of the plot before the actual bombing.[5]

The key to Howe's story is Elohim City, a community founded by Robert Millar, a right-wing preacher. It was a common meeting place for militant white supremacists over the years, including members of The Order, a racist gang who murdered Jewish radio talk show host Alan Berg and staged a series of high-profile bank robberies in the early 1980s. As *Time* magazine confirmed on February 24, 1997, "The city's guest list over the years has been a veritable Who's Who of the radical right."

There are a number of obvious links between Elohim City and the bombing. One of Millar's followers was Richard Snell, a former leader of a racist group called The Covenant, the Sword and the Arm of the Lord (CSA). In the early 1980s, Snell and a number of other white supremacists had plotted to blow up the Alfred E. Murrah building in retaliation for the death of Posse Comitatus leader Gordon Kahl. On the morning of the 1995 Oklahoma City bombing, Snell was executed for killing a black Arkansas State trooper and a pawnshop owner he thought was Jewish. As documented by the June 16, 1996 issue of the *Village Voice*, Snell knew something big was going to happen: "In the days before his execution on April 19, 1995, Snell, according to one prison official, reportedly said, 'There was going to be a bomb, there was going to be an explosion' the day of his execution."

Elohim City was also a hideout for a gang of racist bank robbers who called themselves the Aryan Republican Army (ARA). Between 1994 and early 1996, the ARA robbed over 20 banks throughout the midwest, stealing approximately $250,000. According to federal documents, at least three meetings to organize the robberies took place at Elohim City.

---

5. Although Carol Howe's allegations were confirmed in open court with BATF memos obtained by her lawyers, the press largely ignored the story. *Newsweek*, ABC News and a small number of other corporate news outlets covered some details, but the ongoing developments were primarily reported by publications long associated with the Far Right, including *The New American*, a monthly magazine published by the John Birch Society. Senior editor William Jasper wrote several well documented stories about Howe and her charges, including "Elohim, Terror, and Truth," which ran on March 31, 1997. "Undercover: The Howe Revelations" was published on September 15, 1997, shortly after Howe was acquitted of all charges. It includes extensive passages from numerous memos Howe filed with her BATF Special Agent Angela Finley, her handler for Elohim City, before the bombing. They confirm Howe saw Tim McVeigh at Elohim City plotting to blow up the Oklahoma City building.

Federal law enforcement officials linked the ARA to the Oklahoma City bombing almost immediately after it happened, saying that McVeigh and Nichols financed the bomb plot with money robbed from banks in the midwest. A little more than a month after the attack, *Newsweek* reported, "the FBI expects to arrest 'a group of major players' within the next several weeks, saying, "investigators are looking closely at a white-supremacist group headed by Robert Millar in Elohim City, Okla." [6] Although the government backed off from this accusation as McVeigh's trial approached, one of the robbers, Michael Brescia, strongly resembles John Doe #2.

As it turned out, Howe was not the only informant within the Christian Identity community. Founder Millar repeatedly shared information with law enforcement officials. During a June 31, 1997 court proceeding, FBI Senior Agent Peter Rickel testified Millar was in regular contact with the agency in the years before the bombing. Millar confirmed that he frequently talked to government officials, telling the *Tulsa World* newspaper that he had answered questions from such agencies as the FBI and the DEA.

Writing about the revelation in the July 1, 1997 issue of the *McCurtain Daily Gazette*, Cash said, "Millar's position as a mole for the FBI could explain why the compound has never been raided. Despite its use as a hideout for gunrunners, drug dealers, bank robbers and suspected members of the conspiracy that bombed the Alfred E. Murrah federal building in Oklahoma City, Elohim City has enjoyed a reputation as a place where fugitives can live without fear of arrest."

Another informant who lives in Elohim City is James Ellison, a former CSA member who helped devise the original Murrah building bombing plan in the early 1980s. A few year later, Ellison testified in court against several members of The Order. Because of this, he was considered a traitor and snitch by all racist leaders—except Millar. On May 19, 1995, Ellison even married Millar's daughter, Angela.

The leader of the ARA was also an informant. Peter Langan, the son of a retired U.S. Marine intelligence officer, and Richard Guthrie, another racist, robbed a Pizza Hut in Georgia in October 1992. A short time later, Langan was arrested by Georgia authorities. Remarkably, the U.S. Secret Service intervened, arranging for Langan to be released on a signature bond. At the time, the Secret Service said that Langan had agreed to find Guthrie, who was suspected of threatening the President. Langan did not turn Guthrie in, however. Instead, the two men formed the ARA, recruited several other members and launched one of the most successful bank robbery sprees in U.S. history.

The Secret Service link has prompted several researchers to wonder whether the ARA was, in fact, a covert government operation. They note that the ARA never encountered any bank guards or other law enforcement officials during any of their robberies. They also note that Langan, Guthrie and the other ARA members were not arrested until after the press began reporting on Elohim

---

6. "More Arrests to Come," *Newsweek*, May 29, 1995.

City. Guthrie was found dead in his prison cell a few days after telling relatives that he was writing a book on the ARA that would embarrass the government. Although the death has been ruled a suicide, the coroner's report has never been released.

Yet another likely informant was Elohim City's security director, Andreas Strassmeier. The son of a high-ranking German official, Strassmeier spent several years in the German army, including a stint as an intelligence officer. He came to the United States in 1989, when the U.S. and German governments were running an operation to stop the flow of neo-Nazi literature from America to Germany, where it is illegal. Strassmeier immediately moved to Elohim City, where Millar put him in charge of security. He is the person McVeigh phoned two weeks before the Oklahoma City bombing with his *Spotlight* calling card. Strassmeier fled the country after his name surfaced in the press.

In the months before the bombing, Howe sent over 70 reports to Karen Finley, her BATF control officer. In her reports, Howe reported that Strassmeier, the ARA members, and a number of other people at Elohim City were planning to bomb federal office buildings, including the one in Oklahoma City. Alarmed, Finley requested that the BATF raid the racist encampment. Her request was turned down after being reviewed by top FBI and Department of Justice officials in February 1995.

Judge Richard Matsch prohibited Howe from testifying about her work at Elohim City at McVeigh's trial, saying her testimony might "confuse" the jurors.

After Howe went public with her story, the federal government indicted her on explosives charges. She went to trial in August 1997, with her attorney, Clark Brewster, arguing she bought the explosives at the direction of the government. Brewster entered Howe's BATF reports into evidence at the trial. In them, Howe says she saw McVeigh meeting with ARA members to plot the bombing. The jury believed Howe and acquitted her of all charges.

The federal government also stood by and watched while a small group of right-wing counterfeiters stole hundreds of thousands of dollars and tied up billions of dollars worth of other peoples' property in the early 1990s. The group, the Montana Freemen, argued that the federally-chartered banking system is unconstitutional. Claiming the right to issue their own bank drafts, the Freemen printed up billions of dollars worth of phony checks and illegal property liens. The government responded by infiltrating the group—but then waited over a year before arresting them on fraud and conspiracy charges.

Although a federal jury convicted the group's top leaders in July 1998, testimony at the trial revealed that the government's informants reinforced the Freemen's belief that their checks and liens were legal and actually helped issue them. According to a story in the July 3, 1998 issue of the *New York Times*, two FBI undercover agents infiltrated the group in 1995. They were Dale and Connie Jakes, a husband-and-wife team who were making a living by working as full-time informants for various law enforcement agencies. Dale was embraced by the Freemen because of his knowledge of explosives, while Connie became the group's unpaid office manager. The Jakes used their positions to monitor the group members and their associates. Among other things, they recorded the names, phone numbers, addresses and license plate numbers of all visitors.

During the criminal trial that followed the arrests, several Freemen said they thought their bogus checks were legitimate because the Jakes said they cashed them to buy office equipment. "They said the FBI falsely encouraged the Freemen when an undercover agent told them he cashed their checks and used the money to buy a copier, computer and radio system for the compound," the *Times* reported. The federal government also admitted that it allowed the Freemen to operate for more than a year—during which time the group issued millions of dollars in bogus checks and phony liens—to keep gathering intelligence on anti-government groups. "The delay not only caused hundreds of thousands of dollars in fraud losses to businesses victimized by Freemen checks," the paper reported, "it also caused deep resentment among the Freemen's rural neighbors."

The federal government was also behind a scandalous plot to set up Malcolm X's daughter, Qubilah Shabazz, on a phony murder conspiracy charge. The frame was engineered by Michael Fitzpatrick, a longtime government snitch, who was paid to romance and railroad the confused and emotionally disturbed young woman.

Fitzpatrick was working for the government even before he graduated from the elite United Nations International School in New York. By 1987 he had infiltrated the Jewish Defense Organization, a violent faction of the militant Jewish Defense League. Fitzpatrick helped the FBI arrest and convict a pair of Zionist teenagers on charges of attempting to bomb an Egyptian government tourist office. After his testimony put the young Jews in jail, Fitzpatrick set his sights on the Revolutionary Youth Movement of the Communist Workers Party, recruiting among the punks who hung out at the CBGB rock club. He also joined the Committee in Solidarity with the People of El Salvador, one of several left-wing organizations disrupted by a secret counter-intelligence campaign run by the FBI.

Fitzpatrick travelled the world during the 1980s, moving in and out of New York, Minneapolis, and even Jamaica. He got married twice, but neither relationship lasted. Fitzpatrick also developed a cocaine habit, and was busted for driving under the influence of a controlled substance in January 1986. Although he got a fine for the driving violation, the drug charge was dropped. Shortly after that, Fitzpatrick began frequenting Back Room Books, an anarchist book store in Minneapolis. After insinuating himself with the collective running the store, Fitzpatrick showed up one day with a gun and asked to stash it in the bookstore's closet. One of the group's members got nervous about the gun and removed it from the premises without telling Fitzpatrick. The police entered the shop a few days later, saying they were looking for a runaway girl. The cops went straight to the closet and seemed disappointed when they didn't find anything. Fitzpatrick never returned to the bookstore.[7]

---

7. Mitzi Waltz, "Michael Fitzpatrick: Agent Provocateur," *PDXS*, February 27, 1995.

Fitzpatrick reportedly continued infiltrating political organizations throughout the late 1980s and early 1990s, even working for an abortion clinic as an escort during a large-scale Operation Rescue protest in Minneapolis. Then, in November 1993, he was arrested again, this time on theft charges. His case did not go to trial, however. Instead, Fitzpatrick suddenly came into a lot of money. Although he filed for bankruptcy in April 1993, declaring a used car as his only asset, by the end of the year he was driving a year-old Jeep Cherokee and a new Jeep Grand Wagoneer. He also had a lot of shiny new credit cards—and a new sweetheart.

Although Fitzpatrick was white, he had known Shabazz for a long time. The two first met in high school in New York. Shabazz told friends that Fitzpatrick reappeared and began courting her in the spring or summer of 1994, traveling and calling between Minneapolis and New York, where she lived. Shabazz was smitten with Fitzpatrick, telling friends she was going to marry an old high school friend in Minneapolis. She moved there in September with her young son.

But Fitzpatrick wasn't planning to marry Shabazz. He was setting her up for the FBI. Fitzpatrick was taping their telephone calls, which started off innocuous enough but soon turned to a disturbing subject—Louis Farrakhan, head of the Nation of Islam. Shabazz had reason to hate Farrakhan. Her father was killed after quitting his job as national spokesman for the organization. Farrakhan had called him a traitor, writing that "such a man is worthy of death." Malcolm X was assassinated two months after Farrakhan's words were published, in the Audobon Ballroom in Harlem on February 21, 1965. Three men with ties to the Nation of Islam were convicted in the slaying. Shabazz saw him killed. She was only four years old at the time.

Rumors started circulating almost immediately that Farrakhan had ordered the hit. Although he was never charged with the killing, the allegations circulated within the black community for many years before reaching a larger audience in Spike Lee's 1992 film, *Malcolm X*. It didn't take long for Fitzpatrick to remind Shabazz of the allegations. After she moved to Minneapolis, he arranged to meet her at a hotel room which had been rigged with a video camera. With Fitzpatrick doing most of the talking, Shabazz admitted that she hated Farrakhan. When Fitzpatrick mentioned killing him, Shabazz put up a steady stream of objections, although she said she wished he was dead. A few days later, on January 12, 1995, Shabazz was arrested by federal agents and charged with trying to hire a hit man to kill the Nation of Islam leader.

The arrest set off a huge public controversy, especially when Fitzpatrick's role was revealed. Prominent African-American leaders across the country blasted the sting operation. Even Farrakhan, the supposed target of Shabazz's plot, came to her defense, claiming the federal government was trying to create dissension in the black community. High-ranking officials in the U.S. Justice Department began waffling about when they first knew of the so-called assassination plot. Five days after Shabazz was arrested, Justice Department spokesman Carl Stern admitted that federal prosecutors in Minneapolis had sent three "urgent" reports on the case to their superiors in Washington, DC, beginning in November 1994. And it was revealed that U.S. Attorney Janet Reno had been briefed on the case before Shabazz was arrested, even though Farrakhan was never notified that his life was supposedly in danger.

Before too long, it was clear that Fitzpatrick was nothing more than a sleazy freelance informant who had set Shabazz up for money. The government refused to drop the charges, however, and Shabazz finally agreed to a plea bargain. She was sentenced to probation and ordered to undergo counseling. According to Ronald Kuby, Shabazz's defense attorney, Fitzpatrick "never worried about his own illegal conduct, because quite correctly he thought that no matter what he did, he would be able to get off by ensnaring someone else." [8]

---

8. Mitzi Waltz, "Policing Activism: Think Global, Spy Local," *CovertAction Quarterly*, Summer 1997.

CHAPTER THIRTEEN

PUNISHING WHISTLEBLOWERS

ALTHOUGH SNITCHES ARE GENERALLY HELD in low regard, there is one kind of informant revered by the public—the whistleblower. Typically, whistleblowers are employees who report their bosses to the authorities for breaking the law. Whistleblowers can also be public employees who turn in abusive, corrupt or wasteful government administrators. Or they can work in the private sector and report on corporate heads who approve unsafe products or intentionally overcharge consumers. Either kind of employee might also go to the press with such accusations.

Whatever the case, the reviled snitch is not the same as the honorable whistleblower. As author Timothy Garton Ash wrote in a review of the book *Accusatory Practices* in the *London Review of Books*, "The former secretly passes information about fellow citizens to the authorities, the latter publicly passes information about the authorities to fellow citizens," he said.

In theory, whistleblowers are thought to be so beneficial that several federal laws have been enacted to protect and reward them. The law which created the Occupational Safety and Health Administration (OSHA) prohibits employers from retaliating against workers who report dangerous or unhealthy working conditions. Both the Civil Service Reform Act of 1978 and the Whistleblower Protection Act of 1989 are supposed to shield federal whistleblowers from retaliation. And the False Claim Act makes private employees who discover fraud in government procurement programs eligible for a bounty equal to between 15 and 30 percent of the penalties assessed against the company.

But, despite these alleged safeguards, most whistleblowers are in fact punished as a result of their complaints. According to a 1989 study published in *Public Administration Review*, 60 percent of all whistleblowers lose their jobs. The U.S. Department of Labor confirmed this finding in 1999. The department reviewed 653 cases where employees reported such hazardous working conditions as exposure to toxic chemicals, the use of dangerous machines, the use of contaminated needles, and the strain of repetitive hand motions. Nearly 67 percent of the employees who filed the complaints were fired.[1]

Under the law, workers who believe they have been dismissed or punished for reporting workplace hazards may file complaints with the U.S. Labor Department. The department is supposed to investigate each complaint, and then file suit against the employers in federal court if it concludes the retaliation was

---

1. Robert Pear, "Clinton Wants to Strengthen U.S. Whistleblower Shield," *New York Times*, March 15, 1999.

illegal. But the 1999 Labor Department review revealed that the government rarely files such suits, even when it finds evidence of retaliation. For example, the department received 2,124 complaints of retaliation in 1997. It only filed 18 cases. The department received 2,474 complaints in 1998. It only took 14 of them to court. "Too many employers feel they can retaliate against whistleblowers with impunity," says Charles N. Jeffress, the Assistant Secretary of Labor in charge of OSHA.[2]

The number of prominent whistleblowers who have been fired—or worse— is significant:

- Frank Serpico was a highly-acclaimed New York City police officer when he testified about corruption within the department before a state commission. His testimony led to the dismissal of several veteran officers and supervisors. A short time later, Serpico was shot in the face during a botched undercover drug raid. The officers backing him up failed to come to his aid or call an ambulance. Although Serpico eventually recovered, he quit the force in disgust.

- Karen Silkwood was a whistleblower who paid the ultimate price for her honesty. She was working at the Kerr-McGee Cimarron River nuclear power plant when she was accidentally contaminated with airborne plutonium in August 1974. Concerned about the company's safety practices, Silkwood began carrying a notebook to report lapses she and other workers observed. On September 26, she shared her concerns with the national leaders of the Oil, Chemical and Atomic Workers Union, who were so alarmed they brought her to testify to the Atomic Energy Commission. On November 5, Silkwood discovered that she had been contaminated again—this time by so much radioactivity that she had to be scrubbed with a painful mixture of Tide and Clorox, and had to supply urine and fecal samples to health inspectors. Baffled by the source of the radiation, the inspectors searched her house and found it to be so contaminated that most of its contents had to be removed and buried. As Silkwood's health began to deteriorate, Kerr-McGee officials insinuated that she had smuggled plutonium out of the plant and dosed herself. On November 13, six days after the contamination was discovered in her house, Silkwood drove to meet a reporter from the *New York Times* with documents she believed would prove her employer was guilty of criminal neglect. Her car veered off a straight road, slamming into a concrete culvert and killing her. The incriminating documents were never found. The story was made into the 1983 movie *Silkwood* starring Meryl Streep.

- One of the most famous of recent whistleblowers is Jeffrey Wigand, a former research director for the Brown & Williamson Tobacco Corporation, America's third-largest cigarette maker. In 1993,

2. *Ibid.*

Wigand blew the whistle on his former employer, claiming that B&W had repeatedly covered up research about the harmful effects of nicotine, and that its former chairman lied under oath to Congress about his beliefs on nicotine addiction. The tobacco company retained a team of private detectives to dig up dirt on their former employee. The resulting 500-page file was turned over to the *Wall Street Journal* and a number of other media outlets. It included a range of allegations, from domestic violence and shoplifting to lying on his resume. The *Journal* concluded that most of the assertions were false or unproven.

- Another well-known whistleblower is Frederic Whitehurst, a former chemist at the FBI's crime lab. Whitehurst filed numerous complaints about sloppiness and corruption at the lab before going public during the O.J. Simpson trial. After initially denying Whitehurst's accusations, the FBI finally admitted he was right and promised to overhaul its lab procedures. The agency retaliated against Whitehurst by transferring him out of the lab, however. Fortunately, he had a good attorney who negotiated a generous settlement with the FBI, allowing the whistleblower to retire from the agency on his own terms.

- Jennifer Long was a career tax auditor with the IRS when she testified before the U.S. Senate Finance Committee about taxpayer abuses in September 1997. She was the only one of seven IRS agents who did not sit behind a curtain or use a voice distortion system to hide her identity when she testified. Long said the agency targets taxpayers it thinks are weak and lack the resources to fight an audit, while ignoring cheaters who have the power or connections to fight back. Although Long had been rated "fully successful" by the IRS for 15 years, the agency moved to fire her on April 16, 1999. She was given a formal notice that her work was so bad she had 60 days to straighten up or she'd be dismissed. "You're fired once they give you that letter," she said in the September 17 issue of the *New York Times*. "They just have to give you 60 days notice." The action was halted the following day, after the chairman of the Finance Committee, U.S. Senator William Roth, called IRS Commissioner Charles Rossotti to protest the apparent retaliation.[3]

- Another government whistleblower who lost her job was Yvette Walton, a New York City police officer. Walton had testified at a City Council hearing that her old unit, the Street Crimes Unit, was hostile to black and Hispanic officers and also violated the rights of minority citizens by searching them without justification. The unit came under intense scrutiny after an African immigrant, Amadou Diallo, was shot dead by four of its officers on February 4, 1999. The City Council held a hearing on the unit on April 19. One of the witnesses was Walton. When she left the hearing room, Walton called her supervisor in the Bronx and was told

---

3. David Cay Johnston, "IRS Looks to Fire Star Witness in Hearings on Abuses," *New York Times*, April 17, 1999.

she'd been fired. A short time later, she received a two-paragraph letter from the department informing her that she'd been terminated but giving no reason. "You are dismissed as a police officer in the Police Department of the City of New York, effective: 1600 hours, April 19, 1999," it said. "I felt like I was terminated for telling the truth," Walton told the *New York Times*.[4]

♦ In December 1998, four white police officers shot and killed Tyisha Miller, a 19-year-old black woman, as she sat in her car in Riverside, California. African-American officer Rene Rodriguez arrived on the scene approximately 40 seconds later, and was shocked to hear the white officers making racially and sexually derogatory comments about Miller, her family, friends and acquaintances. Rodriguez reported the remarks to his superiors at the Riverside Police Department, then was surprised when other officers retaliated against him with intimated threats. His life was even put in danger by officers who deliberately refused to provide backup support in dangerous situations. By March 1999, Rodriguez was so stressed out that he was placed on administrative leave, then denied pay and health benefits, nearly forcing him and his wife into bankruptcy. His plight was reported on an October 1999 edition of 6o *Minutes*, prompting black newspaper columnist Earl Ofari Hutchinson to write, "The shabby treatment of Rodriguez makes a huge mockery of the claim by officials that they want employees of public agencies, especially police departments, to report abuses and misconduct and will reward them when they do so. When they turn their backs on credible whistleblowers, it's a powerful deterrent for others who witness misconduct and abuse."

♦ John Carman worked for the U.S. Customs Service for 15 years. Before that, he worked for the Secret Service, the U.S. Mint and the San Diego Police Department. For much of that time, he complained to superiors about illegal activity on the part of other employees, including drug dealing, smuggling, payoffs, bribery and more. One of the first complaints concerned 150 kilos of cocaine, seized in a drug raid, that was reported missing. "You don't just lose a load of 150 kilos of cocaine," Carman told reporter David M. Bresnahan for an October 29, 1999 story on the *WorldNetDaily*. Although Carman complained directly to Internal Affairs investigators, the U.S. Department of Justice, and even the White House, none of his accusations were ever taken seriously. Instead, agency officials and employees retaliated against him. In one chilling incident, Carman was working in an enclosed room on the Mexican border, inspecting cars traveling between the two countries. Someone turned off the blowers which were removing the exhaust gas from the room where Carman was working and he almost died. He believes it was a co-worker. There were other threats as well, including

---

4. Michael Cooper, "Hooded No More, Officer Charges She Was Fired as a Whistleblower," *New York Times*, April 26, 1999.

numerous death threats. Carman finally resigned from the Customs Service after negotiating a settlement with agency officials—an agreement which he says the agency is not honoring. According to Carman, corrupt officials refuse to release his employment records to potential employers, preventing him from getting a new job.[5]

◆ Sheryl Hall, a federal civil servant, was repeatedly threatened and punished for speaking out about a politically-oriented computer system installed in the Clinton White House. She helped install the new recordkeeping system, officially known as the White House Office Database. At one point, Hall told the political appointees in charge of the database that it violated federal laws against using government resources for fundraising. For that, she was cut out of the decision-making process and branded as "disloyal," memos from top Clinton aides show. Then she was demoted from her post as chief of the Information Systems and Technology branch of the Executive Office of the President. She lost her authority over the system just before a supposed technical "glitch" stopped the computers from storing incoming e-mail messages to senior White House aides in the fall of 1996. When Congress began investigating the problem, Hall testified about her opposition to the fundraising system. A few days later, someone broke into her White House office and stole her files on the database. When she told her superiors about the break-in they didn't seem very concerned. Neither did the Secret Service.[6]

Ironically, even whistleblowers who succeeding in sparking investigations are frequently disappointed by the outcomes. A good example is Marc Holder, a Swiss attorney who served on the board of the International Olympic Committee. Holder created an international scandal when he charged that many Olympic officials have been bribed over the years by private businesses, public officials and others hoping to bring the international sporting events to their cities. After Holder went public with his allegations, the IOC expelled six members and four others resigned. In addition, several businessmen were arrested on bribery charges in Salt Lake City. But, interviewed by *Facts* magazine in November, Holder said the IOC was still corrupt. "There is one IOC member who has a theory that everybody has their price," the magazine quoted him as saying.

Given all these problems, why do people continue to blow the whistle on their employers? To a large extent, most whistleblowers are idealists. According to the 1989 study reported in *Public Administration Review*, they believe in absolute moral standards, have a strong sense of individual responsibility and hold a fierce commitment to upholding moral principles.[7]

5. David M. Bresnahan, "Former Customs Agent Alleges Corruption, Blows Whistle on Drug Deals, Smuggling, Payoffs, Bribes," *WorldNetDaily*, October 29, 1999.
6. Paul Sperry, "E-mail Whistleblower's Office was Burglarized," *WorldNetDaily*, March 28, 2000.
7. "Whistleblowers: Saint or Snitch?," *Credit Union Executive*, January–February, 1992.

Many whistleblowers believe they can get their stories out by going to the press. But this is a risky assumption, as demonstrated by the experiences of former Brown & Williamson Tobacco Corporation scientist Jeffrey Wigand. Before he was fired, Wigand was interviewed by the CBS News program 60 *Minutes*. In the interview with Mike Wallace, Wigand said that company CEO Thomas E. Sandefur Jr. lied to Congress when he claimed ignorance about the addictive nature of nicotine.

Wigand had been reluctant to conduct the interview. He was persuaded to come forward by producer Lowell Bergman, despite considerable risk to Wigand's career and personal life. But CBS executives refused to air the most serious allegations in the interview at the last minute after network attorneys said Brown & Williamson could sue them. Instead, Wallace went forward with a weak story in which Wigand was not identified and his remarks were heavily censored. Bergman was infuriated by the decision and leaked the story to several New York newspapers. Humiliated, 60 *Minutes* finally aired the original story nearly three months later. Bergman resigned in disgust.

The incident served as the basis for *The Insider*, the 1999 film by director Michael Mann. "This was a corporate blunder," CBS producer Don Hewitt told the *Washington Post* just before the film was released. "Nobody here at 60 *Minutes* was in agreement with the corporation. Short of a bunch of guerrillas with guns taking over the CBS transmitters, there was no way for us to put it on the air the first time. CBS owns the means of getting that story to the public."

The Public Broadcasting System aired a documentary on controversial stories killed by establishment media outlets in mid-October 1999. As reported in "Fear and Favor in the Newsroom," during the Persian Gulf War NBC News President Michael Gartner ordered his news director not to run video footage of civilian causalities in Iraq which contradicted official claims of U.S. military "surgical strikes." Then Gartner fired the reporter who shot it, six-time Emmy winner Jon Alpert. A short time later, the *New York Times* buckled under industry pressure and killed an exposé of billion-dollar cost overruns at a nuclear-power plant by award-winning reporter Frances Cerra and took her off the story. In 1995, the media giant Cox Enterprises ordered *Atlanta Journal-Constitution* executive editor Bill Kovach to stop reporting on alleged bribery schemes and racist lending practices at the Atlanta-based Coca-Cola company. Kovach resigned.

The airing of this documentary does not mean that PBS is a refuge for whistleblowers, however. As reported by the *San Francisco Bay Guardian*, several public TV outlets, including San Francisco's KQED, the most-watched public station in the country, refused to support the documentary for fear of offending corporate sponsors. "Our public TV executives' response has been appalling, and you can't help but think that the message of the film was the reason why," Randy Baker, co-producer and writer of the 90-minute film, told the newspaper.

CHAPTER FOURTEEN

BRAVE NEW SCHOOLS

IF YOU WANT TO SEE THE FUTURE of the Snitch Culture, all you need to do is visit America's public schools. Snitching is almost a required subject these days. Students are encouraged to spy on one another, with many schools paying cash for tips on potential troublemakers. Uniformed police officers roam the halls looking for squealers. High-tech video cameras are built into the walls and ceilings. Anonymous telephone tip lines take reports on any child who seems a little different. School administrators even check personal Internet websites maintained on home computers by their students.

And the information gathered through this surveillance network is not ignored or forgotten. These tips frequently trigger prompt and drastic responses, even for the most insignificant offenses. Under newly-adopted Zero Tolerance policies, students are routinely kicked out for such minor things as bringing aspirin to school, muttering vague threats, shoving matches, even writing school papers which teachers find offensive.

Largely as a result of these new snitch programs and policies, suspensions and expulsions have skyrocketed in recent years. The number of suspended students almost doubled from 1.7 million in 1974 to 3.2 million in 1998.[1]

The new school surveillance systems are the result of the same forces at play in the larger society. They are being pushed by the federal government, with the active assistance of state and local police. The private sector is developing new informant programs with the enthusiastic support of the corporate media, which routinely exaggerates the risks faced by students, teachers and administrators. In an attempt to prevent a few children from causing trouble, all students are under the microscope, all at the mercy of snitches.

Students have always been watched in the American public school system, of course. The education bureaucracy has traditionally been concerned about more than academic behavior—it has also watched students' social behavior. Files are opened on each and every student, files which record everything from attendance to vaccinations to incidents of disruptive behavior. These files follow each student from school to school, and are stored for years after graduation.

But schools began watching their students much more closely after the federal government got into the act. The U.S. Constitution does not give

---

1. "Projected Student Suspension and Expulsion Rate Values for the Nation's Public Schools by Race/Ethnicity and Gender," Office for Civil Rights, U.S. Department of Justice, June 2000.

Washington, DC any role in the nation's education system. Primary and second-ary schools are funded at the state and local levels, and overseen by locally-elected school boards. But the federal government has worked its way into the schools over the years, originally by protecting the civil rights of minority students, and offering money for specific programs approved by Congress and administered by the U.S. Department of Education. Although the amount of federal money is very low—less than 10 percent of total operating costs in most cases, with much of the money going for lunch programs—the amount of influence is very large, and growing every year.

President George Bush authorized the federal government's first comprehen-sive attempt to take control of the public school system, pushing a set of achieve-ment targets which are commonly called Goals 2000 because they were supposed to be met by the year 2000. They included such laudable-sounding proposals as raising the high school graduation rate from 86 to 90 percent, along with such pie-in-sky objectives as making U.S. students the first in the world in math and science. The National Governors' Association (NGA) endorsed these goals, which essentially authorized federal, state and local governments to identify and treat all students "at risk" of failing to meet them.

One goal specifically required schools to spy on their students. It called for making schools free of drugs, guns and violence—a goal which can only be achieved if students are willing to inform on classmates suspected of using drugs, carrying guns or engaging in violent conduct. Congress passed lots of new legislation to help the schools set up such monitoring programs, including the Safe and Drug Free Schools Act, which provides money for local school districts to hire uniformed police officers to patrol the campuses.

But, as intrusive as these programs were, they were nothing compared to what happened after Columbine, in large part because of the public hysteria fueled by the extensive and largely inaccurate media coverage. The ferocity of the April 20, 1999 attack shocked the nation. Eric Harris and Dylan Klebold killed 12 classmates and a teacher before taking their own lives. But even before the final bodies had been removed from the school, President Clinton went on national TV to urge students to report any anti-social classmates to the authorities, telling them they should not be worried about being labeled snitches.

Using the Columbine shootings to call for more snitching was hypocritical at best. Harris and Klebold had already been identified as troublemakers. After being arrested and convicted on theft charges, the two teenagers had been placed in a government-run anger management program. One of their classmate's parents had provided the Littleton police department with disturbing rants downloaded from Harris' Internet website. The officer assigned to Columbine knew both Harris and Klebold by sight, and he was keeping tabs on them.

In the confused days and weeks following the killings, the corporate media offered numerous theories about the motives behind them. Harris and Klebold were described as goth rockers, cross dressers and neo-Nazis, none of which was true. They were reported to be members of a high school clique called "The Trenchcoat Mafia," which was also false. The press said they listened to Marilyn Manson and "racist" black metal music, which was also false. Various experts also blamed the killings on video games and movies with violent themes, such as *Natural Born Killers* and *The Basketball Diaries*.[2]

Only a few researchers pointed out that the Columbine shootings were an aberration, a bizarre incident which ran completely counter to the national trends. Less than one percent of all murders in the country occur on school property. Children are far more likely to be killed at home by their parents. "Studies show that people think most kids [who are murdered] are killed by other kids," says Jason Ziedenberg, policy analyst at the Justice Policy Institute in Washington, DC. "In reality, less than three percent of kids are killed by other kids. Most are killed by their own guardians."[3]

More than that, violent juvenile crime has been going down, not up, in recent years. According to the FBI's Uniform Crime Reports, the rate of violent crime has been falling for more than a decade. Juvenile arrests for serious and violent crimes fell nearly 11 percent from 1997 to 1998, doubling the 5.4 percent decline for adults. Although juvenile crime had been dropping steadily since 1993, federal officials say this was the most significant decrease in recent years.[4]

"You have a horrific incident like the Columbine shootings, and that paints a picture of a continuing problem that has not gone away," Shay Bilchik, head of the U.S. Department of Juvenile Justice and Delinquency Prevention, told the *New York Times* when the 1998 statistics were released. "But people are shocked when you try to tell them that juvenile crime is actually going down."

Such sobering statistics were lost in the media-driven hysteria, however. Instead, schools rushed to create new snitch programs and other security measures, spurred on by the federal government and its allies. In August 1999, the NGA released a report titled "Making Schools Safe" which says that school officials should be aware of the following six "risk factors" in the lives of their students:

- Arrest of the father.
- Arrest of the mother.
- Documented involvement with child protective services.
- Major family transition, meaning one parent either leaving or returning to the home since the student's birth.

---

2. On December 20, 1999, *Time* published an exclusive story based on videotapes Eric Harris and Dylan Klebold made of themselves before the shootings. In the tapes, Harris and Klebold say they hate everyone, including "niggers, spics, Jews, gays, fucking whites." Harris indicated his favorite CD was *Bombthreat Before She Blows* by KMFDM, an anti-racist industrial band. They wanted Steven Speilberg, the Jewish director of *Schindler's List*, to make a movie of their lives.
3. Author's interview with Jason Ziedenberg, April 18, 2000.
4. Eric Lichtblau, "Youth Crime Rates Plunge," *Los Angeles Times-Washington Post* News Service, October 18, 1999.

- Special education services received by the student.
- Early history of delinquent or criminal activity, meaning that the student was arrested before the age of 14.

The NGA report states that the officials are supposed to pay special attention to all students with three of these six factors.[5] Within two months, *Time* reported it was not unusual for school administrators to know "which girl's parents are breaking up, and which boy chafes at his big sister's accomplishments."[6]

The Columbine-inspired crackdown actually began immediately after the shootings, and it was largely driven by snitches. Several students in Ohio were suspended for contributing to a gothic-themed website. Another Ohio student, nine-year-old martial arts enthusiast Karl Bauman, was kicked out of school for writing "You will die an honorable death" as part of a class assignment. A South Carolina student was suspended for creating a website criticizing the ROTC with the statement, "They can all eat feces and die!" In Georgia, Antonius Brown, a Stephen King fan, was suspended for writing a private journal entry fantasizing about school violence. Virginia student Kent McNew was kicked out for having blue hair. In Arizona, a 13-year-old was sent to detention for carrying an electronics magazine which included ads for guns. A Utah high school student was suspended for "gang activity" because he wore a T-shirt identifying himself as a vegan—someone who doesn't eat meat or consume dairy products. In Virginia, Chris Bullock was arrested and charged with "threatening to burn or bomb" his school after he wrote a fictional story about a student who announced he had a nuclear bomb strapped to his chest. And in South Carolina, three students who wore black coats to their high school were searched by police and suspended. The police interrogated one student about the chemistry textbook in his bag, implying that it might be used to build a bomb.[7]

"In some schools, teenagers have been branded as snitches for voicing suspicions or telling of overheard threats, while students have been arrested for casual remarks made on a school bus, or threats mumbled in response to a teacher's reprimand," the *New York Times* reported.

By the end of the school year which included the Columbine shootings, over 3 million students had been suspended or expelled, many for doing or saying things which had never been considered a problem before. Although

5. "Making Schools Safe," National Governors Association and National Institute of Justice, August 1999.

6. Nancy Gibbs, "A Week in the Life of a High School," *Time*, October 25, 1999. In the story, *Time* reports that some schools have formed teams of "monitors," students specifically charged with spying on their classmates. The principal at Webster Grove High School in St. Louis, Missouri chose 60 students for her Principal's Student Leadership Group and charged them with "reporting any incidents or smoldering resentments that might lead to trouble. Kids who look or act different at Webster know the walls have ears."

7. Robert McFadden, "Violence, Real and Imagined, Sweeps Through the Schools," *New York Times*, April 30, 1999; Kim Brooks, Vincent Schiraldi and Jason Ziedenberg, "School House Hype: Two Years," Justice Policy Institute/Children's Law Center, April 2000.

there's no way to know how many of these students were punished as direct result of the post-Columbine crackdown, the number is undoubtedly substantial. During the last few weeks of the school year, American Civil Liberties Union offices across the nation were swamped with complaints from students and their parents. "It seems to have become a witch hunt," said Ann Beeson, a staff attorney at the ACLU's national headquarters in New York. "I'm sure we've gotten hundreds of phone calls." [8]

The hysteria didn't die down over the summer vacation. To the contrary, many schools across the country spent the summer months creating new snitch programs. The most significant one was developed in North Carolina, where Governor James B. Hunt commissioned a high-tech system called WAVE AMERICA. Hunt unveiled the system during a well-attended press conference on February 10, 2000. At the time, he stressed that the system would be used to keep guns out of the schools. But even a casual review of the WAVE AMERICA program reveals it will do more than that. Built around a 24-hour anonymous telephone tip line and supported by a sophisticated multi-media advertising campaign, it is designed to take reports on any student suspected of acting even a little different, or holding unpopular political beliefs.

And, as the name suggests, WAVE AMERICA will soon be offered to every school district in the country.[9]

Several private companies were providing school tip line services when Hunt commissioned the program. Security Voice, Inc., based in Columbus, Ohio, was already servicing over 2,000 school districts by the start of the 1999 school year. Company employees listen to all tips left on the lines, then transcribe the accusations and fax them to the school district where they originated. Going by the name Safe School Helpline, the program costs $1.80 per student. "We can identify kids who may be a threat because kids many times know best," Missouri school superintendent David Rock said about his district's contract with Security Voice. "They have hunches. They hear other people talking. It's absolutely a great resource. It's an early detection system." [10]

But Hunt chose to go with another company to run WAVE AMERICA—the Pinkerton Services Group, a division of the largest private security firm in the world. PSG was selected because of its experience running AlertLine, the tip line service for private companies staffed around the clock by Pinkerton "communication specialists." PSG also brought professional advertising and public relations types into the project. The final package includes colorful brochures and posters distributed to all schools, along with a colorful Internet webpage, <www.waveamerica.com>. Specifically designed to attract children and teenagers, the webpage features free e-mail accounts, scholarship contests, movie reviews, book recommendations and links to non-profit organizations

8. "ACLU: Swamped with Student Complaints," AP, May 9, 1999.
9. Author's interview with Tamera Park, public relations director, Pinkerton Services Group, February 24, 2000.
10. Noelle Crombie, "Estacada Schools Join Trend of Safety Hot Lines," *Oregonian*, August 13, 1999.

offering college scholarships. It also has a digital snitch function, allowing anyone to even e-mail their tips.[11]

Although PSG describes WAVE AMERICA as an effective tool for reducing school violence, the promotional material encourages people to report students who don't appear to pose much of a threat. A category called "Early Warning Signs of Violence" urges parents and students to turn in students for such normal adolescent behavior as "social withdrawal" and "low interest in school." Some of the "Early Warning Signs" seem to be politically motivated. Students who express "intolerance for difference or prejudicial attitudes" are also supposed to be reported, along with any who have "inappropriate access to, possession of and use of firearms."

And if those categories aren't broad enough, the promotional materials also urges students, parents and teachers to report "anything else harmful to you or your school."[12]

Although North Carolina chipped in $205,000 get the program off the ground, PSG plans to raise all of the other operating expenses from private corporations. International Paper contributed to the cost of producing the brochures, and negotiations are currently underway with banks and other businesses for the rest of the money. Potential sponsors are being promised banner ads on the WAVE AMERICA website, which public relations director Tamera Park describes as "market branding."[13]

PSG is offering corporate sponsors another benefit as well. Park says students will be able to use their plastic WAVE AMERICA cards to qualify for discounts at participating stores. In a phrase straight out of the McCarthy Era, Park says this is the "loyalty card" program.

The private funding will allow PSG to offer the WAVE AMERICA program to all school districts across the country free of charge. Although director Park says there is no firm time schedule, the program could conceivably go national within a few years.

Ironically, in 1967, a California history teacher named Ron Jones conducted a classroom experiment which he called The Third Wave. Using principles drawn from Nazi Youth programs, Jones turned his students into informants. PSG officials denied knowing anything about the experiment. (See Case Study Three: The Third Wave Experiment, for more information.)

Other schools installed metal detectors and posted video cameras in hallways and classrooms. A typical example is Gresham Union High School, located in a small but growing town within easy driving distance of Mt. Hood in northern Oregon. From the outside, the large, beige brick building looks like something straight out of *Andy of Mayberry*. But it is wired with 32 video cameras that peer down every hallway and monitor such popular gathering

---

11. Author's interview with Reid Hartzoge, press aide, North Carolina Governor Jim Hunt, March 3, 2000.
12. WAVE AMERICA press kit, January 2000.
13. Author's interview with Tamera Park, public relations director, Pinkerton Services Group, February 24, 2000.

spots as the parking lot, the lunch room and the bleachers which overlook the football field. Most of the cameras are concealed behind white metal shields bolted to the ceilings.

Although casual visitors probably don't even notice the cameras, the students know they are being constantly watched. "Everywhere you turn, there's a camera, and it feels like you're being followed," senior Jassim Albaker complained to a student reporter.

Digital images from the cameras are continuously fed into two computers in the school's security office. The computers look like large TV cable converter boxes. Black monitors sit on top of each computer, each screen displaying 16 images from throughout the school. The set-up cost $93,000, with $15,000 coming in the form of a federal grant routed through the police department.

The computers can store several weeks' worth of images, which can be retrieved with just a few strokes of the keyboard. School officials can punch up the images from any camera at any time, view them, and print out a picture of any scene which can be given to the police or posted at the school.

The video feed is also sent directly to the Gresham Police Department, which has its own set of monitors for surveying the school. The police can even send the images to monitors in the department's SWAT van, allowing officers to see what's happening in the school if they ever have reason to approach it.

Although no one has ever been killed or even seriously hurt at Gresham Union High School, Assistant Principal Paul Boly said administrators decided to install the video surveillance system anyway, just in case. "What we want to do is create the atmosphere that we are thoughtful and prepared," says Boly.[14]

Officials at Permian High in Odessa, Texas went even further. They entered into a contract with Sandia National Laboratories, an ultra-high-tech private security company in Albuquerque, New Mexico. The company has 30 years experience locking down top-secret nuclear facilities, including weapons labs. Sandia started advising schools in 1991 at the direction of Congress. By 1992, they were deploying scanners which record the unique features of a human hand to identify grade school students. Four years later, the company overhauled a high school in Belen, New Mexico, outfitting it with video cameras, drug-testing kits, metal detectors, mobile Breathalyzers and ID badges. Permian got all of that, plus explosive-sniffing dogs and portable metal detectors for random searches.[15]

The result of these new snitch programs and surveillance systems was predictable—an increase in the number of students suspended or expelled for petty (or imaginary) offenses. Shortly after the start of the 1999–2000 school

---

14. Author's visit to Gresham High School and personal interview with Assistant Principal Paul Boly, April 18, 2000.
15. S.C. Gwyne, "Reaching New Heights in School Security," *Time*, August 23, 2000. After listing various security systems being installed in the nation's schools, Gwyne then said, "Ironically, all this comes amid statistical signs of an overall decrease in school violence. A recent study published in the Journal of the American Medical Association showed a 30 percent decline from 1991 to 1997 in the number of students carrying weapons to school and a 14 percent decline in student fights."

year, seven-year-old Lamont Agnew was suspended for 10 days from an Illinois school for bringing nail clippers to class. Shameka Johnson, a 16-year-old junior, was expelled from the school for a year when district officials found a can of pepper spray on her key chain on October 21. On November 22, a 7-year-old boy at Leif Ericson Scholastic Academy in Chicago was arrested by the police and charged with aggravated assault for threatening to get his brother to come in and shoot his teacher and classmates. On January 5, 17-year-old Sarah Boman was expelled from her Missouri high school for an art project depicting the inner turmoil of a fictional madman. In early March, a 12-year-old Omaha middle school student was kicked out of school after bringing a pair of blunt-nosed safety scissors to class. On March 7, a 7th-grader named Savannah Halfacre was arrested at her Lebanon, Oregon school after classmates said she talked about bringing a gun to school. Halfacre insists she said "gum," not gun. Nevertheless, the 11-year-old was handcuffed, hauled off in a police car and charged with disorderly conduct.[16]

Perhaps the most ridiculous incident occurred on March 15 at Wilson School in Sayreville, New Jersey. Four kindergarten students were playing cops and robbers during the lunch recess on March 15. "Boom!" one of the six-year-olds shouted in a tiny voice, pointing his finger at another child. "I have a bazooka and I want to shoot you." Several other children quickly ran to their teachers to say what was happening. The principal had told the students to report all incidents of violence, and they were eager to tell on their classmates. Administrators suspended the four children who were playing the game, sparking cries of outrage from their parents and others in the waterfront community of 35,000 people. Pressed to justify the suspensions, assistant district superintendent Dennis Fyffe dug his heels in and cited the Littleton shootings. "In light of what happened at Columbine, I'm going to take the more conservative view and avoid a catastrophe rather than have a tragedy," he said.[17]

But how are overworked school counselors and administrators supposed to know which students are merely acting up, and which pose an actual threat to themselves or others? Once again, the private sector offers a dubious answer—MOSAIC 2000, a computer profiling system developed by Gavin de Becker, Inc., a leading threat assessment company. Administrators are supposed to run the program on students who are reported by their classmates, parents, teachers and other school employees. According to de Becker, the computer program ranks students on a scale ranging from safe to homicidal.[18]

"Threat assessment" is a benign-sounding euphemism for a service which requires a tremendous amount of intelligence-gathering, including the recruitment and use of informants. Big corporations and wealthy individuals hire threat assessment firms to determine if they are at risk, from whom, and what they

16. "Different Does Not Mean Dangerous," ACLU press release, June 2000.
17. Ibid.
18. Francis X. Clines, "Computer Project Seeks to Avert Youth Violence," New York Times, October 24, 1999; Jon E. Dougherty, "Computer to Identify Violence-Prone Children," WorldNetDaily, December 15, 1999.

should do about it. MOSAIC 2000 was developed in response to a closed-door Threat Assessment Symposium organized in Washington, DC by the FBI. The gathering brought together school administrators, law enforcement officials, and private businesses which provide threat assessment services. According to published reports, the symposium participants agreed that many of the students involved in school shootings did not meet the stereotypes of "troubled children." They did not come from broken families or live in poor, crime-ridden neighborhoods. By the end of the symposium, the participants agreed that new techniques were needed to determine which students have the potential for such violence in the future. One of the companies at the conference, de Becker, had provided such services to both private companies and public agencies for more than a decade.

On the company's Internet website, founder Gavin de Becker, a Senior Fellow at the UCLA School of Public Policy, and author of the bestseller *Gift of Fear*, describes threat assessment as a behavioral science, suggesting that such anti-social behaviors such as rage and violence can be studied, analyzed, categorized and broken into a series of understandable traits. People who exhibit some or all of these traits can then be ranked on an objective, accurate scale. Based on this theory, his company has produced a number of computer-based ranking programs which are supposed to evaluate people who have the potential of acting violently—and to determine which ones pose a genuine threat to themselves or others.

The computer programs go by the copyrighted name MOSAIC. All of them were designed with heavy input from current and former law enforcement officials. For example, de Becker has served on the President's Advisory Board at the U.S. Department of Justice and co-chairs California's Domestic Violence Council Advisory Board. Robert Martin, the company's vice-president, is a former Los Angles Police Department commanding officer who ran the Special Investigations Unit of the Detective Headquarters Division. Charles Cogswell, another high-ranking corporate officer, was a colonel in the U.S. Army's Intelligence Division. David Batza served in a Military Police unit that managed difficult offenders, while Bill McCrory was with the U.S. Secret Service, in charge of technical countermeasures for the President of the United States.[19]

Some of the first MOSAIC programs were developed for intelligence and law enforcement agencies, including the CIA, the Defense Intelligence Agency, the U.S. Marshals Service, the Los Angeles District Attorney's Office, and numerous police forces.

On October 24, 1999, the *New York Times* reported that the de Becker company's MOSAIC 2000 program was modified for the schools in cooperation with the Bureau of Alcohol, Tobacco and Firearms. According to BATF associate director L. Vita, the nation's schools need the program to deal with the threat posed by good students who feel victimized by bullies in the school system. "They're the hard ones for the school administrators to identify. It's easy to pick out the

---

19. Gavin de Becker, Inc. Internet website.

gang members with tattoos. It's these other people that kind of surprise administrators, and these are the ones they really need to identify," she said.[20]

As developed by de Becker and the BATF, the MOSAIC 2000 program is triggered by informants. Once school administrators are told that a certain student may pose a threat, they answer a lengthy series of questions about that student. The answers are then run through a computer program, which ranks the threat posed by the student on a scale from 1 to 10, with 10 being most potentially violent.

According to de Becker's promotional material, the MOSAIC 2000 program is to be used "only in situations that reach a certain threshold." But the situations described by the company on its Internet website are vague and subjective. One is, "a student makes a threat." Another is, "teachers or students are concerned a student might act out violently." All a school snitch has to do is say another student is acting strangely to trigger a MOSAIC 2000 review.

And what kind of information must school administrators gather to run a student through a MOSAIC 2000 review? In some cases, personal information about the student's parents and friends. Here's an example about firearms, taken directly from the company's promotional materials. Once a student is identified as posing a potential threat, school officials are supposed to decide which of the following situations best describe the student:

- No known possession of a firearm.
- Friends known to have ready access to a firearm.
- There are firearms in the home.
- There are firearms in a home frequented by the student.
- The student owns his own firearm.
- The student recently acquired a firearm.

The ACLU immediately recognized the problem of using computers to determine whether someone poses a threat to themselves or others. "We are understandably hesitant about any program designed to classify students or anyone else in society as potentially dangerous based on supposedly credible data fed into a black box," Raymond Vasvari, legislative director of the Ohio chapter of the ACLU, told the *Times*.

Despite such concerns, the MOSAIC 2000 program was reportedly in use by at least 25 school districts across the country by the end of the 1998–1999 school year.

One month after the MOSAIC 2000 program was unveiled, the concept had moved completely from the private sector to the federal government's primary domestic police agency. On November 9, *The Denver Post* reported that the FBI was developing its own student threat assessment program for use by the public schools. According to the story, the agency's National Center for

---

20. Francis X. Clines, "Computer Project Seeks to Avert Youth Violence," *New York Times*, October 24, 1999.

the Analysis of Violent Crime had identified about 60 "risk factors" to help identify potentially violent students.[21]

Although the FBI did not release its list of risk factors to the paper, Special Agent Mary Ellen O'Toole said that teachers might want to ask "if Johnny is the type of student who has a fragile ego, doesn't handle feedback well, is narcissistic, thinks the world centers around him, blames others for what happens to him." Among other risk factors cited in the story: "Does he have problems expressing anger? Does he show an inordinate fascination with violent movies, books and music? Has he talked or written about committing violent acts?"

O'Toole told the paper that schools will need to gather a lot of personal information about all students to make the profiling system work. "You've got to go below the surface," she said. "We're saying look at the student's behavior, his personality, the family dynamics, the school dynamics and other social issues such as drugs and alcohol. Look at the total student and everything that impacts him, and not just on one day. People's personalities come through only when you see them in a lot of situations."

As with MOSAIC 2000, the FBI's profiling system will require school authorities to learn such personal information as which families own guns. "A student may brag all he wants, but does he have access to weapons, experience with guns?" O'Toole asked. "If the answer is yes, that would raise a bit of a red flag."[22]

The post-Columbine crackdown has had another predictable effect—despite the fact that Harris and Klebold were white, black students are being punished at far greater rates than whites. Federal law requires the Civil Rights Office of the U.S. Department of Education to collect information on suspensions and expulsions by race. In June 2000, the office released a report which showed that nearly one out of eight black schoolchildren were suspended in 1998, while only one out of 30 white students received such punishment. Although blacks made up about 17 percent of all students in 1998, they accounted for 33 percent of all suspensions. In contrast, whites made up 63 percent of all students but only 50 percent of suspensions.[23]

The same disparities were found among the 87,000 students who were permanently expelled—31 percent were black. Only Hispanics were treated proportionally, comprising 15 percent of all students and 14 percent of all suspensions and expulsions.

Two years earlier, the department issued a report titled "The Condition of Education 1997" which revealed that almost 25 percent of all black male students were suspended at least once over a four-year period.

"Suspension rates are skyrocketing, especially for minorities," says Johanna Wald of the Civil Rights Project at Harvard University.[24]

---

21. Janet Bingham, "FBI Puts 'Risk List' Out for Schools," *Denver Post*, November 9, 1999.
22. *Ibid.*
23. Anjetta McQueen, "African-American Students Suspended from School at Higher Rate than Whites," AP, June 15, 2000.
24. Author's interview with Johanna Wald, June 4, 2000.

These official reports confirm similar findings by smaller studies conducted by a number of private, non-profit policy institutes in recent years. The Applied Research Center in Oakland, California collected suspension and expulsion data for the 1998–1999 school year from 10 city school districts. In a report titled "Facing the Consequences: An Examination of Racial Discrimination in U.S. Public Schools," ARC found that the Union High School District in Phoenix, Arizona suspends or expels black students at an astonishing 22 times the rate of whites. All the districts studied showed suspension/expulsion rates for African-American students at between 1.4 and 4 times the rate of whites.

"If racial equality were a required course, most U.S. public school systems would receive a flunking grade," the report said.

Significantly, studies found that most black students aren't being suspended or expelled for violence. To the contrary, as the researchers at ARC discovered, they are being kicked out for such subjectively defined offenses as "disrespect" and "defiance of authority," versus the more objective categories such as "fighting" and "physical assault."

But more than that, a large number of these suspensions and expulsions defy common sense. For example, at the beginning of the 1999–2000 school year, students on a school bus in Mississippi were throwing peanuts at one another. A peanut accidentally hit the white female bus driver, who immediately stopped the bus and called the police. After the police arrived, the bus was diverted to the courthouse, where children were questioned. Five African-American males, ages 17 and 18, were then arrested for felony assault, which carries a maximum penalty of five years in prison. Although the criminal charges were eventually dismissed, all of the students were suspended from the school's bus program and dropped out of school because they could not find alternative transportation. "I [would have] gone to college," says one former student. "Maybe I could have been a lawyer."

This story may seem unbelievable, but it is typical of what is happening to students in the public schools under snitch-driven Zero Tolerance policies. And it is where the rest of the country is headed. Federal and state lawmakers refer to their version of these policies as mandatory minimum sentences.

Part Three
The Shape of Things to Come

CHAPTER FIFTEEN

INFILTRATING THE ANARCHISTS

THE SOUND OF BREAKING GLASS signalled a dramatic change in the focus of the government's political surveillance programs in late 1999. After spending most of the decade spying on the right-wing neo-Patriot movement, law enforcement agencies abruptly shifted gears and declared brick-throwing anarchists to be the newest threat to the American way of life. Accordingly, they began to run COINTELPRO-style operations against a coalition of radical labor, environmental, and human rights organizations. Police photographed suspected activists, entering license plate numbers into their computer databanks. Undercover operatives infiltrated meetings and disrupted protests. Even the Pentagon was involved, dispatching its Delta Force anti-terrorism commandos to identify and secretly videotape suspected leaders. By early August, calls were underway for a full-blown federal investigation into the movement, raising the specter of a government-orchestrated Green Scare along the lines of anti-Communist witch hunts of the 1950s.

The shift was a direct result of the massive protests which disrupted the World Trade Organization conference in Seattle. Over 50,000 demonstrators jammed the streets, snarling traffic and preventing WTO delegates from reaching their meetings. When the authorities tried to break up the protests, a small group of the most militant activists struck back, vandalizing businesses in the downtown core and clashing with police throughout the city. Much like the urban riots of the early 1960s, the intensity of the confrontations caught political leaders and law enforcement officials off guard, prompting the most significant change in the direction of the Snitch Culture in the past 20 years.

Although the size and intensity of the Seattle demonstrations surprised the corporate media, the movement behind them had been growing for years. Neo-Patriots weren't the only ones complaining about international trade deals such as NAFTA and GATT during the 1990s. So were a number of left-wing organizations, ranging from academic think tanks such as the International Forum on Globalization to Earth First! and other grassroots radicals. Although the press occasionally covered their issues, most reports presented them as isolated stories. In fact, sweatshop protesters were in contact with the young environmentalists camped out in old growth forests in the Pacific Northwest, the Free Mumia Abu-Jamal crowd was concerned about the fate of the Brazilian rain forest, and they were all boning up on the World Bank and the International Monetary Fund (IMF).

The vast majority of these activists are pacifists who advocate non-violent civil disobedience. But a small number practice "monkey-wrenching" and other acts of economic sabotage aimed at animal research centers, fur farms, timber companies, mining corporations and genetically-modified food labs. So-called eco-terrorists have committed over 100 major acts of arsons, bombings, and sabotage since 1980, causing nearly $43 million in damages in the 11 contiguous Western states alone. The attacks ranged from the 1981 torching of a $180,000 herbicide-spraying helicopter on the Oregon coast to the August 1999 vandalism of an animal experimentation lab in Orange, California which caused $250,000 in damages. The largest single act of eco-terrorism was a fire which burned down the Two Elks Lodge restaurant at the Vail Mountain ski resort on October 19, 1998. A group called the Earth Liberation Front claimed responsibility for the $12 million arson, charging that an expansion of the ski resort threatened a lynx habitat.[1]

Most of these attacks received little press coverage, in part because they took place in remote forests and isolated farm communities. But, beginning in 1996, young activists with similar political views began vandalizing property in Eugene, a laid back university town of 150,000 people in Oregon's lush, green mid-Willamette Valley. Similar incidents had occurred in other cities over the years, including San Francisco. But the Eugene confrontations generated national media coverage, in part because they seemed so out of place.

Some of the first clashes took place in the city's Whitaker area, a working-class neighborhood a short walk west of the downtown core. When the city moved to shut down an alternative bookstore and music club called Icky's Tea House, a number of its supporters responded by vandalizing nearby businesses which had complained about the noise. They called themselves anarchists. "Those folks quite often got a rock through their window," said Marshall Kirkpatrick, an outspoken Eugene anarchist.[2]

The attacks continued after the city finally closed Icky's for health violations. Among other things, a van owned by a police officer who lived in the neighborhood was spray-painted with the anarchist symbol and the words "Die Pig." Then, in the summer of 1998, a wealthy couple opened an upscale

---

1. Although no single law enforcement agency tracks so-called eco-terrorism, the *Oregonian* ran the first-ever comprehensive series of articles on the topic from September 26–30, 1999. Reporters Bryan Denson and Jim Long contacted numerous police agencies, timber associations, fur lobbies and other industrial organizations for reports of environmentally-oriented crimes. The two reporters spent 10 months verifying or debunking each incident as an act of eco-terrorism by poring over thousands of pages of police files, court records, government reports and news accounts, and by interviewing more than 200 people, including police, victims and a few activists convicted of some crimes. Borderline cases were not included.

    The series documented over 100 major acts of arsons, bombings and sabotage since 1980, causing $42.8 million in damages in the 11 contiguous Western states. Since 1996 alone, the West has seen 33 substantial incidents, with damages reaching $28.8 million. "The crimes are typically intended to disrupt logging, the recreational use of the wilderness, or the use of animals for food or research," the reporters wrote.

2. Author's interview with Marshall Kirkpatrick, January 28, 2000.

restaurant called the Blair Island Cafe. A clean, colorful eatery with Mediterranean-style pasta and seafood, the restaurant was a stark contrast to the older taverns and co-op bakeries in the area. The first window was broken in August. When it was replaced, another was broken. More vandalism followed, followed by fliers urging attacks on "yuppie gentrifying scum." The cafe closed its doors a short time later.[3]

It wasn't long before the confrontations moved downtown. In October 1998, anti-sweatshop demonstrators marched on a Nike store built next to a popular shopping mall called The 5th Street Public Market. A small group of masked protesters broke off from the larger group, charged into the Nike shop and trashed the place, breaking windows and throwing thousands of dollars worth of running shoes and sports gear into the street before ducking outside and escaping the police. The incident shocked most local residents. Eugene is where two University of Oregon track stars, Bill Bowerman and Phil Knight, started Nike in the 1960s.

The confrontations continued the next year, culminating in a June 18 riot at the end of a "Reclaim the Streets" march. Dozens of masked anarchists sparked the confrontation by vandalizing downtown businesses, breaking windows, knocking over trash bins and spray-painting anti-corporate slogans everywhere. Bricks and bottles rained down on the police, who had not prepared for the violence. The skirmishes continued for hours, with demonstrators splitting into factions, racing through the streets, doubling back and continuing their attacks. A 7-11 store lost its beer to the mob, which then marched on a Taco Bell chanting "We want free Gorditas" before breaking all its windows. The police finally chased a large group of protesters into the Whitaker neighborhood, where residents poured out of their houses and began yelling at the cops to leave.

Before it was over, 15 people had been arrested and three officers had received minor injuries. To the anarchists, the June 18 riot was a major victory, a blueprint for how even a small group of committed activists can spur a larger crowd to action and frustrate the police for hours—which is exactly what happened in Seattle, six months later.

By the time the protesters trashed downtown Eugene, the World Trade Organization had already scheduled its annual meeting for November 30 through December 3. The growing coalition of anti-corporate organizations had spent months planning their demonstrations. Thousands of activists from around the country were planning to travel to Seattle, including approximately two dozen Eugene anarchists. An informant tipped the police off to the anarchists' plans. The Eugene police contacted the FBI. Federal law enforcement officials reviewed the police reports on the Eugene riot and immediately began spying on the activists and their organizations. As the *Seattle Weekly* reported, "Sources say . . . that police and 30 other local, state and federal agencies have been aggressively gathering intelligence on violent and nonviolent protest groups

---

3. Kim Murphy, "A Revolutionary Movement Hits Small-Town America," *Los Angeles Times*, August 3, 1999.

since early summer (FBI agents even paid personal visits to some activists' homes to inquire about their plans)."[4]

Even the military got involved. According to the *Weekly*, the Pentagon sent members of the top-secret Delta Force to Seattle to prepare for President Clinton's arrival. As the paper put it, "the elite Army special force, operating under its cover name of Combat Applications Group (CAG), was in Seattle a week in advance of the Clinton visit to scope out possible terrorist acts. Under the control of the Joint Special Operations Command (JSOC) at Fort Bragg, North Carolina, the contingent took up residence in a Regrade motel and fanned out downtown dressed as demonstrators, some wearing their jungle greens."[5]

The preparations didn't work. Thousands of protesters overwhelmed the police on the opening day of the conference, shutting down the center where the main meetings were scheduled to be held. The police overreacted and began macing and tear-gassing protesters who were preventing the WTO delegates from entering the center. The anarchists saw their opening, joining with a number of other militants and attacking such corporate icons as McDonalds, Nike Town, the Gap and Starbucks, smashing windows, toppling shelves, spraying graffiti and provoking a massive police crackdown.

The mayor of Seattle declared a state of "civil emergency," essentially a local version of martial law. Washington's governor called out 300 state troopers and two divisions of the National Guard to secure the blocks around the downtown convention site. A "Protest-Free Zone" was declared around the conference headquarters, allowing the police to exclude anyone merely wishing to express their First Amendment rights. Police dressed up in military-style riot gear chased protesters through the streets for the next few days. Thousands of people were sprayed with pepper gas, clubbed with ballistic batons, and shot with rubber-coated bullets and steel pellet-filled "beanbag" shotgun rounds. Many of the victims were innocent bystanders and business owners who simply didn't get out of the way fast enough.

The chaos was broadcast around the world. TV viewers saw police firing at protesters at point blank range. One cop went out of his way to kick an empty-handed protester in the groin. Another cop ripped a gas mask off a pregnant foreign reporter and struck her.

Delta Force troops were in the middle of the confrontations, working to identify protest leaders. "Some Deltas wore lapel cameras, continuously transmitting pictures of rioters and other demonstrators to a master video unit in the motel command center which could be used by law enforcement agencies to identify and track suspects," the *Weekly* reported.

The WTO conference ended in disarray, a victory for the protesters and a major embarrassment for the Clinton Administration. Four days later, Seattle Police Chief Norm Stamper resigned in disgrace.

---

4. Rick Anderson, "Delta's Down With It: The Justice Department and the Elite Delta Force Pushed for Seattle Crackdown Against WTO Protesters," *Seattle Weekly*, December 23, 1999.
5. *Ibid.*

The corporate media immediately fell into line, portraying all anti-corporate protesters as violent thugs to justify the coming crackdown. Although the police shot demonstrators with tear gas canisters, images of black-clad anarchists smashing windows dominated the post-riot news reports. The December 13 issue of *Newsweek* linked the anarchists to Ted Kaczynski, the Unabomber. *60 Minutes* traveled to Eugene for a story on the new domestic terrorists. "They came to Seattle with violence in their hearts and destruction on their minds," the CBS News show warned viewers.

Even the advocacy groups joined in, with the Southern Poverty Law Center linking the anti-corporate protesters to the same Far Right conspiracy it had railed against throughout the 1990s: "Right alongside the 'progressive' groups that demonstrated in Seattle—mostly peaceful defenders of labor, the environment, animal rights and similar causes—were the hard-edged soldiers of neofascism." The SPLC also ridiculed the anti-globalization movement in general, saying, "They despise capitalism, with its tendency to concentrate wealth and to make people and economies more and more alike—turning the planet into what is seen as a bland and materialistic McWorld. They pine for nations of peasant-like folk tied closely to the land and to their neighbors. They fight for a pristine environment, a land unsullied by corporate agriculture and urbanization. They detest man-centered philosophies, seeing animals as no less important than humans. They reject rationalism in favor of a kind of mystical spirituality. Above all, these mainly young people—in some ways, the descendants of the 'back-to-the-land' hippies of the 1960s—favor decentralization." [6]

The government's abrupt shift from right- to left-wing activists was accompanied by a wave of false alarms and bogus reports. A rumor spread that the Eugene anarchists were planning to drive up the freeway to Portland and disrupt that city's downtown New Year's Eve party. The local police went on high alert, fencing off the site and installing security gates to detain and search partygoers. The U.S. Marshals Office opened a number of temporary holding cells in an old downtown federal building. The FBI set up a command center in the basement of the nearby Mark O. Hatfield Federal Courthouse. Heavily-armed federal agents gathered in the basement on New Year's Eve. Police in full riot gear patrolled the perimeter. None of the anarchists showed up. The informant was wrong.

Another bogus tip sparked a similar panic in Tacoma, Washington a few months later. The local steelworkers union had called for a March 25 rally at the Kaiser aluminum plant. Labor and environmental activists from throughout the Pacific Northwest were planning to attend. Then Eugene authorities contacted the Tacoma police and reported that some of the anarchists were allegedly heading their way with a bomb. The police contacted union organizer Jon Youngdahl, who called off the protest. No bomb-carrying anarchist was ever found.

---

6. "Neither Left Nor Right," *Intelligence Report*, Klanwatch Project, Southern Poverty Law Center, Spring 2000.

These incidents occurred as federal authorities were bracing for the next major anti-globalization protests, set for the World Bank and IMF meetings scheduled to begin on April 16, 2000 in Washington, DC. As the activists began planning their demonstrations, they were targeted by federal, state and local officials. Their meetings were infiltrated, their public gatherings disrupted, their phones tapped, and police were posted outside their homes and offices. Even the corporate media took note of the harassment. "Some protesters think they are being watched. They are correct," the *Washington Post* reported on April 10, quoting Executive Assistant Washington Police Chief Terrance W. Gainer as saying, "If it's an open meeting and it says, 'Come on over,' then anybody's welcome."

Three days later, *USA Today* reported government agents were going undercover online to thwart the protesters. "[T]hey have been monitoring 73 Internet sites where the groups have been exchanging messages to learn more about their plans. Sometimes, officers have even gone online posing as protesters," the paper said, adding that police were physically following suspected anarchists throughout the capitol city. "They have been monitoring the movements of nearly two dozen self-proclaimed anarchists who have arrived in Washington."

As a result of this surveillance, all 3,500 DC police officers were put on alert, along with an unknown number of law enforcement agents from at least 12 federal and state agencies, including the FBI and BATF. The authorities spent over $1 million on new body armor and bulletproof shields. They set up three mass detention centers where arrested protesters would be taken. They removed 69 mailboxes where bombs could be hidden.

"They ain't burning our city like they did in Seattle," Police Chief Charles Ramsey told *USA Today*. "I'm not going to let it happen. I guarantee it."

The authorities started cracking down on the activists the week before the IMF/World Bank meetings were scheduled to begin. On April 13, seven activists driving to a planning meeting were pulled over and arrested. Police seized 256 PVC pipes, 45 smaller pipes, 2 rolls of chicken wire, 50 rolls of duct tape, gas masks, bolt cutters, chains, an electrical saw, and lock boxes. According to a *Washington Post* account of the incident, a Secret Service agent frisked one passenger, showing a photo that had been taken of him earlier.

The police justified the arrests by saying the materials and tools found in the van were "implements of crime." The accusation struck National Lawyers Guild President Karen Jo Koonan as absurd. "These activists construct signs, puppets, sound stages, and other tools for expressing their political views," she wrote in a letter to U.S. Attorney General Janet Reno. "They were in fact arrested for possession of implements of First Amendment activity. We have been told by an MPD officer that the FBI directed them to make this arrest."

But the police claim it was made for a specific purpose—a purpose which would soon become clear. It is illegal for the police to spy on anyone simply because of their political beliefs. But political activists can be monitored if the police believe they are planning to commit crimes, no matter how petty. The police claimed the items seized from the van were 'instruments of crime" to justify their surveillance. It was a claim that would be heard repeatedly in the days, weeks and months to come.

On the morning of April 15, law enforcement authorities unexpectedly raided a warehouse that served as the demonstrators' headquarters. According to eyewitness accounts, the agencies involved in the raid included the BATF, the Washington Metropolitan Police Department and the Washington Fire Department. Saying the warehouse violated fire codes, the authorities threw all the activists out and closed the building. Then the authorities claimed they found weapons in the warehouse, physical proof that violent crimes were being planned. According to the police, the evidence included a Molotov cocktail, balloons filled with acid, and a lab for producing explosives and pepper spray. In a later retraction, the police admitted they'd only found oily rags and a kitchen, but not until after the warehouse was shut down. Police also kept all the signs, banners and giant satiric posters under construction inside, depriving the demonstrators of their most effective means of communicating their causes.[7]

By the morning of Saturday the 16th, the police had cordoned off 50 blocks around the headquarters of the World Bank and the IMF. The first mass arrests happened that afternoon when thousands of protesters marched downtown. The police blocked their way, then isolated and arrested approximately 635 activists, far more than the total arrested during several days of rioting in Seattle. "What makes the situation all the more maddening is that such actions are apparently being taken based on the ridiculous view that every protester or activist is an anarchist time bomb waiting to go off—a view apparently buttressed by unspecified police 'intelligence' that may or may not be true," reporter Jason Vest wrote in the online SpeakOut.com website.[8]

7. Tim Ream, "Unrestrained Stories: False Police Claims of Protester Violence," <http://la.indymedia.org/>, August 9, 2000.
8. From the very beginning, the new anti-corporate globalization movement knew the establishment press would not accurately report on its issues or protests, so activists set up their own Independent Media Centers (IMC) in all of the cities where major protests occurred. "Six global corporations control all the media in this country," Eric Galatas of Free Speech TV said in a <www.phillyimc.com> report. "We had a saying in Seattle: We were trying to break through the information blockade." These reports documented some of the first law enforcement efforts to infiltrate the organizations and disrupt their demonstrations, repeatedly forcing the mainstream media to revise its coverage. For example, after the major TV networks reported that Seattle police did not fire rubber bullets at protesters, that city's temporary IMC posted photos of the rubber bullets on the Internet, prompting the "professional" news agencies to change their stories.
      Additional stories on police infiltration and harassment during the Washington DC protests by reporter Jason Vest were posted on Speakout.com. Among other things, Vest, a former *Business Week* editor and *Village Voice* reporter, discovered that activists at George Washington University were under surveillance. "We know they're reading our e-mails,

The authorities quickly revealed that they were obsessed with identifying the protesters. Those who provided identification were fined $50. Those who didn't were fined $300.

Demonstrators clashed with police during the next few days. The federal government gave all non-essential employees in Washington, DC the day off on Monday, resulting in a partial government shut-down, which is far more than the neo-Patriot movement was able to achieve at any point in the 1990s. By the time it was over, even the IMF had released a communique acknowledging the protesters had made its policies a matter "of growing public debate." As the ABC Evening News reported on Monday, "The demonstrators outside the building did their best to be heard. The delegates inside the building said they got the message." [9]

---

and I'm fairly convinced my phone is tapped too," GW student Dan Calamuci told Vest over a phone line replete with loud, regular clicking noises. "Last week, we did a speakout— just seven of us with a bullhorn—at the corner of 21st and H. Within a few minutes, five cops showed up, three of whom were undercover, or trying to be—talking into cell phones saying, 'We have three guys and four girls on the corner and this is what they're saying.' "

9. WTO officials also said they heard the protesters' message after the Seattle demonstrations. But Bruce Silverglade of the Center for Science in the Public Interest discovered the truth when he managed to get into a day-long high-level seminar titled "After Seattle: Restoring Momentum to the WTO." Speakers included Clayton Yeutter (former Secretary of Agriculture), Robert Litan (former Associate Director of the White House Office of Management and Budget), Lawrence Eagleburger (former Secretary of State), and Luiz Felipe Lamreia, the foreign Minster of Brazil. Silverglade wrote a length essay on the gathering, which was edited and posted by Sam Smith in the April 7, 2000 issue of the *Progressive Review*:

"As it turned out, I got a lot more than I bargained for. The seminar turned out to be a strategy session on how to defeat those opposed to the current WTO system. Apparently, no one knew who I was (perhaps my graying temples and dark suit helped me blend in with the overwhelming older male group of attendees) and I did not speak up until the end of the meeting.

"The meeting was kicked off by a gentleman named Lord Patterson who was Margaret Thatcher's Secretary of State for Trade and Industry. He began by stating that our number one job is to restore confidence in the WTO before embarking on any new rounds of trade negotiations. So far, so good, I thought.

"But he then proclaimed that non-profit groups have no right to criticize the WTO as undemocratic because the groups themselves do not represent the general public. (I wondered which groups he was talking about, because organizations that are gravely concerned about the impact of the WTO on environmental and consumer protection, like the Sierra Club and Public Citizen, have hundreds of thousands of members). He then stated that we must never have another WTO meeting on U.S. soil because it was too easy for advocacy groups to organize here and security could not be assured. He added that President Clinton's speech during the WTO meeting in Seattle, in which the president acknowledged the protesters' concerns, was 'disgraceful' and stated that it was also disgraceful that delegates to the WTO meeting in Seattle had to survive on sandwiches and couldn't get a decent meal during three days of social protest. The Lord finished his speech by recalling better times having tea with Maggie, and stating that the staff of the WTO Secretariat should not be balanced with people from developing countries just because of the color of their skin. After a few words with the chairman of the meeting, Lord Patterson added, 'Oh, I hope I have not offended anyone.'

The full extent of the government's surveillance operation was not revealed until May 4, when the Paris-based *Intelligence Newsletter* carried a story titled "Watching the Anti-WTO Crowd" which reported that U.S. Army intelligence units were monitoring the anti-corporate protesters. Among other things, the newsletter discovered that "reserve units from the U.S. Army Intelligence and Security Command helped Washington police keep an eye on demonstrations staged at the World Bank/IMF meetings . . . [T]he Pentagon sent around 700 men from the Intelligence and Security Command at Fort Belvoir to assist the Washington police on April 17, including specialists in human and signals intelligence. One unit was even strategically located on the fourth floor balcony in a building at 1919 Pennsylvania Avenue with a birds-eye view of most demonstrators."

The newsletter also charged that much information being collected about the protesters was being fed into the RISS computers. According to the report, the government is rationalizing this surveillance by claiming the protesters are terrorists: "To justify their interest in anti-globalization groups from a legal stand-point, the authorities lump them into a category of terrorist organizations. Among those considered as such at present are Global Justice (the group that organized the April 17 demonstration), Earth First!, Greenpeace, American Indian Movement, Zapatista National Liberation Front and Act-Up."

In early May, *In These Times* confirmed the government spy operation. The progressive magazine quoted Robert Scully, executive director of the National Association of Police Organizations, as saying that law enforcement agencies were "successful in infiltrating some of the groups . . . and had firsthand, inside information of who, when, why and where things were going to happen."

Even before the Washington, DC protests began, organizers began planning to bring their message to the Republican and Democratic Presidential conventions, scheduled for July and August in Philadelphia and Los Angeles. Police representatives from both cities traveled to the nation's capitol for the April demonstrations, consulting with the feds on how to identify and handle

---

". . . Under the banner of rebuilding public confidence in the WTO, [former Agriculture Secretary] Yeutter concurred with his British colleague's suggestion that the next WTO meeting be held in some place other than the U.S. where security can be assured. He further suggested that the WTO give the public little advance notice of where the meeting would be held, to keep the protesters off balance. He said that the protesters' demands for greater transparency in WTO proceedings was a misnomer because the protesters didn't really want to participate in WTO proceedings—all they wanted was to get TV coverage and raise money for their organizations.

"The day ended with the usual Washington reception. During dessert, the foreign minister of Brazil lamented that if the next WTO meeting had to be held in an out-of-the-way place, he preferred that it be held on a cruise ship instead of in the middle of the desert. He then gave an impassioned speech in which he opposed writing core labor standards into the WTO agreement and defended child labor by describing how in one region of Brazil, more than 5,000 children 'help their families earn a little extra money' by hauling bags of coal from a dump yard to a steel mill. He stressed, however, that the children do not work directly in the steel mill. He was greeted by a hearty round of applause."

the protesters. Federal officials also traveled to the convention cities, setting up surveillance operations in advance.

Once again, private advocacy groups stepped forward to demonize the growing movement. In late June, the Philadelphia City Council adopted an ordinance making it illegal for protesters to wear masks. Violators would face a $75 fine. It was crafted with the help of the local chapter of the Anti-Defamation League, and was modeled after a Georgia law aimed at combating the Ku Klux Klan— essentially linking the anti-globalists to the Far Right once again.[10]

By late May, the corporate media was openly writing about the intelligence-gathering operations. Previewing the Republican convention, the *Philadelphia Inquirer* said, "The Secret Service is checking rooftops. The FBI is monitoring the Internet. And city police are getting ready to play cat and mouse with protesters . . . 'Virtually every resource that the FBI has available will be put into play,' said Thomas J. Harrington, the assistant special agent-in-charge in the FBI's Philadelphia office."

Throughout June, activists from several groups reported at least five instances in which unidentified men were seen photographing people entering and leaving protest planning meetings. On June 29, a reporter with the *Philadelphia Inquirer* observed two men dressed in casual clothes watching activists arrive for a meeting at the offices of the Women's International League for Peace and Freedom. The pair sat on the hood of a maroon Plymouth, taking pictures of the activists as they came and went. Both men refused to answer any questions from the reporter. Police spokeswoman Lt. Susan Slawson flatly denied her agency was doing anything that would violate its policy against political intelligence-gathering, saying, "[W]e are in no way violating it." But then the reporter traced the license plates on the Plymouth to the police department. Confronted with proof of his agency's role in the surveillance operation, department spokesman David Yarnell reluctantly admitted the activists were right. "We were watching. We were making surveillance efforts. It's just prudent preparations for anything," he confessed. "This is just outrageous," responded organizer Michael Morrill, "If this is in fact going on, and city officials are lying about it, I wonder what else they're doing." [11]

In fact, they were doing a lot more. As eventually reported by the *Philadelphia Inquirer* ("State Police Infiltrated Protest Groups, Documents Show," September 7, 2000), four undercover agents with the Pennsylvania State Police infiltrated the downtown warehouse where protesters were painting banners and assembling large puppets and floats. The four men—who identified themselves only as Tim, Harry, George and Ryan—claimed to be union carpenters from Wilkes-

10. David Morgan, "Republican Convention Host City Adopts Anti-Mask Law," *Reuters*, June 22, 2000.

11. "Philadelphia Police Admit Spying on Activists," *The Philadelphia Inquirer*, July 21, 2000. In its story, the paper also reported that Philadelphia police traveled to New York and photographed demonstrators at a May 1 protest. This revelation prompted the Center for Constitutional Rights to threaten to sue the New York Police Department for violating a 1985 consent decree prohibiting the police from photographing political demonstrators.

Barre. The infiltrators later reported that the protesters were planning to break the law by using their puppets and floats to block traffic. These petty claims were used by the Philadelphia police to secure a search warrant for the warehouse. In language straight out of the McCarthy Era, affidavits supporting the search warrant claimed funds for one key protest group "allegedly originate with Communist and leftist parties and from sympathetic trade unions" or from "the former Soviet-allied World Federation of Trade Unions."

The allegations came from the Maldon Institute, a Baltimore-based, right-wing think tank. Founded in 1985, the organization publishes reports on international political developments which are read by the heads of governments, cabinet members, opinion shapers and decision-makers around the world. At the time of the Republican convention, the organization's director was longtime anti-Communist zealot John Rees (see Chapter Eight: Private Intelligence Networks, for more information). Jack Lewis, a state police spokesman, said the Maldon Institute routinely supplies e-mail reports to police departments. "I'm told by our intelligence people that the Maldon Institute is a private organization that provides intelligence information to police departments. We have found in the past that the Maldon Institute generally presents reliable information," he told the *Philadelphia Inquirer*. Asked to release the report the organization provided on the protesters, Lewis said, "The department does not believe it has an obligation to provide the public with all information it receives as part of its intelligence-gathering operation, whether or not the department pays for that information."

Over 70 activists in the warehouse were arrested when the police raided it on July 31. Before the raid, police officials publicly claimed the activists were storing weapons in the building, including C4 explosives and acid-filled balloons. No explosives or acid were found, however.

The raid set off street protests, during which 15 police officers were injured in scuffles, and more than 25 police cruisers and other city vehicles were vandalized by protesters who also overturned dumpsters, smashed windows, and sprayed graffiti on downtown buildings. Before the end of the day, more than 350 people were arrested, including 19 charged with such felony offenses as assault. Most were jailed and kept imprisoned on high bails. Hundreds were still behind bars days after the convention ended, complaining of deplorable conditions and brutal treatment.

The day after the delegates went home, Philadelphia police commissioner John Timoney called a press conference and announced that he and his intelligence officers had uncovered a vast left-wing conspiracy. He claimed outside agitators had conspired to cause violence and property damage at the convention. He called on the federal government to investigate this subversive plot, saying, "There is a cadre, if you will, of criminal conspirators who are about the business of planning conspiracies to go in and cause mayhem and cause property damage in major cities in America that have large conventions or large numbers of people coming in for one reason or another." [12]

---

12. "Police Claim Protest Leaders have Orchestrated Violence," AP, August 5, 2000.

One of the alleged conspirators was John Seller, director of the Ruckus Society, a Berkeley-based organization which trains political protesters in civil disobedience tactics. He was arrested while walking down the street and talking into a cell phone outside the Police Administration building. Although all of the charges filed against Sellers were misdemeanors, one of them was for carrying an "instrument of a crime," the police excuse for spying on him. His bail was set at $1 million, far more than all but the most dangerous felons are required to post.

In seeking the high bail, District Attorney Cindy Mertelli produced a 27-page "dossier" on Sellers. She called him "a real risk of danger to the community," noting he had been "involved in Seattle, a situation with almost dead bodies." Although none of the charges levied at Sellers involved violence or even vandalism, Mertelli said he "sets the stage to facilitate the more radical elements and intends to do the same in L.A.," where the Democrats were set to meet in early August.[13]

Shortly after bail was set, CBS News was reporting that Philadelphia police had pinpointed the "ringleaders" of the most violent protests. Sellers was identified as one of the ringleaders.[14]

"We know they had a list of things they were going to do, and they set about doing it," Timoney said at an August 2 news conference, signalling that at least some of his information came from infiltrators. "I intend on raising this issue with federal authorities. Somebody's got to look into these groups."

Although a judge soon lowered the bail, the local news media immediately embraced the police version of events. The day after Timoney's press conference, the *Philadelphia Inquirer* congratulated the police for their restraint, crediting their excellent intelligence-gathering work. The paper also said that what appeared to be a spontaneous melee on August 1 was in fact a carefully choreographed assault, the result of a conspiracy.[15]

Timoney's conspiracy theory got a boost when it was embraced by Bruce Chapman, president of the Discovery Institute and a former U.S. Ambassador to the United Nations Organizations in Vienna. Writing in the *Washington Times*, Chapman claimed several left-wing political organizations had conspired to cause violence in Seattle, Washington, DC, Philadelphia and Los Angeles— including the Direct Action Network, Global Exchange, the Rainforest Action Network, the Foundation for Deep Ecology, and the International Forum on Globalization, which he described as "an umbrella group for 55 organizations opposed to globalization and high technology." Chapman said several of the most prominent organizations were funded by Douglas Tompkins, who he described as "a businessman who nurses an intense anger at modern technology and international trade." Chapman ended his piece by calling for a federal investigation of Tompkins, the organizations, and "the rioters."[16]

---

13. David Morgan, "Police Chief Wants Feds to Investigate Protest Movement," *Reuters*, August 3, 2000.

14. *Ibid.*

15. *Ibid.*

16. Bruce Chapman, "Lessons of Rioting—Look to the Funders Behind the Riots," *Washington Times*, August 7, 2000.

Protesters faced a similar surveillance and harassment campaign in Los Angeles. On July 13, the *Los Angeles Times* printed a guest editorial by Mayor Richard Riordan which warned of violence by "international anarchists." In the piece titled "A Fair Warning to All: Don't Disrupt Our City," Riordan said the protesters coming to town had attended "training camps where they have learned strategies of destruction and guerrilla tactics." Before too long, the authorities and media were talking about the protesters in terms which had previously been reserved for domestic terrorists. On July 23, the *Los Angeles Times* reported the Secret Service and other government agencies were warning that a biological agent might be released in or around the Staples Center, where the convention was scheduled to be held. "We have purchased a lot of equipment, specialized masks and gowns," said Dr. Robert Splawn, medical director of the California Hospital Medical Center, the closest hospital to the center.[17]

LAPD detective Darryl Butler also implied the Eugene anarchists were already in town. He claimed police had arrested a handful of people for taking pictures of downtown buildings from rooftops and other unusual places, and that their addresses all traced back to Oregon.[18]

On August 7, the Southern California chapter of the ACLU wrote a letter to Police Chief Bernard Parks and Deputy City Attorney Debra Gonzales on behalf of several groups coordinating the upcoming demonstrations. In the letter, ACLU attorney Dan Tokaji complained that police were watching the four-story protest headquarters building around the clock, constantly videotaping the building and recording license plate numbers of cars used by protesters. He also alleged police were selectively enforcing traffic laws near the building, and had repeatedly entered it without producing search warrants. "They've crossed the line separating legitimate security preparations from unlawful harassment . . . The mere potential for a disturbance does not justify the suspension of our constitutional rights," the letter said.[19]

When the city didn't respond, the ACLU went to federal court on August 11 and obtained a temporary restraining order to prevent the police from raiding the building without a warrant. In its complaint, ACLU lawyers cited 22 separate incidents of surveillance and harassment. Although U.S. District Court Judge Dean Pregerson granted the injunction, he did not bar police from keeping the protest headquarters under surveillance if they had "probable cause."[20]

But the injunction didn't stop the police from infiltrating the protest organizations. On August 12, a group called The Youth Are the Future! We

---

17. "Los Angeles Braces for Chance of Convention Germ Attack," UPI, July 24, 2000. Stressing the terrorism angle, the story also said, "The federal government has chipped in by sending trained personnel from the Centers for Disease Control to Los Angeles with special computer software that will quickly track symptoms of emergency room patients and determine if they match up with the signs of a disease that would be found in a biological weapon, such as anthrax or the plague, or are deathly ill due to natural causes."

18. Michelle DeArmond, "L.A. Warned on Democratic Convention," AP, July 26, 2000.

19. "DNC Protesters Complain of Police Harassment," MSNBC, August 8, 2000.

20. "Judge Bars LAPD From Raiding Activist HQ," *Reuters*, August 11, 2000.

Demand a Better World! held a meeting at Luna Sol Cafe, planning to participate in the next day's Mumia Abu-Jamal protest march. Shortly after the meeting broke up, uniformed police officers rushed through the cafe's door and threw three of the main speakers up against a wall. Several of the meeting's participants also jumped up and helped with the arrests, revealing themselves to be undercover officers. After checking the identities of the three activists, the officers let two go and hauled the third one away in handcuffs.[21]

By the time the Democratic National Convention began on August 18, there were an untold number of undercover officers and other infiltrators among the protesters. The infiltrators included members of the LAPD's Anti-Terrorism Division who were already spying on political dissidents in the Los Angeles area. As reported by the *Los Angeles Times*, "[S]ome of these undercover officers met before going out on the streets in their work clothes: T-shirts and shorts, bandannas, thong shoes and sneakers. They even are allowed to break department policy by wearing beards and keeping their hair long. One wore a 'Free Mumia' bandanna, a reference to a Pennsylvania inmate on death row for killing a police officer. His face was unshaven, his hair tousled."

Among other things, these "scouts" mingled with protesters at the various demonstrations, using cell phones to file continuous reports and allowing commanders to make "real time" decisions on deploying riot gear-equipped squads around town. Police used tips provided by these infiltrators to justify arresting 42 animal rights protesters on August 15. Authorities claimed the protesters had materials which could be used in "homemade flamethrowers," a charge strongly denied by the activists. A Superior Court judge released 40 of them after a hearing two days later.

"It's standard operating procedure: infiltrate and disrupt," protest organizer Lisa Fithian told the *Times*. "They are potentially trying to incite problems in the midst of our demonstrations. We're not doing anything illegal; we're not doing anything wrong."

By the time the Democrats went home, even the protesters were beginning to concede the snitch-fueled tactics were beginning to hurt the anti-globalization movement.

"A disturbing trend is developing regarding police pre-emptive response to mass protest. In numerous situations since WTO protests in Seattle in late 1999, police have issued misinformation claiming unsubstantiated evidence of violent plans by protesters gathering for mass actions. The false information is then used as a pretext for unwarranted police actions. The misinformation concerning protester plans have ranged from chemical weapons to bomb-making. None of the numerous claims of violent plans have been substantiated. Nonetheless, many media outlets appear to have been predisposed to repeat information provided by police without fact-checking or seeking responses from the organizations accused. The damage to free speech and the mass protest movement

---

21. "Police Arrest Youth at March Planning Meeting," Sheri Herndon, <sheri@speakeasy.org>, August 13, 2000.

has been extensive," activist/journalist Tim Ream wrote in an August 10 dispatch from Los Angeles, noting that nearly 2,500 protesters had been arrested since November 30, 1999. "In addition, activists are scared. Anyone who has been involved in the mass protest movement through a major event of the last six months has friends who have been brutalized at the hands of the system."

CHAPTER SIXTEEN

THE COMING GLOBAL SNITCH CULTURE

AT THE BEGINNING OF THE 21ST CENTURY, America has been transformed into the most sophisticated, pervasive surveillance society in the history of the world. Dictators such as Adolph Hitler and Joseph Stalin may have relied on informants to maintain order, but their regimes lacked high-tech monitoring systems which can track people on a minute-by-minute basis. Nor did the Nazi or Soviet governments possess computers which can send the most personal information on anyone across the country at the stroke of a key. And no previous empire had anything like Echelon, the spy-in-the-sky capable of intercepting virtually every e-mail, phone call, and fax transmission.

But this isn't enough for the architects of the Snitch Culture. They are working hard to create a global surveillance system capable of tracking every man, woman and child on the Earth. Although a number of other nations routinely spy on their citizens (including democracies in Europe, dictatorships in the Balkans, and fundamentalist nations in the Middle East) this worldwide monitoring network is being pushed most aggressively by the U.S. federal government, with the full and active cooperation of the United Nations.

The Central Intelligence Agency and the National Security Agency have conducted international surveillance operations since they were first created in 1947. The CIA and NSA have close working relationships with intelligence agencies in allied countries, including Scotland Yard, Interpol and Israel's Mossad. But in recent years, the FBI has also begun sending its employees abroad, opening 43 offices around the world before the end of 1999. Its agents are currently hunting terrorists in the Middle East, war criminals in the Balkans, and drug dealers in Columbia.[1] And it is beginning to identify an international left-wing conspiracy as the newest threat to the American way of life.

In August 2000, the *Central and Eastern European Review* reported that FBI Director Louis Freeh and Czech Interior Minister Stanislav Gross met to discuss launching a joint operation, in advance of the annual meeting of the World Bank and the IMF set for September 26 in Prague. At the time, thousands of left-wing European activists were planning to protest the gathering, and Czech Prime Minister Milos Zeman had declared "the largest threat to stability in the country is the extreme left."

The corporate media fully supports the effort to create a global surveillance network. The establishment press continuously cranks out stories about drug-dealing Columbian revolutionaries, millionaire Muslim terrorists, murderous

---

1. "U.S.-Backed Raids Break Up Columbia's Biggest Heroin Ring," *Oregonian*, April 13, 2000.

Russian Mafia members, and numerous other foreign threats allegedly facing the free world. Hollywood movies such as *The Peacekeeper*, the first film from the politically-connected Dreamworks Studio, emphasize that only an international strike force can protect the country from worldwide terrorism.

These efforts are accompanied by an all-out federal assault on the Internet. Despite the global nature of the World Wide Web, Washington is obsessed with finding ways to monitor and control it. Apparently the free flow of news, opinions and information makes politicians, bureaucrats and law enforcement officials nervous. The political establishment has spent years trying to portray the Internet as little more than a cesspool of pornography, unfounded conspiracy theories and bomb-making instructions. The purpose of this propaganda campaign is obvious—to create public support for government regulation of the Internet, including the power to monitor all transmissions and shut down those it deems offensive. The private advocacy groups have jumped on board, with watchdog organizations such as the Anti-Defamation League releasing reports characterizing the Internet as a recruiting tool for white supremacist and neo-Nazi organizations.

The corporate media has responded with lurid stories about online molesters trolling for young victims, pedophiles swapping digital kiddie porn, and international criminals using encrypted e-mails to plot worldwide reigns of terror. For example, on June 1, 2000, *USA Today* published a half-page story which linked the Russian Mafia to the Internet. Headlined "Hackers: Pirates Thrive in Russia's Underworld," the piece charged that Russian gangsters were using computers to wreak havoc around the world: "Russia has only about 1.5 million Internet users, a small number compared with the estimated 110 million in the U.S. But among them are some of the world's busiest digital vandals, pirates, thieves and spies. Their victims include the wealthy and powerful: Microsoft, whose software is widely pirated here, America Online, the Pentagon, Citibank."

Such stories provide cover for federal efforts to control the World Wide Web. Much of this work is being pushed by the FBI through a top-secret, international organization it established in 1993. Operating under the innocuous title of the International Law Enforcement Telecommunications Seminar (ILETS), the group has met every year to plan how to make the telecommunications systems "interception-friendly." Details of plans to force ISPs all over the world to install secret Internet interception "black boxes" on their premises was reported in 1999.[2]

By October of that year, members of the international Internet Engineering Task Force were complaining that the FBI was pressuring it to build "surveillance-friendly" features into the infrastructure of the global communications network. Created in 1986, the 15-person IETF sets the protocol standards for moving digital information around the world. As reported by Wired News, the FBI wanted the task force to build electronic "trapdoors" into e-mail communications

---

2. "The Spy in Your Server," <www.mediachannel.org>, August 10, 2000.

programs to give police investigators easy access to supposedly confidential messages. The ACLU warned, "What law enforcement is asking . . . is the equivalent of requiring the home building industry to place a 'secret' door in all new homes to which only it would have the key."[3]

The campaign against an unfettered Internet reached new heights just after the start of the New Millennium. Over the course of a few days in early January, a handful of the most popular websites were struck with "denial of service" attacks. Amazon.com, eBay and several other large online retailers were effectively shut down for several hours each. The attacks didn't cause any lasting damage, nor did they pry into any customer accounts. Nevertheless, U.S. Attorney General Janet Reno used them to call for the end of Internet anonymity and the creation of a new online network of law-enforcement agents with the power to operate across multi-jurisdictional lines. "There is a dark side of hacking, crashing networks and viruses that we absolutely must address," Reno told the National Association of Attorneys General during a conference at Stanford University on January 10.[4]

Reno introduced the new unit as LawNet, and said that it would utilize computer geeks and law enforcement officials from all levels of government. "I envision a network that extends from local detectives to the FBI to investigators abroad," she said. Among other things, Reno explained that LawNet investigators would have the power to evade the jurisdictional red tape that complicates the prosecution of Internet-related crimes.

Deputy U.S. Attorney General Eric Holder went even farther on February 29. Speaking before a joint session of legislators from both the House and Senate judiciary committees gathered on Capitol Hill, Holder charged that such common Internet practices as anonymous re-mailers and free trial accounts are preventing the government from catching online criminals. "A criminal using tools and other information easily available over the Internet can operate in almost perfect anonymity," Holder told the panel, adding that the Justice Department is reviewing "whether we have adequate legal tools to locate, identify and prosecute cyber-criminals."

Little more than a week later, on March 9, 2000, Reno released an official report which complained that some private Internet companies are not keeping sufficient records to trace criminal activity. The report was written by the White House "Working Group on Unlawful Conduct on the Internet," which she chaired. Among other things, it called for modifications to the Privacy Protection Act of 1980, which prevents law enforcement agencies from seizing the work of American journalists, scholars and writers. The report complained the law "may now apply to almost any search of any computer. Because computers now commonly contain enormous data storage devices, wrongdoers can use them to store material for publication—material that the PPA protects—while

---

3. Declan McCullagh, "Wiretapping the Net: Oh, Brother," *Wired News*, October 12, 1999.
4. Thomas C. Greene, "Janet Reno Proposes Online Police Squad," *The Register*, January 13, 2000.

simultaneously storing (in a commingled fashion) child pornography, stolen classified documents, or other contraband or evidence of crime. With the advent of the Internet and widespread computer use, almost any computer can be used to 'publish' material. As a result, the PPA may now apply to almost any search of any computer."

Speaking at a press conference to announce the report, Reno said, "The Internet has provided our world with unparalleled opportunities. At the same time, the Internet is providing criminals a vast, inexpensive and potentially anonymous way to commit crime."

The federal government has already recruited influential international organizations into its assault on the Internet. One is the Group of 8 industrialized nations. Commonly known as G-8, it is comprised of the leaders and finance ministers of France, Germany, Japan, United Kingdom, United States, Italy, Canada and Russia. In May 2000, a G-8 subgroup convened a meeting between top law enforcement and computer industry officials in Paris to discuss responses to cyber-crime. One of the issues discussed was a proposal that ISPs be required to keep logs of all of their users' activities online for up to one year.

But the federal government isn't waiting. Echelon, the NSA's information vacuum cleaner, is already patrolling the Web. The February 1999 European Union report on Echelon detailed how the NSA collects and analyzes data from the Internet. The report presented evidence the NSA had struck deals with Microsoft, Lotus, and Netscape and other Internet companies to alter their software and develop products to capture data of interest. According to a former NSA employee, by 1995 the agency had installed "sniffer" software to collect traffic at nine major Internet exchange points. The NSA's National Computer Security Center uses "bots" to visit targeted sites every day and download all their new files.

The report went on to accuse the U.S. government of "lying" about the true extent of Echelon's operations.[5]

The federal focus on the Internet is reflected in the skyrocketing number of search warrants seeking citizens' online data. The number of search warrants issued against AOL subscribers alone increased more than eight times between 1997 and 1999, according to a study by USA Today. "The warrants, served by state and local investigators, were aimed at discovering the identity and activities of AOL subscribers," the paper reported.[6]

But the most significant international organization in the creation of the Global Snitch Culture is undoubtedly the United Nations, which has enthusiastically embraced the concept of fighting international wars against global crime, drug trafficking and terrorism—the same pretexts used to spy on millions of law-abiding Americans over the years. The U.N. has evolved over the years from an international debating society to the precursor of a One World Government, complete with its own laws and military force. In 1999 alone, the number

5. Constant Brand, "EU: Wider Probe of U.S. Spies," AP, April 7, 2000.
6. "Search Warrants for Online Data Soar," USA Today, July 28, 2000.

of U.N. peacekeepers, military observers and peace officers nearly tripled from 13,000 to more than 35,000, with their cost rising from 1 billion in 1999 to an estimated $3 billion in 2000.[7]

Nowadays, U.N. officials routinely call for global police initiatives against crime, drug trafficking, the sale of women and children, and various other human rights abuses, all requiring millions of snitches to enforce. For example, on April 10, 2000, U.N. Deputy Secretary-General Louise Frecehtte formally called for a Global War on Crime. "No country alone can cope successfully with the growth of transnational crime. If criminals are going global, those fighting them must also launch a global effort and create effective networks of technical, legal and judicial cooperation or they will always be one step behind."[8]

The same conference produced a call for controlling the Internet, with Frecehtte citing the threat posed by global organized crime networks. "To them, opening borders means it is easier to traffic in women and children for forced labor and prostitution, to smuggle drugs and arms, and to escape justice," she said. "Open economies mean more businesses to extract bribes from and new shares of illegal markets to be won. Technological progress means new opportunities for child pornography, falsification of documents and money laundering."

One of the most outspoken advocates for expanding the U.N.'s powers in recent years has been Pino Arlacchi, head of the orgaization's Office of Drug Control and Crime Prevention. Under Arlacchi's leadership, the U.N. is creating its own satellite monitoring system to identify narcotic cultivators around the world. The European Space Agency offered to provide the satellites and technical expertise to monitor the drug crops in early 1999, with the European Commission agreeing to pick up much of the estimated $15 million-a-year cost. The surveillance will concentrate on five countries which grow almost half of the world's coca leaf, Afghanistan, Myanmar, Columbia, Peru, and Bolivia. "For the first time the international community will have a very reliable instrument to measure the extent of illegal crops," he said.[9]

Speaking before a high-profile New York press briefing in July 2000, the former Italian prosecutor said the international body should be given "universal jurisdiction" to prosecute a broad range of crimes, including drug trafficking, money laundering, and all criminal activity on the Internet. Under international law, the only crimes that now qualify for universal jurisdiction are genocide and crimes against humanity. Arlacchi said the others should be added because they cross national borders, saying, "It is extremely difficult to route a case into a precise jurisdiction, so we believe this problem is encouraging us to go in the direction of universal jurisdiction." Speaking about the Internet, he said it was being used by drug traffickers to find new customers and argue against existing

7. Colum Lynch, "U.S. Falls Further Behind in Its Debt to United Nations," *Los Angeles Times-Washington Post* News Service, *Oregonian*, August 9, 2000.
8. "Organized Crime on Globalization Bandwagon," UPI, April 10, 2000.
9. Christopher Wren, "U.N. to Create Own Satellite Program to Find Illegal Drug Crops," *New York Times*, March 28, 1999.

drug laws. "The Internet is more and more important in providing exchanges of information, in expanding the market, particularly the final market, and we are very worried about it," he said.[10]

Arlacchi's statements represent the first step toward codifying recommendations set forth in the 1997 annual report prepared by the U.N. International Narcotics Control Board. Published shortly after the passage of California's Medical Marijuana Initiative, this document criticizes member nations which allow open, public discussions of global anti-drug strategies. Article III of the 1988 U.N. Convention Against Illicit Traffic in Narcotic Drugs and Psychotropic Substances compels all signatories to prosecute citizens for "publicly inciting or inducing others by any means" to use drugs. The report denounces countries which have yet to "establish such conduct as a criminal offense under its domestic law," specifically stating that the "successful campaigns for the 'medical' use of cannabis in Arizona and California in the United States of America" violates the 1988 treaty.

But the plan to use the U.N. to create a seamless global surveillance system was not publicly acknowledged until early September 2000, when the organization held a Millennium Summit at its New York headquarters. During several days of public speeches and private meetings, world leaders discussed proposals to create a standing army, a global police force, and an international justice system. "The time has come to replace the present system with an entirely new contract between the U.N. and its member states," British Prime Minister Tony Blair told the gathering. Among other things, the delegates discussed the need for the U.N. to have its own "intelligence capacity"—a euphemism for a Global Snitch Culture.

---

10. Cletus Nelson, "Silencing Dissent: The Global Information War," <www.disinfo.com>, July 10, 2000. In the piece, Nelson notes, "After subjecting the public to an unrelenting barrage of urine tests, roving wiretaps, 'no knock' searches, and other invasive measures to advance its 'zero tolerance' Drug War agenda, the police state apparatus is opening a new front in this scorched earth battle: the marketplace of ideas. The architects of this free speech threat won't be found among Washington's wing-tipped Mandarin class, but rather within the ranks of the United Nations ruling elite." Additional information on the Pino Arlacchi press conference can be found at <www.drcnet.org/wol/143.html#unagain>.

CHAPTER SEVENTEEN

STOPPING SNITCH ABUSE

STOPPING THE SPREAD of the Snitch Culture looks impossible, given how many government agencies, private employers, and non-profit advocacy groups are currently gathering and swapping information. And how can anyone slow its growth on the international level, since the United Nations is not even a democratically-elected body? But, over the years, populations have repeatedly woken up to the harm caused by informants and forced them to be reined in.

The delantors of ancient Rome eventually became so abusive they were banned. The colonial governor of Massachusetts put an end to the witch hunts. Congress enacted but then repealed mandatory minimum sentences for marijuana. Publicity about COINTELPRO forced the FBI to curtail its political surveillance programs, at least temporarily.

More recently, Canadian citizens won a major victory in May 2000 when they forced their government to dismantle a huge computer database containing detailed information on virtually everyone in the country. Called the Longitudinal Labor Force Files, the databank was maintained under the direction of Canada's human resources minister, Jane Stewart. The files reportedly contained information on 33 million Canadians, including ethnicity, movements in and out of the country or from province to province, and sensitive data about their health and taxes. The data came from a number of different agencies, including Canada Customs and Revenue, under a secret information-sharing agreement.

Canadians first learned about the database in mid-May, 2000. Privacy Commissioner Bruce Phillips revealed that Stewart had created the files by combining the information she received from other agencies with her own department's jobs and welfare data. According to Phillips, some files contained up to 2,000 pieces of information.

Stewart originally claimed the files were needed for policy research purposes, saying that the information was never shared with any other agency. But the press quickly discovered that law enforcement agencies, including the Canadian Security Intelligence Service and the Royal Canadian Mounted Police, had access to them. The revelations ignited a huge public outcry. Over 18,000 Canadians called to ask the department what kind of information it was holding on them. Opposition leaders in the House of Commons demanded that the files be destroyed. On May 28, Stewart announced she was dismantling the entire system, acknowledging there were "public concerns about privacy in this era of constantly changing technology."[1]

Such victories, however small or fleeting, show that fighting the surveillance society is not as hopeless as it may seem. As law professor Clifford S. Zimmerman put it, "The mishandling of informants has recurred in a somewhat cyclical pattern since the earliest days of the English common law. The pattern typically starts with widespread informant use, which is then curtailed after publicized misconduct or mishandling."[2]

Another such cycle may be underway. Public opinion polls show privacy is rapidly emerging as one of the hottest political issues of the early 21st Century. A Rasmussen Research poll taken in late July revealed that 71 percent of Americans who were familiar with the new Carnivore computer system believe the FBI is "very likely" or "somewhat likely" to use it to spy improperly on private citizens. Sixty-two percent of those polled believe "the President or members of Congress" would have no qualms about asking the FBI to monitor private citizens as a way to intimidate or harass political opponents, compared to just 23 percent who said the FBI would only use Carnivore for lawful, proper investigations.[3]

Writing about the privacy issue in early June 2000, the *New York Times* said, "It encompasses far more than Peeping Toms or even hackers invading websites or intercepting cell phone conversations. Not only are people frightened that information about their personal peccadillos could turn up in hostile hands, but also that the thieves could cash in on their financial data. Increasingly, people confess to pollsters, they are suspicious of companies that have access to their financial and health care records, and are frightened that the information will be used against them. They are no less wary of what the government could do with such data."[4]

Even politicians are growing wary of some intelligence-gathering programs. Lawmakers in 11 states balked at expanding their DNA databanks in the last half of 1999. Although all 50 states originally agreed to join the FBI's computer network, these legislators either defeated or failed to act on laws requiring more of their citizens to submit DNA samples to the authorities.[5]

Some courts have already begun challenging the unbridled power of informants. On July 1, 1998, three judges on the 10th Circuit Court of Appeals issued a ruling which cut to the heart of the traditional relationship between law enforcement agencies and snitches. Ruling on an appeal brought by a woman convicted of conspiracy to distribute cocaine, the judges decreed that federal law prohibits

1. "Canada Dismantles 'Big Brother' Files," UPI, May 29, 2000.
2. Clifford S. Zimmerman, "Toward a New Vision of Informants: A History of Abuses and Suggestions for Reform," *Hastings Constitutional Law Quarterly*, Fall 1994.
3. "Most Fear FBI Abuse of 'Carnivore,'" *WorldNetDaily*, August 2, 2000.
4. Richard Berke, "What Are You Afraid Of? A Hidden Issue Emerges," *New York Times*, June 4, 2000.
5. Richard Willing, "As Police Rely More on DNA, States Take a Closer Look," *USA Today*, June 6, 2000.

the government from offering anything of value to witnesses in exchange for their testimony—in other words, paying snitches with money or reduced sentences.

The woman, Sonya Singleton, was convicted in part because of the statements of an alleged co-conspirator, Napoleon Douglas, who had entered into a formal plea-bargain agreement with prosecutors for leniency in exchange for his testimony. In its ruling (165 F3rd 1297), the panel declared that the promise of leniency violated a federal law against bribing witnesses. Section 201(c)(2) of the United States Code, reads in part, "Whoever . . . directly or indirectly, offers or promises anything of value to a person, for or because of the testimony under oath or affirmation given or to be given by such person as a witness at trial . . . before any court . . . shall be fined under this title or imprisoned for not more than two years, or both."

This was not the first time that a criminal defendant cited this law to prevent cooperating witnesses from testifying against them. Previous courts had always ruled the statute applied to everyone except federal prosecutors. But the panel disagreed, arguing that it did not exempt prosecutors. Instead, the judges held that the promise of leniency was nothing more than a bribe, an illegal attempt to buy testimony. "The obvious purpose of the government's promised action was to reduce his jail time, and it is difficult to imagine anything more valuable than personal physical freedom," the panel said.

In its decision, the judges ruled that the law not only could, but should be applied to the government. "The judicial process is tainted and justice cheapened when factual testimony is purchased, whether with leniency or money," they said. "Because prosecutors bear a weighty responsibility to do justice and observe the law in the course of a prosecution, it is particularly appropriate to apply the strictures of [the law] to their activities."

After the ruling was issued, prosecutors across the country attempted to portray it as the death knell for criminal justice. If the ruling had been allowed to stand, it would have undoubtedly changed how the government deals with informants. Plea bargain agreements would have been all but eliminated, greatly restricting the government's ability to prosecute crime.

The full 10th Circuit Court of Appeals overturned the panel's ruling on January 8, 1999 (144 F3rd 1342). Writing for the majority of the court, Chief Justice Porfilio cited the Webster's Third New International Dictionary's definition of the term "whoever" as "whatever *person: any person.*" Justice Porfolio argued that federal prosecutors are not "persons," but representatives of the United States government. "The United States is an inanimate entity, not a being," he wrote, noting that plea-bargains date back to English common Law, the foundation of this country's system of justice.

The original three judges continued to disagree, however, issuing a dissenting opinion which reasserted their original conclusion. "Criminal judgements are accepted by society at large, and even by individual defendants, only because our system of justice is painstakingly fair," they wrote, arguing that preventing prosecutors from bargaining for testimony would maintain "the integrity, fairness and credibility of our system of justice."

At the very least, the controversy proves that the proper role of informants in the American justice system is still up for debate.

Informants also came in for a public drubbing when the death penalty re-emerged as a public issue in late 1999. Because of advances in DNA testing, a growing number of convicted criminals were being exonerated. Eleven inmates were released from Death Row in Illinois by the fall of 1999, prompting the *Chicago Tribune* to publish an exhaustively-researched series of stories which found that almost half of the state's 285 death-penalty convictions had been based on faulty evidence, with much of it coming from jailhouse snitches who cut deals with prosecutors to reduce their own sentences. Two more inmates were freed from Death Row a few weeks later, pushing the total to 13, one more than the number of murder convicts executed in Illinois since the death penalty was reinstated in 1977. Governor George Ryan responded by declaring a moratorium on executions in his state.

"There seems to be a growing awareness that the death penalty is just another government program that doesn't work very well," Stephen Bright of the Southern Center for Human Rights told the June 12 issue of *Newsweek*.[6]

But it wasn't only Death Row inmates being proven innocent by new DNA tests. So were convicted muggers, rapists and robbers. Many of them were freed through the efforts of the Innocence Project, a New York-based non-profit organization started by Barry Scheck, a well-known and media-savvy criminal defense attorney. By June 2000, Scheck's organization had freed nearly 100 inmates around the country, approximately a dozen of them from Death Row.

This is the first time in the history of the country that so many convicted criminals have been proven to be innocent. As the numbers continue to grow in coming years, even law-and-order conservatives will be forced to concede that the criminal justice system is seriously flawed, and that lying snitches are a significant problem for even law-abiding Americans.

So what can be done about the Snitch Culture? The first step is to accurately identify the problem. Although people commonly complain about "snitches," "rats," "stool pigeons" and "tattletales," informants are absolutely essential for solving many, if not most, serious crimes, including murder cases which aren't eventually overturned by DNA evidence. The real problem is snitches who lie, manufacture evidence, or prompt otherwise innocent people to commit crimes. Government agencies, private employers, and private intelligence networks also create problems when they use informants to attack people for activities that aren't crimes, such as holding unpopular political views. The problem is informant *abuse*, not informants per se.

Here are a few suggestions for reforming the informant system without preventing the police from solving crimes, prohibiting employers from firing

---

6. Jonathan Alter, "The Death Penalty on Trial," *Newsweek*, June 12, 2000.

dishonest workers, or interfering with the open exchange of controversial opinions:

1 .Stop the war mentality.

Politicians, police officials, and the media frequently refer to law enforce- ment activities as "wars"—the War on Crime, the War on Drugs, the War on Youth Violence, and so forth. But law enforcement is not war. Every- thing is allowable in war, including spies who lie, cheat, steal—even kill— to fulfill their missions. In a war, the enemy has no rights. But American citizens do, even those suspected of the most heinous crimes. It's long past time for peace on the homefront.

2 .Repeal all mandatory minimum sentences.

In their zeal to look tough on crime, politicians have enacted numerous mandatory minimum sentences for many crimes—and the vast majority of them are unreasonable. Mere possession of a small amount of crack cocaine can result in 20 or more years in prison. Under these laws, the only way to qualify for a lesser sentence is to provide "substantial assistance" to prosecutors to solve other crimes—in other words, to turn snitch at the direction of the prosecutor. This gives prosecutors too much power, and all but forces criminal defendants to make up stories to avoid the lengthy minimum sentences. Instead, judges should be given more discretion in sentencing.

3 .No asset forfeitures until after criminal convictions.

Under the current federal asset forfeiture law, a mere accusation of criminal activity can allow the government to seize a suspect's money and property. Because the government benefits financially from such seizures, it has a strong incentive to act on tips from even the most unreliable informants. The government has even kept the assets of suspects who were never formally charged with any crimes. The law should be changed to allow the government to seize a suspect's money and property only after he is convicted of a crime, and only *after* the government has proven his money and property was generated by the criminal activity.

4 .Limit payments to informants.

Snitches have too many financial incentives to lie. At the present time, informants can make millions of dollars by lying to the authorities. The temptation to make up a story is simply too great. According to a recent report by the U.S. Department of Justice, approximately 29 percent of the total revenue from all assets seized in 1996 (the latest year for which figures were available) were used to fund the forfeiture program expenses, much of which went to informants. Rewards should be limited to specific, reasonable fees—not a percentage of the property seized or multi-million dollar payments.

5. Make law enforcement agencies and others liable for misconduct committed by their informants.

Under current Supreme Court rulings, governments are not liable for the actions of their informants. Even though an informant may be working directly for an agency, his "handler" is not presumed to be able to control his behavior. This is why people who are victimized by informants cannot successfully sue law enforcement agencies they are working for, making the agency less concerned about the behavior of the informants than they should be. The laws should be changed to make the agencies liable for any harm caused by their informants. At the very least, that would encourage officials to screen their informants more carefully. The same would be true for private employers and private non-profit agencies.

6. Prevent private advocacy groups from providing non-criminal information to law enforcement officials.

Police are prohibited by law from collecting information on anyone simply because of their political beliefs. But the FBI and other agencies get around this restriction by accepting such information from politically-oriented private intelligence networks, including the Anti-Defamation League, the Southern Poverty Law Center and the Maldon Institute. Police agencies should be prevented from accepting personal information on citizens from these "surrogate snitches."

7. Stop building a global police state.

It's hard enough to fight against lying snitches in the American criminal justice system. Even Constitutional guarantees, U.S. Supreme Court rulings, and hundreds of federal and state laws do not prevent prosecutors from using dishonest informants. But these problems will be many times worse in the global police state which is currently being constructed by the United Nations and its supporters. Even though the U.N. has adopted numerous human rights treaties, it does not guarantee a fair trial to anyone accused of violating the international laws it is currently developing. For example, in June 2000, a weeklong U.N. Women's Conference called for tough measures to combat the international sex trade. Similar U.N.-sponsored gatherings have demanded new laws to stop global trafficking in drugs and small arms. As laudable as these goals sound, such laws will take millions of snitches to enforce—and there are no international safeguards against lying snitches and *agent provocateurs*. Few other nations have anything resembling our Bill of Rights, and neither does the International Court which has begun prosecuting war criminals. Until these problems are addressed and solved, the United States should refuse to participate in—let alone push—international law enforcement efforts.

None of these reforms would prevent the effective use of informants to solve serious crimes. Mandatory Miranda warnings didn't stop the U.S. prison population from topping 2 million in early 2000. As the dissenting judges in the final Singleton ruling wrote, "[E]xperience has proven that the government, just like the private citizens it regulates and prosecutes, can live within the rules. No one would suggest that the criminal justice system has ceased to function because the Court or Congress has effectuated constitutional or statutory guarantees designed to promote a more reliable outcome in criminal proceedings."

Ironically, without such reforms, the country will soon become like the totalitarian regimes it defeated in World War II and bankrupted with the Cold War. Americans will lose their rights without firing a shot, without even knowing they are under assault until it's too late. And there won't be anywhere to run and hide, either.

Part Four
Case Studies)

THE REAL LEGACY OF MCCARTHYISM

HOW MUCH REAL EFFECT can snitches have on America, given the sheer size and complexity of the country? Consider this—informants were used to create the Cold War, reversing years of social progress and plunging the country into a dangerous and costly nuclear arms race. Red-baiters such as FBI Director J. Edgar Hoover and U.S. Senator Joseph McCarthy exploited disillusioned socialists, politically-motivated infiltrators, seasoned criminals, *agent provocateurs*, and a host of other shady characters to create the illusion of a looming Communist Menace which must be fought at all costs. Conservative politicians and law enforcement officials used this scare to reshape American political, cultural and intellectual life after World War II, abandoning the liberal reforms that started under FDR's New Deal, stifling creativity and artistic expression, and officially adopting the military strategy of Mutually Assured Destruction, appropriately known as MAD.

As Navasky put it in *Naming Names*, "The morale of the United States' newly reliable and devoted civil service was savagely undermined in the 1950s, and the purge of the Foreign Service contributed to our disastrous miscalculations in Southeast Asia in the 1960s and the consequent human wreckage. The congressional investigations of the 1940s and 1950s fueled the anti-Communist hysteria which eventually led to the investment of thousands of billions of dollars in a nuclear arsenal, with risks that boggle the minds of even those who specialize in 'thinking about the unthinkable.'" [1]

Although Navasky was writing about the Red Scare of the 1950s, the propaganda campaign against Communism actually began in 1917, and it relied on snitches, too. Shortly after the Russian Revolution, the federal government and a number of state legislatures held extensive public hearings to assess this new menace. They focused largely on the alleged threat to national security posed by subversives, broadly defined to encompass the various factions of anarchists, communists, and socialists on the left.

One U.S. House investigation, conducted by the Senate Overman Committee in 1919, began as a probe into wartime German propaganda by brewing companies but evolved into a study of "Bolshevik propaganda." Similar hearings were conducted by some state legislatures, including New York's Lusk Committee, which was also launched in 1919. Although some of the investigations lasted only a few months, others ran for many years.

---

1. Victor S. Navasky, *Naming Names*, New York: The Viking Press, 1980.

In 1930, the U.S. House ordered an investigation into "Communist Propaganda in the United States." Its committee, chaired by Congressman Hamilton Fish, featured testimony from a variety of public and private surveillance organizations, all of whom were eager to prove that left-wing radicals were conspiring to take over the labor movement and overthrow the government. Much of the information was provided by government undercover agents and private citizens who had infiltrated left-wing organizations.[2]

The Fish Committee was succeeded by the McCormack-Dickstein Committee in 1934, and then by the Special Committee on Un-American Propaganda Activities. Also called the Dies Committee after chairman Martin Dies, it was given a one-year mandate to investigate "un-American propaganda" and "un-American propaganda activities." The committee was extended each year until 1945, when it was succeeded by the permanent House Un-American Activities Committee (HUAC). Unlike the previous committees, HUAC was not only charged with the traditional committee powers of considering and proposing legislation, it was also given the power to subpoena witnesses and cite them for contempt if they refused to appear and answer questions.

In the late 1940s, the California Legislature's Joint Fact-finding Committee on Un-American Activities, chaired by State Senator Jack Tenney, charged that Communists had infiltrated Hollywood and were putting subversive messages in films. In 1947 and again in 1951, the Congressional HUAC looked into the allegations. Approximately 60 percent of the Hollywood insiders called before the committee were screen-writers, while actors made up roughly 20 percent of the witnesses. When the first subpoenas were issued, Hollywood decided to fight back. Defense committees were formed and many of the witnesses agreed they would not admit whether they or anyone they knew were Communists, arguing that the U.S. Constitution guarantees freedom of association. The resulting hearings were a fiasco for the defiant witnesses, however. They looked like they had something to hide, and ten screenwriters—The Hollywood Ten—were charged with contempt of Congress on November 24, 1941. A few days later, movie producers meeting at the Waldorf Astoria hotel announced that "no Communists or other subversives will be employed by Hollywood." The Hollywood Ten made an appeal to the courts, but it was rejected and they eventually served one-year prison sentences.

One of the pivotal moments in the Red Scare was the Alger Hiss case. Two grand juries investigated Soviet espionage in the United States in 1947 and 1950, eventually focusing on Hiss, a high-ranking U.S. State Department official. A snitch named Whittaker Chambers accused Hiss of being a Communist and passing sensitive U.S. documents on to him. At the time, Chambers was a senior editor at *Time* magazine who admitted having been a Soviet agent from 1934 to 1938. Although Hiss adamantly denied the charges, he was eventually convicted of perjury and served three years in prison. A young, first-term California

---

2. Frank Donner, *The Age of Surveillance: The Aims & Methods of America's Political Intelligence System*, New York: Alfred Knopf, 1980.

congressman named Richard Nixon was tapped to run for Vice President after holding the highly publicized hearings on Chamber's allegations.[3]

HUAC returned for a second round of hearings in 1951. According to the *Encyclopedia of the American Left*, the proceedings were a charade: "The political views of those called were already known and the people they were asked to name as comrades were also known. The hearings amounted to a kind of ideological exorcism. Witnesses were expected to state that they had been misled or confused in the past and were now regretful. They could prove their sincerity by naming others who had been with them in Communist organizations or at Communist functions."

Some Hollywood insiders went along with the committee, denouncing their association with the Communist Party and naming names. The most famous informant was film director Elia Kazan. A former member of the legendary Group Theater of the 1930s, Kazan helped establish the Actors Studio along with Lee Strasberg in the late 1940s. It introduced "method acting" to American cinema and produced such talents as Marlon Brando, Julie Harris, Lee J. Cobb, Montgomery Clift, Shelley Winters and James Dean. Kazan was the force behind such powerful films as *A Tree Grows in Brooklyn* (1945), *Gentleman's Agreement* (the 1948 indictment of anti-Semitism), *A Streetcar Named Desire* (1951), and *East of Eden* (1955).[4]

Kazan appeared before the committee twice. The first time was in January 1952, when he answered all questions but refused to name the people he knew to be members of the Communist Party from the summer of 1934 to the spring of 1936, when he worked in the Group Theater and was also a party member. Then Kazan changed his mind and returned to the committee in April, naming eight other former Theater members he knew to be Communists more than 16 years earlier. Although Kazan testified in secret, his remarks were released the next day. (Many film critics believe Kazan intended his classic 1954 film *On the Waterfront* as a defense of his snitching.)

Nearly 90 percent of those identified to the committee lost their jobs in Hollywood (at least temporarily), including actors Zero Mostel, Sam Jaffe, and Lee Grant, nominated for an Oscar for her role in the 1951 film *Detective Story*. Charlie Chaplin, a British citizen, was not allowed to re-enter the United States following a trip to Europe. Even technical workers lost their jobs because Roy Brewer, the head of the Hollywood craft unions, was anti-Communist. Dozens of those on the blacklist lost their spouses, and even more went broke. Mental and physical afflictions were common. Clifford Odets never wrote well again, and the untimely deaths of John Garfield, J. Edward Bromberg, Canada Lee and half a dozen others have been attributed to their committee appearances.[5]

3. Josh Getlin, "Grand Jury Testimony from Hiss Case Will be Released," *Los Angeles Times-Washington Post* News Service, *Oregonian*, May 14, 1999.
4. Dan Georgakas, "Hollywood Blacklist," *Encyclopedia of the American Left*, Urbana and Chicago: University of Illinois Press, 1992.
5. Victor S. Navasky, *Naming Names*, New York: The Viking Press, 1980.

The most famous public hearings into Communism began in January 1953 when Republican U.S. Senator Joseph McCarthy was named chairman of the Senate Permanent Investigations Subcommittee. McCarthy had made Communism a political issue in his first campaign for a Wisconsin U.S. Senate seat. In 1946, he charged that his Democratic opponent, Howard McMurray, had been endorsed by the *Daily Worker*. In April 1947, McCarthy told the *Madison Capital Times* that his top priority was "to stop the spread of Communism." In 1949, the FBI provided McCarthy with a 100-page report alleging extensive communist penetration of the State Department. Although the report had been circulating around Capitol Hill without provoking any response, McCarthy decided to make it a major political issue. Speaking before the Ohio County Women's Republican Club on February 9, 1950, he said that "today we are engaged in a final, all-out battle between communistic atheism and Christianity."

McCarthy blamed the Communist take-over of China and other countries on "the traitorous actions" of the State Department's "bright young men," and he specifically named John S. Service, Gustavo Duran, Mary Jane Keeney, Julian Wadleigh, Dr. Harlow Shapley, Alger Hiss, and Dean Acheson. The line from the speech that made McCarthy famous was, "I have in my hand 57 cases of individuals who would appear to be either card-carrying members or certainly loyal to the Communist Party, but who nevertheless are still helping to shape our foreign policy."

The Democrat-controlled Senate did not embrace McCarthy's crusade. Instead, in February 1950, it referred the charges to a subcommittee of the Senate Foreign Relations Committee chaired by Senator Millard Tydings. After 31 days of hearings, the Tydings Committee concluded that McCarthy's charges were a "fraud" and a "hoax," and it said that the individuals on his list were neither communist nor pro-communist.

McCarthy did not back down, however. He continued to claim the government was being taken over by Communists in numerous public speeches, including a 60,000-word address on the floor of the U.S. Senate on June 14, 1951, later published as a book entitled *America's Retreat From Victory*. Two years later, after the Republicans took control of the Senate, McCarthy was finally given the authority to conduct his own hearings.

During 1953 and the first three months of 1954, the Senate Permanent Investigations Subcommittee held 199 days of hearings and examined 653 witnesses. These individuals first appeared in closed-door executive sessions and were given the opportunity to confess and snitch. A total of 83 witnesses refused to answer questions about Communist or espionage activities, on constitutional grounds, and their names were made public.

Many people lost their jobs after being identified as current or former members of the Communist Party by McCarthy and his committee. They included 32 people who were dismissed by General Electric after the committee heard testimony from two witnesses—William H. Teto and Herman E. Thomas—that the company's plants were riddled with Communist spies. The president of General Electric issued a policy statement expressing concern about "the possible danger to the safety and security of company property and personnel whenever a General Electric employee admits he is a Communist or when he asserts before a competent investigating government body that he might incriminate himself by giving truthful answers concerning his Communist affiliations or his possible espionage or sabotage activities."

McCarthy's snitch-fueled crusade had a dramatic effect on public discourse. "Since political activities could get you in trouble, prudent folk avoided them," Ellen Schrecker lamented in her 1995 essay, *The Impact of McCarthyism*. "Instead, to the despair of intellectuals, middle class Americans embraced social conformity. A silent generation of students populated the nation's campuses, while their professors shrank from teaching anything that might be construed as controversial."

Schrecker relays the following incident as typical: "In the late 1950s, a group of graduate students at the University of Chicago wanted to have a coffee-vending machine installed outside the Physics Department for the convenience of people who worked there late at night. They started to circulate a petition to the Buildings and Grounds Department, but their colleagues refused to sign. They did not want to be associated with the allegedly radical students whose names were already on the document. This incident—and it is not unique— exemplifies the kind of timidity that came to be seen, even at the time, as the most damaging consequence of the anti-communist furor."

As the hearings proceeded, McCarthy was denounced by many Democrats, and even much of the news media began to grow wary of his ever-wilder accusations. Then, responding to tips from civilian employees, the committee began looking into whether the U.S. Army had been infiltrated by Communists. The Army suspended or discharged 35 people as security risks, but when these cases reached the Army Loyalty and Screening Board at the Pentagon, all but two were reinstated and given back pay. McCarthy demanded the names of the 20 civilians on the review board, setting the stage for his demise.

In March 1954, the Eisenhower Administration publicly attacked McCarthy, accusing his staff of seeking preferential treatment for a committee consultant named G. David Schine, who had been drafted the previous November. A special committee was appointed to investigate the charges. Beginning on April 22, the special committee held 36 days of televised hearings. The defining moment came when McCarthy was attacking an associate of Joseph N. Welch, the chief attorney for the Army. Welch stood up, faced the senator, and said, "Until this moment, Senator, I think I never really gauged your cruelty or your recklessness. Let us not assassinate this lad further, Senator. You have done enough. Have you no sense of decency, sir, at long last? Have you no sense of decency?"

This was the beginning of the end for McCarthy. On December 2, 1954, the U.S. Senate voted 67-22 to condemn him for "conduct contrary to Senatorial traditions." Publicly humiliated, McCarthy began drinking heavily and was frequently hospitalized. He died on May 2, 1957, at the Naval Medical Center in Bethesda, Maryland of peripheral neuritis.

Mainstream historians say that McCarthy died a defeated man. But in fact, his anti-Communism crusade was a resounding success. From the 1950s on, American foreign policy was based on the principal of fighting Communism around the world. That policy sent U.S. troops to South Korea and Vietnam, and it was used to justify the covert supply network which funded the contra rebels in Nicaragua.

"Opposition to the Cold War had been so thoroughly identified with Communism that it was no longer possible to challenge the basic assumptions of American foreign policy without incurring suspicions of disloyalty," Schrecker wrote. "As a result, from the defeat of Henry Wallace in the fall of 1948 until the early 1960s, effective public criticism of America's role in the world was essentially non-existent. The insecurities bred by McCarthyism afflicted the State Department for years, especially with regard to East Asia. Thus, for example, the campaign against the loss of China left such long-lasting scars that American policy-makers feared to acknowledge the official existence of the People's Republic of China until Richard Nixon, who was uniquely impervious to charges of being soft on Reds, did so as President in 1971. And it was in part to avoid a replay of the loss-of-China scenario that Nixon's Democratic predecessors Kennedy and Johnson dragged the United States so deeply into the quagmire of the Vietnam War."

Congress continued holding anti-Communist hearings well after McCarthy's death. For example, in 1967, Arkansas Senator John L. McClellan was authorized to conduct an investigation into the urban riots which were hitting major American cities. McClellan was reportedly convinced that Communist and other agitators were stirring up inner-city blacks, and his committee ultimately warned about a "master plan" to overthrow the government pushed by a nation-wide conspiracy of subversives. Aided by testimony from no fewer than 63 undercover agents, the McClellan Committee put together a series of "power structure charts" of such left-wing organizations as Students for a Democratic Society (SDS) and the Black Panther Party. Chicago Police Sergeant Joseph P. Grubisic, head of the Intelligence Unit, provided the committee with up to 300 names of alleged agitators, proving that the Communist threat is real and "poses a major threat to the peace and security of our Nation."

HUAC also took up the issue of urban riots. In 1968 the committee contracted with an informant to write a booklet about the Communist conspiracy to stir up blacks. For $1,000, Phillip A. Luce, a former member of the Marxist Progressive Labor Party, gave the committee enough information to publish "Guerilla Warfare Advocates in the United States." Among other things, the 61-page tract claimed that American Communists received "guerilla training instructions in Spain during the civil war of 1936–1939."

In 1969, HUSC came under the leadership of Missouri Representative Richard Ichord and was renamed the House Internal Security Committee

(HISC). It was also given a new mandate, ensuring "internal security" by monitoring organizations that sought to overthrow the U.S. government by "any unlawful means" and establish a "totalitarian dictatorship." The committee was also charged with policing the activities of any group that used illegal means "to obstruct or oppose the lawful authority of the Government of the United States in the execution of any law or policy affecting the internal security of the United States."

HUAC/HISC conducted five investigations into peace activists and student radicals between 1968 and 1972. The reports are full of information provided by undercover agents and snitches, including logs, surveillance reports, and internal documents from the organizations.

One of the major investigative committees authorized by Congress was the Senate Internal Security Subcommittee (SISS), launched as an arm of the U.S. Judiciary Committee in 1951. Almost 20 years later, in 1970, the subcommittee held a series of hearings on the "Extent of Subversion in the New Left," followed by the publication of a 400-page study titled "Report on the SDS Riots, October 9–11, 1969." It also included a great deal of material from informants.

Many of the informants who appeared before the congressional committees were working for the FBI or other federal law enforcement agencies. One, FBI informant Gerald Wayne Kirk, testified on the SDS. Some of the informants, however, worked directly for the committees. For example, an SISS operative attended the Labor Day 1967 National Conference for a New Politics held in Chicago. He broke into the organization's headquarters, and also rifled files at the offices of the Mississippi Freedom Democratic Party, stealing a card index to prove the organization was supported by Communists. Several committee spies reportedly infiltrated left-wing protest groups at the 1968 Democratic Convention in Chicago.[6]

A lot has happened since the Red Scare of the 1950s. Public revulsion to government abuses revealed during the Watergate Scandal eventually prompted Congress to disband their special investigative committees. The Soviet Union has fallen. Chinese sweatshop workers make shoes for Nike and clothes for Disney. Far Right extremists replaced subversives as the official domestic political threat in the 1990s. But the hard feelings created by McCarthyism are still with us.

On January 7, 1999, the Motion Picture Academy of Arts and Sciences proposed giving film director Elia Kazan an honorary Oscar for lifetime achievement. The proposal was first made by actor and former Academy president Karl Malden, who had worked with Kazan in *A Streetcar Named Desire* and *On the Waterfront*. Although all 39 members of the Academy's board approved the award, the vote set off a wave of protests across the country, a direct reaction to Kazan's decision to name names in 1952. A victim of the Hollywood blacklist, screenwriter Bernard Gordon, formed the Committee Against Silence, which denounced the award in *Variety* and the

---

6. Church Committee Report, U.S. Government Printing Office, 1976.

Hollywood Reporter. Maureen Dowd attacked Kazan and the Academy in a *New York Times* column titled "A Streetcar Named Betrayal." Shortly before the March 21 awards ceremony, former blacklisted screenwriter Abe Polonsky told *Entertainment Weekly*, "I'll be watching, hoping someone shoots him. It would no doubt be a thrill in an otherwise dull evening."

Heavy security prevented serious trouble at the March 21 Academy Awards ceremony. Although protesters chanted anti-Kazan slogans outside the Dorothy Parker Pavilion, only a handful of audience members refused to applaud when he walked on stage to accept his Oscar. Still, the depth of the anger directed toward Kazan was remarkable, considering that nearly 47 years had passed since he testified before the committee—a clear demonstration of how snitches can divide the country, even after the issues they raised have long since passed into near-irreleveance.

COINTELPRO ABUSES

SOME OF THE FEDERAL GOVERNMENT'S most abusive surveillance operations occurred under the FBI's Counter-Intelligence Programs, commonly called COINTELPRO. Running from August 1956 to April 1971, they utilized thousands of informants and undercover operatives to monitor and harass a broad range of political activists, including communists, pacifists, civil rights protesters, black militants and white supremacists. Although the FBI claims to have ended the COINTELPRO operations, the same basic infiltration and disruption techniques are still being used against political dissidents.[1]

All of the COINTELPRO operations were created under the direction of FBI Director J. Edgar Hoover. Three programs began between 1956 and 1964, followed by two more in 1967 and 1968. The FBI authorized over 2,300 "actions" as part of these operations, including 715 which were specifically designed to disrupt organizations or create tensions between two or more groups. The major COINTELPRO operations were as follows:

- COINTELPRO-CPUSA was launched in August 1956 against the Communist Party USA. It quickly grew to encompass other people and organizations which the FBI suspected of being "Communist-influenced," including the National Committee to Abolish the House Un-American Activities Committee and numerous civil rights leaders. The CPUSA operation involved 1,338 agency-approved actions, more than half of the COINTELPRO totals, reflecting Hoover's obsession with fighting Communism. Informants were involved in nearly all of these operations, which ranged from identifying party members to disrupting meetings with calls for violence to instigating police raids on Communist Party USA offices around the country.
- The "SWP Disruption program" was formally begun in October 1961. Although originally targeted at the Socialist Workers Party, a Marxist splinter group, it also gathered information on other organizations which co-sponsored events with the SWP, such as peace marches during the Vietnam War. Remarkably, when the SWP sued the FBI over the surveillance program, the government revealed that over 1,300 informants had provided information against the small, inconsequential group.

---

1. Much of this chapter is drawn from the 1976 Church Committee report, which remains one of the most authoritative sources on the COINTELPRO operations. Frank Donner's *Age of Surveillance* was another significant source.

- The "Klan-White Hate Groups" program was authorized in September 1964. It was directed at 17 Klan organizations and 9 "hate groups," including the American Nazi Party. The FBI ultimately recruited or sent over 2,000 infiltrators into these organizations. Informants were elected to top leadership positions in over half the Klan units under investigation. As a September 2, 1965 letter from the FBI to a White House assistant put it, "Particularly significant has been the high-level penetration we have achieved of Klan organizations. At the present time, there are 14 Klan groups in existence. We have penetrated every one of them through informants [and] currently are operating informants in top-level positions of leadership in seven of them."
- The "Black Nationalist-Hate Groups" program was launched in August 1967. The FBI's second-largest COINTELPRO operation, it targeted a wide range of black organizations, from the militant Black Panther Party to non-violent Southern Christian Leadership Conference and most African-American student organizations on college campuses. An internal FBI memo said the project was needed to "prevent the *rise of a 'messiah'* who could unify and electrify the militant black nationalist movement." [Italics in the original.]
- The "New Left" program, approved in May 1968, was launched in reaction to the student protests at Columbia University. The term "New Left" was never defined by the FBI, and the operation soon expanded to collect information on a broad range of youth and anti-war groups, ranging from Students for a Democratic Society to the Women's International League for Peace and Freedom, the Inter-university Committee for Debate of Foreign Policy and, remarkably, all employees and students at Antioch University (described in FBI memos as the "vanguard of the New Left"). Internal FBI memos reveal Hoover was so horrified by the sexual mores of the New Left that he instructed his agents to be on the alert for "mounting evidence of the moral depravity" of the movement's leaders.

Stewart Albert is a longtime peace activist who saw COINTELPRO's effect on the peace and civil rights movement. He helped organize protests and wrote for a number of underground newspapers throughout much of the 1960s and 1970s, working with well-known activists as Jerry Rubin and Abbie Hoffman. He was also an unindicted co-conspirator in the Chicago 7 trial which grew out of the protests at the 1968 Democratic Party convention.

According to Albert, the anti-war movement disintegrated after being infiltrated by informants, including undercover police officers and right-wing freelancers. "Some of the informants were caught in the act, some surfaced as witnesses during trial, some were revealed years later in Freedom of Information requests, and some were never discovered," Albert recalls. "The informants changed the entire culture of the movement, It started out very open and trusting, but, after we realized we had been infiltrated, people became paranoid, fearful, and distrustful. Before too long, the movement became just like the society it was protesting." [2]

Although all COINTELPRO operations used informants, the most out-of-control snitches worked against African-American political organizations such as the Black Panther Party. Many were *agent provocateurs*, helping law enforcement officials set up black activists on bogus charges and occasionally prompting violent confrontations with the police.

One of the best known victims is Geronimo Pratt, the former leader of the Los Angeles Black Panther Party. Framed for a murder he did not commit in 1969, Pratt served 25 years in California state prisons before being released in 1997 after a judge overturned his conviction. The judge ruled that prosecutors intentionally and illegally failed to tell Pratt's attorneys that the key witness against him, Julius Butler, was an informant for the FBI, the LAPD and the Los Angeles District Attorney's office. [3]

The government continued to withhold information about Butler throughout the appeals process. Richard Held coordinated the FBI's "Key Black Extremists" operation in the early 1970s. When questioned about his relationship with Butler by Pratt's attorneys, Held said, "I don't recall really knowing much about the case at all anyway." In fact, Held was Butler's "control agent" and met with him at least 33 times. In addition, Held wrote a memo to FBI Director Hoover on January 28, 1970 which read in part, "I request Bureau approval . . . to attack, expose and ridicule the BPP . . . operation number one is designed to challenge the legitimacy of the authority exercised by Elmer Gerard Pratt." [4]

A notable *agent provocateur* from that era was George W. Sams Jr., a seriously disturbed and violent black man who spent two years in an institution for the mentally retarded before becoming an FBI informant. Sams infiltrated the New Haven, Connecticut chapter of the Black Panther Party in 1969 and quickly landed a position as a security enforcer. Shortly after that, he accused another member, Alex Rackley, of being an informant. Sams and a number of other Panther members then kidnapped Rackley and tortured him to death. The killers, including Sams, were arrested and charged with murder. Sams pleaded guilty and became a government witness against his accomplices. He was pardoned after serving four years and given a new identity in the government's Witness Protection program. He was jailed for violating his parole in 1997 after being arrested on a series of violent assault charges.

---

2. Author's interview with Stew Albert.
3. Don Terry, "Ex-Panther Wins Fight for Freedom," *New York Times* News Service, *Oregonian*, February 18, 1999.
4. Noelle Hanrahan, "America's Secret Police," Redwood Summer Project, P.O. Box 14720, Santa Rosa, CA 95402.

William O'Neill was an FBI informant who became the "Captain of Security" for the Chicago chapter of the Panthers. He was paid about $30,000 from 1969 to 1972, in addition to such expenses as car maintenance and insurance fees. He helped arrange an FBI wiretap at the Panther headquarters which caught him arranging a drug deal (he was not arrested). Acting as an *agent provocateur*, O'Neill tried to convince other members to engage in armed robberies with explosives which he had bought and stored. A June 4, 1969 police raid based on an O'Neill tip yielded a list of the organization's financial contributors, the chapter's treasury and eight arrests on explosives charges, which were quickly dropped. A November 13 police raid erupted in a shoot-out during which two Chicago police officers were killed. Six days later, again acting on information provided by O'Neill, the police raided a Panther apartment where charismatic leader Fred Hampton was staying. The police fired over 180 rounds during the raid. The Panthers fired one shot. When the smoke cleared, Hampton was dead and several other Panthers were seriously wounded. A 1976 civil suit filed by the families of the victims and the survivors of the raid exposed secret details about the FBI's involvement in the raid, and about the agency's COINTELPRO efforts against black dissidents.

In January 1970, an FBI informant named Alfie Burnett was released from a King County, Washington jail where he was being held on robbery charges. Burnett was freed when he agreed to provoke black activists to commit violent acts so the police could arrest them. Although Burnett was not able to set up any high-ranking Panther members, he persuaded his best friend, an unemployed veteran named Jimmy Davis, to bomb a building for $75. The police were waiting and Davis was killed in an ambush on May 14. The Seattle police blamed the FBI. "As far as I can tell, Davis was a relatively decent kid," said a police intelligence commander. "Someone set this whole thing up. It wasn't the police department."

These and other FBI-run operations resulted in 28 fatalities over an 18 month period, incapacitating the leadership of the Black Panther Party through deaths, imprisonments and flights to foreign countries.

The COINTELPRO operations might have continued uninterrupted but for information gathered during a March 8, 1971 break-in at the FBI's field office in Media, Pennsylvania. Confidential documents were stolen and circulated within the underground press, eventually reaching NBC reporter Carl Stern, who filed a Freedom of Information Act request with the U.S. Department of Justice for all documents concerning COINTELPRO. The Justice Department released a few reports in the fall of 1973, generating an outcry over the previously-unknown domestic surveillance programs.

The controversy eventually prompted the U.S. Senate to appoint a special committee to investigate the federal government's domestic surveillance programs. Chaired by Senator Frank Church, it was formally titled the Select Committee to Study Government Operations With Respect to Intelligence Activities. It was the first substantial inquiry into the intelligence community since World War II, and no similar study has been conducted since.

The Church Committee's investigation lasted a year. Its final report was released in April 1976. The committee agreed to withhold most of the names of those targeted for investigation, yet still the report is replete with examples of government abuses.

Although most of the report focuses on COINTELPRO operations, the committee also discovered that other federal agencies were spying on American citizens in the 1950s, 1960s and 1970s, including the NSA, the CIA and various intelligence branches of the armed forces. In its final report, the committee identified the following domestic surveillance programs operated by these agencies:

- The NSA's "Watch List" program was started in 1967 to intercept "any information on a continuing basis" concerning foreign governments or individuals attempting to influence U.S. "peace" and "Black Power" groups. By 1969 the program had been expanded to include all "Information on U.S. organizations or individuals who are engaged in activities which may result in civil disturbances or otherwise subvert the national security of the U.S."

- Operation CHAOS was created by the CIA in 1967 in response to President Johnson's persistent interest in the extent of foreign influence on domestic dissidents. The first CHAOS instructions to CIA station chiefs in August described the need for "keeping tabs on radical students and U.S. Negro expatriates, as well as travelers passing through certain select areas abroad." The program was eventually expanded to monitor all "radical students, antiwar activists, draft resisters and deserters, black nationalists, anarchists and assorted 'New Leftists'" traveling abroad.

- Project MERRIMACK, also created in 1967, involved the infiltration of CIA agents into Washington, DC-based anti-war and civil rights groups. Although the stated purpose of the program was to obtain early warnings of demonstrations, the collection requirements were soon broadened to include general information about the leadership, funding, activities and policies of the targeted groups.

- Project RESISTANCE was a broad CIA effort to obtain general background information on radical groups across the country, particularly on college and university campuses. Also created in 1967, the project authorized CIA field offices to obtain information from state and local police departments, many of which were already using informants to monitor the groups.

- In the early 1960s, after U.S. military troops were used to control racial disturbances and enforce court orders in the South, Army intelligence units began collecting information on civilian political activity in all areas where it believed civil disorders might occur. Then, after the Army was used to quell civil disorders in Detroit and to cope with an antiwar demonstration at the Pentagon in 1967, the Army Chief of Staff approved a recommendation for "continuous counterintelligence investigations" to obtain information on "subversive personalities, groups or organizations" and their influence on urban populations in promoting civil disturbances. The "collection plan" specifically targeted as "dissident elements" the civil rights movement and the anti-Vietnam/anti-draft movements.

The report also provides details on such controversial black budget operations as the CIA's MKULTRA mind control program, which, among other things, gave LSD to unsuspecting research subjects.

The committee summed up the problems created by domestic surveillance abuses in terms which still apply today:

> Too many people have been spied upon by too many Government agencies and too much information has been collected. The Government has often undertaken the secret surveillance of citizens on the basis of their political beliefs, even when those beliefs posed no threat of violence or illegal acts on behalf of a hostile foreign power. The Government, operating primarily through secret informants, but also using other intrusive techniques such as wiretaps, microphone 'bugs', surreptitious mail opening, and break-ins, has swept in vast amounts of information about the personal lives, views, and associations of American citizens. Investigations of groups deemed potentially dangerous—and even of groups suspected of associating with potentially dangerous organizations—have continued for decades, despite the fact that those groups did not engage in unlawful activity. Groups and individuals have been harassed and disrupted because of their political views and their lifestyles. Investigations have been based upon vague standards whose breadth made excessive collection inevitable. Unsavory and vicious tactics have been employed—including anonymous attempts to break up marriages, disrupt meetings, ostracize persons from their professions, and provoke target groups into rivalries that might result in deaths. Intelligence agencies have served the political and personal objectives of presidents and other high officials. While the agencies often committed excesses in response to pressure from high officials in the Executive branch and Congress, they also occasionally initiated improper activities and then concealed them from officials whom they had a duty to inform.

The information unearthed by the Church Committee should have sparked a huge national controversy, focusing public attention on the government's willingness to ignore the Bill of Rights, spy on Americans simply because of their political beliefs, and worse. But by the time the hearings started, the corporate press was too busy congratulating itself over the far less significant Watergate Scandal.

Contemporary political histories tend to blur the two scandals. But the special congressional committee which investigated Watergate concentrated on smaller (though still disturbing) incidents, such as existence of a White House "enemies list" and the June 17, 1972 burglary at the Watergate office building and apartment complex. In fact, Nixon resigned before the Church Committee was even created.

All of the federal intelligence agencies which appeared before the committee swore they no longer operated such domestic intelligence programs. The FBI said its COINTELPRO operations all ended in the early 1970s, and the CIA and Pentagon made the same claims. By the time the committee released its final reports in April 1976, Congress had already passed the Privacy Act as a hedge against the government spying on people because of their political beliefs. The revelations in the report were so shocking, however, that the U.S. Department of Justice issued a new set of guidelines to further restrict political snooping.

But, as documented throughout this book, the FBI quickly figured out how to get around the new restrictions. And they did not even cover such intelligence-gathering agencies as the Bureau of Alcohol, Tobacco and Firearms. Even after the new guidelines were issued, the BATF continued using undercover operatives to provoke confrontations between political radicals and law enforcement agencies. One resulted in the scandalous Greensboro Massacre.

In the mid-1970s, a BATF agent named Bernard Butkovich infiltrated an American Nazi Party unit in Forsyth County, North Carolina. He encouraged the members to commit a variety of illegal acts, offering to procure hand grenades and teach bomb-making classes. Then the Far Left Communist Workers Party scheduled a "Death to the Klan" rally in Greensboro for November 3, 1979. Butkovich urged the neo-Nazis and various Klan members to bring weapons to the rally. "I wouldn't go without a gun," he told them.

A shoot-out erupted when the racists arrived at the rally. Five CWP members were killed and nine wounded. Nine neo-Nazis and Klansmen were indicted on federal charges. Butkovich's role was revealed during the trial, prompting the *Greensboro Record* to report, "Although tighter surveillance restrictions were placed on the FBI and CIA in recent years, most of the limitations have not extended to the Treasury Department's Bureau of Alcohol, Tobacco and Firearms." The July 14, 1980 story ran under the headline, "Rules Differ for ATF Agents Involved in Undercover Work."

And those rules have never applied to the CIA or NSA.

THE THIRD WAVE EXPERIMENT

RON JONES IS ONE OF THE FEW Americans who understands how easily this country could turn into Hitler's Germany, Stalin's Russia or Mao's China. He has seen how a single leader can turn the people against each other with his own eyes. The leader was him.

Today Jones is a professional writer and storyteller who works with handicapped children in San Francisco. But in 1967, he was a rookie high school history teacher having trouble convincing his students how easily Adolph Hitler and his National Socialist Party rose to power in pre-WWII Germany. So Jones conducted an experiment in his Palo Alto, California classroom. One Monday he introduced his students to a new motivational program which he called The Third Wave.

Jones didn't tell his students, but he made up the program himself, basing it on Nazi Youth principles. For the next few days, Jones drilled the students on the proper ways to sit at their desks, read their books, and answer questions. He also had them chant inspirational slogans such as "Strength through discipline, strength through community, and strength through action."

As the experiment progressed, Jones gave the program a salute, an upraised hand curved in the shape of a wave. Membership cards were issued, and some of the students were appointed as "monitors." It was their job to tell Jones which students did not support the program.

But the experiment soon spun out of control. Some students physi-cally attacked anyone who questioned it. And many of the students began ratting on each other, telling Jones which of their classmates were breaking school rules, smoking, drinking, doing drugs and having sex. "Students were becoming like the Gestapo and giving me personal information I could use against other students in class," he recalls.[1]

Jones was shocked how quickly his students began acting like young Nazis. "I was pretty naive," he admits. "I'd graduated from Stanford and thought I could teach simulations very well. But I was pretty ignorant and naive, actually."

At the end of the week, Jones stopped the experiment. He showed his class a film on the Hitler Youth movement and told them it was the model for the Third Wave. Some of the students cried when they realized how easily they had gone along with it.

"Through the experience of the past week, we have all tasted what it was like to live and act in Nazi Germany," Jones told his class. "We have learned

---

1. Author's interview with Ron Jones, April 8, 2000.

what it felt like to create a disciplined social environment. To build a special society. Pledge allegiance to that society. Replace reason with rules. Yes, we all would have made good Germans."[2]

The experience radicalized Jones. He was soon fighting with school administrators over student and civil rights issues, and he eventually quit teaching altogether to form an experimental theater company. Years later, Jones wrote about the Third Wave experiment for the Spring 1976 issue of *CoEvolution Quarterly*. The essay, titled "Take as Directed," caught the attention of television producer Norman Lear, who helped turn it into an ABC-TV Afterschool Special called *The Wave*. The broadcast was well received, winning Emmy, Peabody and Golden Globe awards.

A novelization of the movie was released by Doubleday/Dell. Translated into German and Danish, it became an international bestseller. The German version, *Die Welle*, became required reading in that country's schools. More than 230 newspapers, magazines and religious publications around the world reprinted parts of the story. Over 40 psychological and educational textbooks published reports on the experiment.

Despite the success of the TV movie and book, Jones was not happy with changes made by the scriptwriters. The teleplay and book revolved around a fictional love affair between two students. Their love makes them the only ones to realize the experiment is dangerous, and gives them the conviction to stop it. In other words, in true TV fashion, it has a happy ending. Love wins. "It didn't happen that way," Jones says. "Love didn't stop The Wave, and it sure didn't stop the Holocaust."[3]

So Jones bought back the rights to his story and turned it into a play called *The Wave*. Various versions have been staged throughout Europe for nearly 20 years. It has been performed in theaters, school auditoriums, libraries, attics and under the stars in Roman ruins, directed as a conventional three-act play, performed as experimental theater, and staged as a rock opera. A German adaptation won the Play of the Year Award in 1990. Two years later, the German government invited Jones to speak at a conference in Nuremberg on the origins and dangers of Fascism. He has returned to Germany and visited other European countries over the years to answer questions about the ramifications of his experiment.

Jones wrote a lengthy essay about what he had learned over the years for the Summer 1993 issue of the *Whole Earth Review*. "The Third Wave is not something I'm particularly proud of, but it became an opportunity to examine our willingness to give up our freedom," he said.[4]

Speaking from his home in San Francisco, Jones is disturbed by how little most Americans know about Fascism. "The American culture is ignorant of

---

2. Ron Jones, "Take As Directed," *CoEvolution Quarterly*, Spring 1976.
3. Author's interview with Ron Jones, April 8, 2000.
4. Ron Jones, "Based on a True Story," *Whole Earth Review*, Summer 1993. *CoEvolution Quarterly* and *Whole Earth Review* are published by *Whole Earth Magazine*, 1408 Mission Avenue, San Rafael, CA 94901. In an April 3, 2000 e-mail to the author, editor Mike Stone said the company still receives many requests for reprints of both essays.

history," says Jones. "We don't take on big issues, like in Germany. They really studied what happens.

"It's scary, having been in Germany because of The Wave," he continues. "Having toured Germany several times and talked to the Germans about this, I've found they're amazed that the United States doesn't study the classroom experiment, don't look at it, try to learn from it."

Jones has thought about Fascism a lot since 1967. He thinks snitching lies at the heart of it.

"I've also been to the former East Germany several times," he says. "One thing that people tell me that's the most frightening thing is, after the Russians left and the West came in, they were allowed to see to all the secret documents that were collected about each person. I had the mayor of one of these towns tell me, 'My wife betrayed me, my best friend turned me in.' These are very, very common comments.

"If you want to know what an environment's like when people tell on each other all the time, ask them." [5]

---

5. Author's interview with Ron Jones, April 16, 2000.

THE NEW GHETTO INFORMANT PROGRAM

IN THE LATE 1960s AND EARLY 1970s, the government's War on Drugs was widely and correctly seen as being politically motivated. Everyone understood that the government was targeting marijuana and such psychedelic drugs as LSD as a way to disrupt the "counterculture"—the youth-based movement united by the civil rights, anti-Vietnam War, environmental and women's movements. The mainstream media described drug users as rebels, not common criminals. Anti-establishment icons from The Beatles to Timothy Leary to Peter (*"Easy Rider"*) Fonda advocated the use of "consciousness-expanding" drugs to develop alternatives to the materialism of consumer society.

Richard Nixon not only ran against Hubert Humphrey for President in 1968, he campaigned against the counterculture, casting it as a dangerous threat to the nation. One of his official acts after taking office was launching Operation Intercept, a massive federal effort to stop marijuana from entering the country from Mexico. Over 2,000 additional U.S. Customs agents were sent to the Mexican border and ordered to search every car coming into the country. The resulting traffic jam shut down every border crossing, disrupting both commerce and tourism, and forcing the White House to abandon the operation after just three weeks.[1]

Nixon responded by increasing the federal focus on the young. He recruited entertainers, including Sonny Bono, to preach the anti-drug message to young people. Nixon even named Elvis Presley a Special Agent of the Bureau of Narcotics and Dangerous Drugs, the forerunner of the U.S. Drug Enforcement Administration.

Politicians are smarter today. Anti-drug programs are no longer presented as serving larger purposes. Aside from a few legalization advocates, hardly anyone talks about marijuana in a political context anymore. The corporate press considers hallucinogenics to be "party drugs," while presenting cocaine, heroin and methamphetamine only as reasons why addicts commit violent crimes. But the truth is, the federal government's drug war is still politically motivated. The most aggressive efforts are directed against young black males, the same group targeted in the government's first broad-based snitch operation, the Ghetto Informant Program.

Instead of warning against urban unrest, the federal government has chosen a drug associated with young blacks, crack cocaine, to justify spying on the

---

1. Ron Mann, *Grass*, Unapix, 2000.

residents of America's inner cities. The result has been more effective at suppressing black activism than any of the FBI's COINTELPRO operations. Instead of trying to identify and silence black leaders, the government has simply slammed a huge percentage of their potential followers in jail. Although blacks make up just 13 percent of the U.S. population, they have accounted for the majority of the nation's prison population since 1995.[2]

The criminal justice system's focus on blacks is so blatantly racist it has been condemned by Human Rights Watch, the same well-respected organization quoted by the corporate press to deplore totalitarian despots in the Balkans and Middle East. "These racial disparities are a national scandal," Ken Roth, executive director of Human Rights Watch, said on June 7, 2000, citing a report which found nearly twice as many blacks are being imprisoned for drug offenses than whites, even though studies show there are five times as many whites using drugs. The report further notes that 67.2 percent of drug offenders sent to prison in 1996, the last year for which complete statistics were available, were black, while only 36.7 percent were white.

"Black and white drug offenders get radically different treatment in the American justice system. This is not only unfair to blacks, it also corrodes the American ideal of equal justice for all," Roth continued.[3]

And snitches are at the heart of this scandal.

Informants have always been the most effective weapon in the government's anti-drug initiatives. "[T]he police have a greater incentive to use informants in drug cases than in many others because they are victimless crimes. Therefore it can be assumed that the police try harder to produce more informants in a case in which drugs are involved—particularly as it currently is prestigious to solve these cases," notes sociologist Malin Akerstrom.[4]

This has always been true, whether the illegal drug is moonshine, marijuana or heroin. But the federal government specifically targeted crack cocaine for special attention after it made inroads into the black community. Congress used the cocaine-related death of a college basketball player named Len Bias as an excuse for this decision. He had been drafted by the Boston Celtics, the professional team in the home district of House Speaker Tip O'Neill. A few weeks after Bias died, Congress passed the Comprehensive Crime Control Act of 1986, dramatically increasing the penalties for crack. Under the guidelines established by the law, the minimum sentence for someone convicted of selling 5 grams of crack is the same as that for a person found guilty of trying

2. "Poor Prescription: The Costs of Imprisoning Drug Offenders in the United States," Justice Policy Institute, July 2000. According to the report, blacks are incarcerated for drug offenses at a rate 14 times higher than that of whites. While the rate of white drug offenders sent to prison doubled from 1986 to 1996, the rate for black offenders quintupled. Even in states that registered an overall decrease in drug incarceration rates, the rates for blacks increased.

3. Steven A. Holmes, "Data Document Racial Disparities in War on Drugs," *New York Times*, June 8, 2000; Gary Fields, "Study: War on Drugs Stacked Against Blacks," *USA Today*, June 8, 2000.

4. Malin Akerstrom, "Snitches on Snitching," *Society*, January/February 1989.

to sell 500 grams of powdered cocaine—a 100 to 1 ratio. According to the U.S. Sentencing Commission, by the end of the 20th Century, the average crack cocaine sentence was 122 months, compared to 79 months for powdered cocaine. Suddenly, minor drug users were facing the kind of penalties traditionally reserved for murderers and criminal kingpins, dramatically increasing their willingness to snitch.

There was only one way to avoid serving the new mandatory minimum sentences—provide the government with what prosecutors consider "substantial assistance" in arresting and convicting other drug dealers and users. In other words, become a snitch. According to a 1995 study by the National Law Journal, "Between 1980 and 1993, the number of federal search warrants relying exclusively on an unidentified snitch nearly tripled, from 24 percent to 71 percent."[5]

Within a few years, inner city black communities were swarming with informants desperate to rat out their friends, associates, even their family members. A good example is Scott Tredwell, an African-American cocaine dealer who worked as an informant in Minnesota, Washington and Oregon. The deal Tredwell cut with the government is typical of professional informants. He was not only paid a regular salary, but received bonuses for every bust he helped set up. In addition, as long as he was informing, the government allowed Tredwell to continue dealing drugs, and to break a number of other state and federal laws, too.[6]

According to federal court documents, Tredwell first began dealing drugs in the St. Paul-Minneapolis area in Minnesota in the late 1980s. He was selling kilograms of powder cocaine, and began doing business with a high-level drug dealing family. Tredwell made thousands of dollars every week dealing cocaine, eventually "fronting" cocaine to distributors who sold the drugs for him.

In 1987, Tredwell stole $20,000 from a member of the drug family and flew to Los Angeles, intending to buy cocaine and bring it back to Minnesota to sell. Unfortunately for him, the police arrested him at the airport with $11,000 in cash. Tredwell originally gave a false name and lied to the police, but he quickly struck a deal and agreed to work as an informant. The police bailed him out, returned his $11,000, and paid to fly him back to Minneapolis.

After he returned home, Tredwell testified before a grand jury as a "cooperating witness." He continued to sell drugs, but soon got scared and fled the area because the word was out that he was a snitch. Tredwell eventually called the police for help and they agreed to continue working with him, even giving him $4,000 to pay off his most recent "dope debt."

Tredwell's next stop on the informant superhighway was Seattle, Washington, where the police gave him a nice apartment, a Cadillac, and a bounty.

---

5. Mark Curriden, "No Honor Among Thieves," ABA Journal, June 1989.
6. United States of America v. Rance Preston, CR 92-155 RE, United States District Court for the District of Oregon.

Tredwell was paid per buy, and his compensation—including car and expenses—totalled over $30,000 within just a few months. During this time, Tredwell filed a tax return that failed to report any of the money the government paid him. After Seattle, Tredwell moved to Portland, Oregon for more of the same. He signed on with the Oregon State Youth Gang Strike Force, which included sworn officers and support personnel from the U.S. Drug Enforcement Administration, the Bureau of Alcohol, Tobacco and Firearms, the Oregon National Guard, the Oregon State Police and the Portland Police Bureau. By 1991, Tredwell had participated in nearly 50 buys, driving his total earnings to over $70,000. The DEA paid Tredwell an additional $21,000 for his Strike Force work.

Tredwell continued breaking the law while living in Portland. According to court documents, he sold cocaine and marijuana, assaulted his girlfriend, and smashed up the car which had been provided for him. Although he was arrested a few times, the charges were always dropped because of his status as an undercover informant. After Tredwell finished testifying in the Oregon trials that grew out of his undercover work, he moved to another state and started informing again.

The result of such operations has been a dramatic increase in the nation's prison population. The number of people locked up in federal, state and local jails has quadrupled since 1980, nearly doubling during the 1990s, largely because of drug busts. "In the Federal system, nearly 60 percent of all people behind bars are doing time for drug violations; in state prisons and local jails, the figure is 22 percent. These numbers are triple the rate of 15 years ago," the *New York Times* reported on March 7, 1999.

The vast majority of people arrested for drug violations are charged with simple possession, not manufacturing or dealing. According to the 1998 FBI Uniform Crime Report, 78.8 percent of all drug arrests are for possession. Only 21.2 percent of the arrests are for manufacturing or dealing.

These trends were confirmed in early 1999 by the non-profit Justice Policy Institute. According to JPI, over one million non-violent offenders were incarcerated in America in 1998. Over the past 20 years, the non-violent prisoner population has increased at a rate much faster than the number of violent prisoners. Since 1978, the number of persons imprisoned for drug offenses increased eight-fold. By 1998, 77 percent of the people entering prisons and jails were sentenced for non-violent offenses.[7]

This is especially true in California, the nation's most populous state. According to the California Department of Corrections, as of June 1999, drug offenders represented 28 percent of the prison population. At the same time, a record 12 percent of prisoners were being held for simple possession.

Worse, according to criminal justice experts, many of the people who have been convicted on drug charges are innocent. The pressure to snitch is so great that a large number of informants simply make up accusations against

---

7. Kim Brooks, Vincent Schiraldi and Jason Ziedenberg, "School House Hype: Two Years," Justice Policy Institute/Children's Law Center, April 2000.

friends, associates—even family members—to escape the long mandatory minimum sentences. "Our rights as citizens [and] the United States Constitution [are] now in the hands of a group of about 15,000 wild, out-of-control informants," Michael Levine, a retired DEA and Customs agent, told the *National Law Journal* for its 1995 article.[8]

Even conservative former prosecutors agree the situation is a national scandal. Stephen Trott was the chief of the Criminal Division of the Justice Department under President Ronald Reagan before being appointed to the U.S. Circuit Court of Appeals. By the late 1990s, he was offering this chilling warning in lectures to federal prosecutors: "Criminals are likely to say and do almost anything to get what they want, especially when what they want is to get out of trouble with the law. This willingness to do anything includes not only truthfully spilling the beans on friends and relatives, but also lying, committing perjury, manufacturing evidence, soliciting others to corroborate their lies with more lies and double-crossing anyone with whom they come into contact, including—and especially—the prosecutor."

All this snitching has had the most devastating effect on the African-Americans. The sheer number of young black males in jail has undermined inner city families far more than the drugs themselves.

Many black leaders understand the cruel irony of the federal government's obsession with crack—much of the cocaine used to manufacture it was shipped into the country with the knowledge and cooperation of the government itself.

Over the years, numerous journalists, researchers and political activists have documented that elements of the U.S. government are deeply involved in the global drug trade. The CIA has worked with drug lords in Southeast Asia and Central America. Government agents have traded guns for drugs in covert operations approved at the highest levels of the White House. A large amount of these drugs—including marijuana and heroin—have gone into America's inner cities over the years. But government-sanctioned cocaine shipments are the most significant. They created the Crack Scare of the 1980s, which was used as an excuse to create huge numbers of new snitches.

One of the first books to document the government's involvement in the narcotics business was *The Politics of Heroin: CIA Complicity in the Global Drug Trade* by Alfred W. McCoy, Ph D., a professor of Southeast Asian history at the University of Wisconsin-Madison. In his book (published in 1972 despite CIA efforts to block publication), McCoy discusses how the CIA first began working with drug lords in Southeast Asia after World War II as part of the Cold War. The CIA used the drug lords and their guerilla armies to gather intelligence about communist activities in such countries as Vietnam and Thailand. In exchange for their reports, the CIA helped facilitate drug shipments into the United States.

As McCoy put it, "To an average American who witnesses the dismal spectacle of the narcotics traffic at the street level, it must seem inconceivable

---

8. Gary Webb, "Dark Alliance," *San Jose Mercury News*, August 18–20, 1996.

that the government could be implicated in the international drug trade. Unfortunately, American diplomats and CIA agents have been involved in the narcotics traffic at three levels: 1) coincidental complicity by allying with groups actively engaged in the drug traffic; 2) support of the traffic by covering up for known heroin traffickers and condoning their involvement; and 3) active engagement in the transport of opium and heroin. It is ironic, to say the least, that America's heroin plague is of its own making."

Elements of the federal government became even more involved in the drug trade in Central America under President Ronald Reagan in the 1980s. A fanatical anti-Communist, Reagan used federal funds to finance and assist the contra rebels who were fighting the Sandinista government in Nicaragua. After the CIA was caught mining the country's harbors in early 1984, Congress began talking about cutting off all federal funds for the secret war against the Sandinistas. In response, Reagan authorized a large-scale covert operation to keep the contras supplied.

The network was put together by Lieutenant Colonel Oliver North, working under the direction of Donald Gregg, the National Security Aide to Vice President George Bush. In May 1984, Duane Clarridge, the CIA officer in charge of the rebels, introduced North to contra leaders at a meeting in Tegucigalpa, Honduras. "If something happens in Congress, we will have an alternative way, and to assure that, here is Colonel North," Clarridge promised the leaders. "You will never be abandoned." [9]

When Congress passed the Boland Amendment cutting off everything but humanitarian aid to the contras, North tapped several veterans of the government's covert operations in Southeast Asia to put the supply network together, including retired Generals Richard Secord and John Singlaub, and former CIA Deputy Director of Operations Theodore Shackley. Together, they created an off-the-shelf operation consisting of CIA mercenaries, opportunistic anti-Communist guerillas, and Central American drug dealers—then cleared the way for the contras to pay for their supplies with cocaine flown directly into airports across the United States. In addition, some of the pilots and other operatives in the supply network stuck private deals with a number of the drug dealers, flying additional loads of cocaine into the country on their own.

At its peak, the CIA-backed network was shipping hundreds of tons of cocaine a year into the country. One Mexico-based drug ring operated by Rafael Caro Quintero and Miguel Angel smuggled four tons a month into the United States in the mid-1980s. Another ring was run out of El Salvador by CIA Bay of Pigs veteran Felix Rodriguez.

The entire operation began to unravel in October 1986 when a C-123 cargo plane carrying guns for the contras crashed in Nicaragua. The only surviving member of the four-man crew, Eugene Hasenfus, was captured by the Sandinistas and publicly confessed to being part of the secret supply campaign.

---

9. Clarence Lusane, "Cracking the CIA-Contra Drug Connection," *CovertAction Quarterly*, Winter 1996–97.

Congress, the U.S. Department of Justice, the FBI, the U.S. Customs Service and a number of other federal agencies all launched investigations into the supply network—investigations which quickly uncovered evidence of the guns-for-drugs trades. The investigations also tied such major players as North, Gregg, Secord, Singlaub and Shackley to the operation. Bush denied any knowledge of the supply network, claiming he was "out of the loop."

As the official investigations ground on, a liberal inter-faith legal center called the Christic Institute sued many of the major players in the contra supply network, including Secord and Singlaub. The 1986 civil anti-racketeering suit charged that former U.S. intelligence agents and anti-Communist crusaders had engaged in "political assassination, gunrunning and drug trafficking." Headed by lead lawyer and chief fundraiser Daniel Sheehan, the Christics unearthed many details of the U.S. government's involvement with the contra rebels. But the organization was also spied on by Roy Bullock, an operative for the private Anti-Defamation League. In late June 1988, federal Judge James Lawrence King dismissed the suit, ruling that Sheehan and the other lawyers had failed to prove their conspiracy theory. Then, in February 1989, the court awarded the defendants millions of dollars in attorneys' fees, bankrupting the Christics.

Although a congressional subcommittee chaired by U.S. Senator John Kerry eventually confirmed that drug dealers were heavily involved with the contra supply network, no one looked at what happened to the cocaine shipped into this country until 1996, when the *San Jose Mercury News* published a series of stories under the title "Dark Alliance." Written by investigative reporter Gary Webb, it focused on a South Central Los Angeles drug dealer named Ricky Ross. As Webb reported, Ross got most of his cocaine from two CIA-backed contra supporters, Danillo Blandon and Norwin Meneses. According to documents discovered by Webb, Ross sold approximately four tons of cocaine in three years. His connection with Blandon and Meneses allowed him to consistently undersell competitors and dominate the South Central market.

Much of the cocaine which Ross acquired was turned into crack before being sold on the streets. Using police documents, Webb was able to show that Ross was one of the first dealers to push crack, promoting it when other dealers showed no interest in the highly-addictive product.

The Mercury News posted the "Dark Alliance" series on the Internet, where it received widespread national attention. Webb's revelations were immediately applauded by African-American leaders, including elected officials such as Democratic Congresswoman Maxine Waters, who had long suspected government involvement in the inner-city drug trade. A coalition of liberal organizations held a demonstration in Los Angeles to protest government-facilitated drug dealing on February 22, 1997. Among the speakers were several former government intelligence agents, including Celerino Castillo, a DEA agent who witnessed CIA drug dealing from El

Salvador in 1986, Ralph McGehee, a former CIA analyst who documented hundreds of references to cocaine in Oliver North's diaries, and Mike Ruppert, a former Los Angeles Police Department narcotics officer who came from a CIA family and who caught agency employees working with heroin and cocaine dealers in 1976.

But Webb was also attacked by larger media outlets such as the New York Times and the Los Angeles Times, which misrepresented his reporting by falsely claiming that he accused actual CIA employees of selling crack cocaine to black Americans. Most of the attacks came from unnamed sources who appeared to be high-ranking CIA officials.

San Jose Mercury News executives caved in to the attacks. Editor Jerry Ceppos wrote a meandering "clarification" in June 1997 which was immediately reported as a "retraction" by the rest of the mass media. Webb was demoted, transferred and, eventually, forced to resign. He was hired as a consultant to the California State Legislature's Task Force on Government Oversight, then went to work on a book on the government's involvement with drug dealers, titled Dark Alliance: The CIA, the Contras, and the Crack Cocaine Explosion. Published in 1998 by Seven Stories Press, it included additional documentation of the relationship between government officials and international drug dealers.

This is the cynical truth about the War on Drugs. Officially-sanctioned factions within the National Security State allow drugs into the country, then domestic law enforcement agencies recruit informants to arrest the people who use them.

THE ASSET FORFEITURE MONEY MACHINE

IN THE EARLY MORNING HOURS of October 2, 1992, a squad of federal, state and local law enforcement officers came roaring down the narrow dirt road to Donald Scott's rustic 200-acre ranch in Ventura County, California. They had been told that Scott, an eccentric, heavy-drinking millionaire, was running a 4,000-plant marijuana operation on the property. When they broke down the door of the house, Scott's wife screamed, "Don't shoot me! Don't kill me!" Her screams brought Scott staggering out of the bedroom, hung-over and holding a .38 caliber snub-nose revolver over his head. When he lowered the gun, he was shot and killed. Later, the lead agent in the case and his partner posed for photographs outside Scott's cabin, smiling and arm-in-arm.

Despite an extensive search of the property, no traces of marijuana or any other illegal drug were found. In the aftermath of the botched raid, Ventura County District Attorney Michael Bradbury launched an investigation into the operation. Although Scott's ranch was in his jurisdiction, no one invited any Ventura Country cops to come along. Instead, the squad was made up of representatives from the U.S. Drug Enforcement Administration, the Border Patrol, the National Park Service, the California National Guard, and the Los Angeles Sheriff's Department. In a 64-page report issued by Bradbury's office in March of 1993, the district attorney said the search warrant for the raid contained numerous misstatements, evasions, and omissions.

But more than that, Bradbury concluded the raid was intended to seize Scott's ranch under asset forfeiture laws, and then divide the proceeds with such participating agencies as the National Park Service, which had put Scott's ranch on a list of property it would like to acquire, and the Los Angeles Sheriff's Department, which funded a large part of its budget with assets seized in drug raids.

As proof of Bradbury's accusation, the report pointed to a parcel map in possession of the raiding party that contained a handwritten note that an adjacent 80-acre property had recently sold for $800,000. In addition, during a briefing conducted the day of the raid, participants were told that Scott's ranch could be seized if as few as 14 plants were found on it.

In January 2000, federal and Los Angeles county officials paid Scott's heirs $5 million to settle a wrongful death suit stemming from the raid.[1]

An important tool in the development of the Snitch Culture is the passage of revised asset forfeiture laws. Beginning in the mid-1980s, these laws have

---

1. Paul Ciotti, "Ranch-Coveting Officials Settle for Killing Owner," *WorldNetDaily*, January 23, 2000.

provided much of the money for paying the ever-growing army of snitches sweeping the country. Although no single agency keeps track of all the money generated through asset forfeiture laws, it is clearly in the billions of dollars a year.

Forfeiture laws are not new. Many colonists fled to America in part because English law allowed the government to seize money and property. A ship owned by John Hancock, the first signer of the Declaration of Independence, was seized by the Crown for failure to pay a tax on its cargo of Madeira wine. James Madison, Thomas Jefferson and other signers of the U.S. Constitution wanted forfeiture laws to be used very sparingly, to seize foreign vessels for failure to pay customs fees, for example. That's why the Bill of Rights protects Americans from illegal searches and seizures. The Fourth Amendment specifically provides that no person shall "be deprived of life, liberty, or property, without due process of law; nor shall private property be taken for public use, without just compensation."

Despite this restriction, however, the federal government has a long history of seizing property allegedly used in criminal activity. As explained by Bruce Benson and David Rasmussen in an article titled "Predatory Public Finance and the Origin of the War on Drugs: 1984–1989" published in *The Independent Review Journal of Political Economy*, through most of the 20th Century, the money generated through such seizures was not targeted toward any specific agency or program. It merely went into the general government fund, where it was mixed with taxes, fees and other revenue sources.

All this changed with the passage of the Comprehensive Crime Control Act of 1984. The law greatly increased the number of seizures by allowing the federal agencies which made them to keep most of the money and property. The law also created an "equitable sharing" provision for state and local governments, allowing them to retain 80 percent of the assets in every case they agree to have prosecuted in federal court. The remaining 20 percent went to the federal government. Spurred on by this incentive, state legislatures began passing their own asset forfeiture laws. In 1984, only eight states allowed real estate to be confiscated. But by 1991, 43 states had passed laws to allow such seizures.

The result was a dramatic increase in the number of asset forfeiture cases— and a dramatic increase in the number of snitches. The financial incentives prompted law enforcement agencies to employ more informants to make more cases, especially against drug dealers and others with large quantities of cash and such saleable possessions as homes, cars, boats, planes and businesses.

"Between 1985 and 1991 the Justice Department collected more than $1.5 billion in illegal assets; in the next five years, it almost doubled this intake. By 1987 the DEA was more than earning its keep, with over $500 million worth of seizures exceeding its budget." [2]

Seizures have ranged from a doctor's savings to a private prison in Louisiana with all 400 inmates, a Houston hotel, a 4,346-acre Florida ranch, a church's Spanish-language radio station, a rare 1970 Dodge Challenger R/T with a 426-cubic inch hemi V-8, and Hollywood Madam Heidi Fleiss' $550,000 Beverly Hills mansion.

2. Eric Blumenson and Eva Nilsen, *The Nation*, March 9, 1998.

Most of these seizures were accomplished through a provision which allows the government to seize property under civil—as opposed to criminal—asset forfeiture laws. A person charged with a criminal offense is entitled to a lawyer. But not under civil law, where the presumption of innocence until proven guilty doesn't apply. As strange as it may sound, under civil seizure law, it is the property which is charged with the offense, not the individual. As *Nexus* magazine said in its June–July 1996 issue, "Even if you are totally innocent, the government can still confiscate your guilty property." And, according to the July 17, 1995 issue of *A-albionic Research*, only three percent of everyone facing civil forfeiture ever gets a trial to recover their property—in large part because the government has usually seized the money they need to hire an attorney.

But even if the property owners can hire a lawyer, they still have the burden of proving that the assets should not be seized. The accused must prove they lacked knowledge and control over the property's unlawful use. In other words, if a drug sale takes place on someone's property, they must prove they were not aware of the sale and lacked the control to prevent it. Over the years, adult parents have lost their homes because their children sold drugs in their bedrooms, and landlords have lost rental houses because their tenants dealt narcotics.

The vast amount of money has corrupted law enforcement agencies across the country. Driven by greed, they have routinely violated the rights of innocent citizens to snatch their cash and property. *The Orlando Sentinel* won a Pulitzer Prize for exposing a Daytona Beach sheriff who seized so many cars from Interstate 95 that Florida rewrote its forfeiture law. *The Arkansas Democrat-Gazette* unearthed a string of forfeiture-related scandals, reporting about authorities who let drug dealers go in exchange for their cash and cars, and a county sheriff who gave seized cars to his deputies. Similar schemes sent Arkansas prosecutor Dan Harmon to jail for 11 years for extortion. In New Jersey, Somerset County prosecutor Nicholas L. Bissell Jr. killed himself in 1997 after being convicted of corruption for spending $1.5 million in seized money.[3]

By the late 1990s, some state legislatures began worrying that their asset forfeiture laws were causing undue hardships for too many people. A number of states passed laws preventing the police from keeping the money and property, instead requiring the assets go to other programs, such as the schools. But a year-long investigation by the *Kansas City Star* discovered that law enforcement agencies are routinely and intentionally circumventing these restrictions. The paper investigated police agencies in more than two dozen states and found that all of them were keeping the money for themselves. "Police and highway patrols across the country are evading state laws to improperly keep millions of dollars in cash and property seized in drug busts and traffic stops," reporter Karen Dillon wrote.[4]

---

3. Frank J. Murray, "Are Asset Forfeitures Penalty—or Piracy?" *Washington Times*, July 23, 1999.
4. Karen Dillon, "Taking Cash Into Custody," *The Kansas City Star*, May 20, 2000.

The May 2000 story revealed that the police are using federal law enforcement agencies to launder the money, taking it in and then kicking it back in apparent violation of state law. As the paper explained, "It works this way: When police seize money, they call a federal agency instead of going to state court to confiscate it. An agency such as the DEA accepts the seizure, making it a federal case. The DEA keeps a cut of the money and returns the rest to police. State courts—and their generally more-restrictive forfeiture laws—are bypassed altogether."

The amount of money involved is enormous. The Department of Justice told the newspaper that it accepted $208,454,000 in seizures from state and local police from October 1996 through March 1999 alone. But the *Star* disputed even that figure as unrealistically low, noting the Justice Department had not published an audited annual forfeiture report since 1996, although the law requires such a report to be produced each year.

These money-laundering schemes create enormous problems for innocent people who want their money or property back. The federal courts have much higher standards of proof than state courts, even for people who are never even charged with a crime.

"The line between a free society and a police state is usually broached in small steps," Roger Pilon, president of the Libertarian-oriented Cato Institute, told the paper.

By 1998, even Congress was beginning to question the wisdom of the new asset forfeiture programs. When the House Judiciary Committee held hearings on abuses of the federal forfeiture law, the members were regaled with horror stories of law-abiding citizens whose lives had been destroyed by abusive government agencies. According to *The Nation*, a pilot testified that the DEA seized his airplane and destroyed his air charter business because one of his customers was a drug dealer. After spending $85,000 in legal fees, the pilot filed for bankruptcy and became a truck driver. A landscaper testified that while on a purchasing trip, he had been stripped of $9,000 by an airport drug interdiction unit, then sent home without a receipt, on grounds that only drug dealers carry so much cash. Legislators also heard the tale of Mary Miller (a pseudonym), a 75-year-old grandmother dispossessed of her home for the sins of her fugitive, drug-dealing son.[5]

Congress finally reacted to the abuses by passing the Civil Asset Forfeiture Reform Act of 2000. It was championed by Republican Representative Henry Hyde (R-Illinois), chairman of the House Judiciary Committee, and supported by a coalition of liberal and conservative organizations including the ACLU, the NRA, the American Bar Association, Americans for Tax Reform, the Marijuana Policy Project and the National Association of Criminal Defense Lawyers. Among other things, the bill imposed the following restrictions on law enforcement agencies:

---

5. Eric Blumenson and Eva Nilsen, *The Nation*, March 9, 1998.

- Requiring warrants or other formal legal procedures to obtain property for forfeiture.
- Eliminating the requirement for claimants to post a bond of at least $250 to preserve the right to contest a forfeiture.
- Shifting the burden of proof in seizures to the government by requiring it to show complicity by a "preponderance of the evidence."
- Providing a uniform definition of the "forfeitable proceeds" of criminal acts.
- Increasing the time during which a person whose assets have been seized may file a claim.
- Requiring the government to comply with strict notice and time requirements.
- Allowing for release of seized property in certain hardship cases.
- Allowing lawyers to be appointed for indigent claimants.
- Requiring payments of reasonable attorney fees in cases where the claimants prevail.
- Allowing claimants to sue the government for harm to seized property while under government control.

"This is a horrible bill," complained Gene Voegtlin, legislative counsel for the International Association of Chiefs of Police. "We know there have been high-profile cases of abuse, but these laws aren't about taking property from innocent grandmothers."

The ACLU said the bill did not go far enough, however. "I think it's a good first start, but these are very modest changes compared to what we really need," said Rachel King, legislative counsel for the organization's Washington, DC office.

Among other things, the ACLU noted the bill does not address the money-laundering charges documented in the *Kansas City Star* series. "As long as this provision and opportunity exists for local police departments, there is going to be strong incentive for police to use forfeiture to increase their budgets," King said. "Stopping adoptive forfeiture would drastically change the process and put teeth into the existing state laws, which are generally stronger than federal law."

THE ADL SPY SCANDAL

THE PUBLIC RARELY SEES how some private, politically-oriented advocacy groups spy on American citizens. A dramatic exception occurred in the early 1990s when the Anti-Defamation League, a well-respected Jewish watchdog organization, was caught building files on thousands of individuals and organizations. The scandal touched on many of the most disturbing elements of the Snitch Culture, including the close relationship between the police and private intelligence networks, the problems caused by rogue cops, and the inability (or unwillingness) of prosecutors and the courts to rein in such activities, even when they clearly violate the law.

Two men were at the heart of the scandal, an ADL undercover operative named Roy Bullock and a dishonest San Francisco police detective named Thomas Gerard. Although their story has all the elements of a spy thriller, they are the bad guys, collecting and maintaining confidential information on thousands of people who never did anything wrong. The ADL wanted these people tracked because of their political beliefs. Much of the information came from supposedly secret law enforcement files, including unverified FBI reports on the Nation of Islam.

Roy Bullock began his life of intrigue as a teenager in the 1950s. Inspired by a book called *Undercover*, he traveled to Moscow with a Communist youth group one summer. After returning from the Soviet Union, Bullock contacted the FBI and told them about everything he had seen on his trip. He also gathered information on several white supremacist organizations, including the National Renaissance Party of New York, bringing his files to the ADL and volunteering to infiltrate right-wing groups. The Jewish organization took him up on his offer, even sending him to Chicago at one time with the approval of the FBI.[1]

Bullock moved to Los Angeles in 1960, becoming a paid, full-time investigator for the ADL. The organization did not pay Bullock directly, but instead routed the money through a local attorney named Bruce Hochman. Bullock's payments started at $75 a week and grew to $2,200 a month by the time the scandal broke in the press.

For most of his career as an ADL operative, Bullock spied on right-wing organizations, including the John Birch Society, the American Nazi Party and the George Wallace for President campaign. Then, in the early 1980s, the ADL

---

1. Many details on Roy Bullock's work for the ADL are drawn from lengthy interviews with him conducted by the San Francisco Police Department during its investigation into the spy scandal. Transcripts of the interviews were released by the D.A.'s Office, along with numerous other documents related to the investigation.

expanded its snooping to left-wing groups. This happened when Richard Hirschhaut became director of the ADL's San Francisco office. At Hirschhaut's urging, Bullock expanded his research to include a broad range of liberal, socialist, gay and anti-apartheid organizations—including Greenpeace, the United Farm Workers union, the Christic Institute, the Communist Party USA, the National Lawyers Guild and ACT-UP, the AIDS activist organization.

As part of his research, Bullock frequently attended political gatherings and joined activist organizations. He also searched through the trash outside of the offices of political organizations, including the Christic Institute, which opposed the illegal, covert U.S. operations against the government of Nicaragua.

Bullock entered much of the information he collected on these groups into his personal home computer. He listed the groups under four headings: "Arab," "Pinko," "Right," and "Skins" (for skinheads). Many of the files included names and personal information on the groups' members. Much of this information came from state and local law enforcement officers, including Larry Siewert, an intelligence officer with the police bureau in Portland, Oregon.[2] But Bullock's most important source was undoubtedly Thomas Gerard, a San Francisco detective with a colorful past.

A bomb squad expert with a sterling reputation, Gerard also dabbled in international undercover work. He took a leave of absence from the SFPD in the mid-1980s to join the CIA in Central America, spending three years working with American-backed forces in El Salvador and other hot spots. After returning to his old job, Gerard was assigned to what was then called the Intelligence Unit, later renamed Special Investigations. His role in this unit demonstrates how the War on Crime, the War on Drugs, and the War on Terrorism are essentially one massive domestic law enforcement initiative. As an SFPD intelligence officer, Gerard investigated both left- and right-wing political organizations. He also tracked groups suspected of terrorism, including some allegedly associated with the Palestinian Liberation Organization. And when crack cocaine became a major public issue in the 1980s, Gerard became an expert on black drug gangs, earning the nickname "the Weatherman" for his ability to predict drive-by shootings and gang violence.

Bullock and Gerard were formally introduced in the San Francisco ADL office in 1986 and immediately hit it off. They soon began swapping information on political activists and organizations. Gerard copied Bullock's computer files, creating a new category of "ANC" for African National Congress. During the next few years, the SF detective ran background checks on various people for the ADL operative. Gerard routinely provided Bullock with criminal background information, motor vehicle records, and other government records covered by state privacy laws.

---

2. The Portland Police Bureau conducted an investigation into Criminal Investigations Division Detective Larry Siewert. Although the investigation confirmed that Siewert swapped information with Bullock, it concluded the detective did nothing wrong, saying all of the information came from public records, even though local reporters had never seen them.

Shortly after they began working together, Gerard talked Bullock into helping him supply information to the government of South Africa. It is not clear how Gerard first came to work for the South Africans, but, according to Bullock, the detective introduced him to a "Mr. Humphries" in 1987 or 1988. He worked for the South African Consulate in New York, and he agreed to pay Bullock several hundred dollars a month for reports on anti-apartheid groups. Humphries was soon replaced by a man known only as "Louie," who continued the arrangement until late 1991. Bullock split the money with Gerard on a 50/50 basis. According to the documents released by the prosecutor, at least some of the information Bullock supplied to the South Africans came from his ADL files. Bullock also provided the ADL with some of the reports he wrote for Humphries and Louie.

Gerard's supervisors eventually began to suspect that he was selling confidential police information to outsiders, notifying the FBI of the possible illegal transactions in 1992. Even though the agency had used Bullock as an informant in the past, it launched an investigation which was subsequently turned over to the San Francisco D.A. When Gerard learned of the probe, he fled to the Philippines and mailed in a letter of retirement. The San Francisco police searched Gerard's houseboat while he was out of the country, discovering hundreds of SFPD intelligence files which had been ordered destroyed as a result of lawsuits brought by civil rights organizations.

The police search also revealed that Gerard may have helped organize death squads in El Salvador and Honduras for the CIA. A briefcase he owned was seized by the San Francisco prosecutor. It included information on such squads, along with photographs of hooded men in shackles.

As a result of the search, the police discovered Gerard's relationship with Bullock. Investigators learned that he had provided information on local Arab-Americans to the ADL operative in violation of California law and SFPD rules. This prompted the police to search the ADL's San Francisco office, where they discovered Bullock's files, along with confidential reports from the Los Angeles Police Department and the FBI. A number of reports on suspected skinheads from the Portland Police Bureau were also found. Altogether, investigators unearthed files on 950 groups and 12,000 individuals.

When the story hit the press, the D.A. released a list of the files. Many of the those named in the files were not aware that they had ever been spied on. The local media was shocked to learn that Gerard had simply taken confidential SFPD files home. Writing about the scandal in early January 1993, the *San Francisco Examiner* quoted an unnamed department source as saying, "A lot of cops have computers and keep intelligence information on their own. The department doesn't know what they have."

The *San Francisco Chronicle* went even further. On May 11, 1993 the paper said, "The secret of eternal life has been found. Once an entry is m official computer files, nothing can dislodge it."

But much of the press quickly focused on the ADL's involveme scandal. They were shocked that a supposedly liberal organization would spy on anyone, let alone other liberals.

The *San Francisco Weekly* ran a cover story on the ADL titled "Spy Masters" on April 28, 1993, accusing the organization of trampling on the rights of law-abiding citizens. The *San Francisco Chronicle* picked up the same theme on May 8 with a story headlined "ADL Critics Say Group Lost Sight of Original Goals." The New York-based *Village Voice* questioned the ADL's actions in a May 11 cover story titled, "The Anti-Defamation League is Spying on You." And, in its July/August 1993 issue, the liberal, Jewish-oriented *Tikkun* magazine published a story on the controversy by Chip Berlet and Dennis King which said, "[T]he special document-trading relationship the ADL apparently enjoys with some police departments and that apparently involves Joseph McCarthy-style obsessions on both sides is not only ethically disturbing, but compromises the integrity of the ADL's research findings."

The ADL initially defended the spying by saying it was necessary to help police prevent hate crimes. "It has been a regular practice of the ADL to trade hate crime-related information with police departments," Bullock's supervisor Hirschhaut told the *Los Angeles Times* on February 26, 1993. "It has always been our understanding and our credo in conducting our fact-finding work that we conduct our work from a high ethical plateau and in conjunction with the law."

As the scandal continued to unfold, however, the ADL went on the attack. In the May/June 1993 issue of the organization's newsletter *Frontline*, ADL National Director Abraham Foxman accused the group's critics of using the "Big Lie" technique. "There is no ADL spy network," he wrote.

Foxman's denials aside, the San Francisco D.A.'s Office was in fact on the trail of a vast "ADL spy network." Journalists learned the organization had agents spying on people in other major American cities, too. "A small group of undercover operatives throughout the nation is being paid by the Anti-Defamation League of B'nai B'rith to spy on pro-Palestinian, black nationalistic and white supremacist groups, according to a San Francisco law enforcement official," the *San Francisco Examiner* reported, noting that investigators had found evidence of contacts with up to 20 other law enforcement agencies. "This Gerard-Bullock thing is the tip of the iceberg—this is going nationwide," the paper quoted another official as saying.[3] A short time later, the *Examiner* quoted a source close to the case as saying, "The ADL is doing the same thing all over the country. There is evidence the ADL had police agents in other cities. The case just gets bigger every day. The more we look, the more people we find are involved."[4] And New York's *Newsday* discovered that Bullock "was just one member of network of 'fact-finders' working out of the ADL's 32 nationwide offices, including New York."[5] No formal investigations were launched against these other operatives, however.

---

3. "Police Said to Aid Spying on Political Groups," *San Francisco Examiner*, March 9, 1993.
4. "A New Target in S.F. Spy Probe," *San Francisco Examiner*, April 1, 1993.
5. *Newsday*, May 3, 1993.

Before too long, the press discovered the ADL was not only spying on political activists, but on journalists, too. *Editor & Publisher* magazine said some of these journalists worked for the *San Francisco Chronicle*, the *Philadelphia Inquirer*, *Mother Jones* magazine, the gay-oriented *Bay Area Reporter* and the San Francisco-based Center for Investigative Reporting.[6]

Also, the investigation revealed that the two men were sharing information with foreign intelligence agencies. In addition to the government of South Africa, Gerard had been selling information on the local Arab-American community to Mossad, Israel's version of the CIA.[7] On February 11, Assistant District Attorney John Dwyer revealed that the ADL files contained the names of two Arab-American U.S. citizens recently arrested in Israel on charges of financing terrorism, prompting Christine Totah, a spokeswoman for the Arab-American Civil Rights Committee, to say, "Everything we have been warning about and pleading about with our public officials—concerning our anxieties over the release of confidential intelligence information being passed onto a foreign government—is unfortunately coming true."

In October 1993, the Arab-American Anti-Discrimination Committee (ADC) filed a class action lawsuit against the ADL, accusing the Jewish organization of violating the civil rights of thousands of American citizens and legal organizations. Plaintiffs named in the suit included the ADC, the National Association of Arab-Americans, the Bay Area Anti-Apartheid Network, the National Lawyers Guild, the Coalition Against Police Abuse, the National Conference of Black Lawyers, the Committee in Solidarity with the People of El Salvador, Global Exchange, the International Jewish Peace Union, the American Indian Movement, the Palestinian Aid Society, the Association of Arab-American University Graduates, and former Congressman Mervyn Dymally.

Albert Mokhiber, the Vice Chairman of the ADC's Board of Directors, spoke at a press conference announcing the suit: "This litigation is not about the Arab-Israeli conflict. It's about civil rights and privacy rights. It is an effort to curtail the so-called privatization of intelligence gathering by law enforcement agencies. In our democratic society, law enforcement officials cannot use private persons and organizations to infiltrate organizations and spy on individuals in a manner which, if done by a law enforcement agency, would violate provisions of the Bill of Rights and state laws. Conversely, a private organization should not be able to obtain from law enforcement officials personal and confidential government information to further its own agenda."

But despite the growing controversy, the scandal ended with a whimper instead of a bang. Gerard returned to San Francisco on May 7, 1993 and was charged with four counts of stealing government documents and one count of conspiracy. The most serious charges against him were dismissed on April 29 after the FBI refused to provide its wiretap and investigative files to the police. On May 27, Gerard pleaded "no contest" to one charge of illegally ac̶─·̶·ᵢₙᵧ

---

6. *Editor & Publisher*, May 8, 1993.
7. "Former S.F. Cop Target of Probe," *San Francisco Chronicle*, January 15, 199?

police computers and was sentenced to a mere 45 days of work in a Sheriff's Department weekend work detail, three years' probation and a $2,500 fine.

Six months later, the San Francisco D.A.'s Office abruptly dropped its criminal investigation, negotiating a quick and quiet settlement with the ADL. In November 1993, the D.A. agreed not to prosecute ADL officials or investigator Bullock any further. In exchange, the ADL donated $75,000 to two anti-hate crime funds administered by the prosecutor's office. A source close to District Attorney Arlo Smith said he was "reluctant to prosecute the case because the Anti-Defamation League does so many good things." [8]

In September 1999, the ADL settled the class action civil suit. As part of the settlement, U.S. Federal District Judge Richard Paez permanently enjoined the organization from engaging in any further illegal spying against Arab-American and other civil rights groups. Paez also ordered the ADL to provide an annual statement for four years explaining the steps it has taken to remain in compliance with the order. The ADL also agreed to pay $25,000 towards a community relations fund to be jointly administrated with representatives of the plaintiff class.

Although ADC spokesman Hussein Ibish said the settlement proved the ADL had "engaged in illegal activities," the ADL issued a statement which denied any wrongdoing and noted there was no court finding of any illegality in the organization's work. [9]

That left only one suit against the ADL, a civil invasion of privacy case filed on behalf of a handful of individuals cited in the files by former U.S. Congressman Pete McCloskey. Although the case has been stalled in the courts for many years, if McCloskey can force Bullock, Gerard and the other major players in the scandal to testify under oath, the public may learn even more about the ADL's vast spy network.

For a complete list of the hundreds of groups found in Tom Gerard and Roy Bullock's computers, check the Snitch Culture page on the Feral House website, <www.feralhouse.com>.

---

8. "Inquiry Into a Jewish Group's Methods is Dropped," *New York Times*, November 17, 1993.
9. Press release, Arab-American Anti-Discrimination Committee, September 24, 1999; "Anti-Defamation League Settles Spying Lawsuit," *Los Angeles Times*, September 28, 1999.

THE PROJECT MEGIDDO FIASCO

THE CLINTON ADMINISTRATION had it both ways on the Oklahoma City bombing. Federal prosecutors argued that only two people, Timothy McVeigh and Terry Nichols, blew up the Alfred E. Murrah federal office building. But President Clinton charged the bombing was just the start of a Far Right terrorist campaign aimed at overthrowing the U.S. government. Exploiting public opinion over the tragedy, he convinced Congress to appropriate hundreds of millions of dollars to the FBI to greatly expand their domestic surveillance programs.

Clinton didn't simply make up this conspiracy theory. He adopted it from a handful of private, politically-oriented advocacy groups. Such so-called civil rights watchdogs as the American Jewish Committee, the ADL, the Coalition for Human Dignity and the SPLC developed this theory in the early 1980s, using it to recruit new members and raise money. Essentially, this theory holds that a growing coalition of Far Right activists have banded together to wage war on the U.S. government. They supposedly range from such traditional racists as Ku Klux Klan members to skinheads and militia followers. The watchdogs argue that this coalition has been on the verge of provoking a race war and bringing down the federal government for more than 20 years.[1]

The ADL made the first formal presentation of this conspiracy theory in a 1980 report on "hate groups" prepared for the U.S. Civil Rights Commission. Although the Commission paid the ADL $20,000 for the report, the federal agency refused to publish it, citing the report's inflammatory writing and outrageous claims. "I would like to raise several policy considerations," acting Commission general counsel Paul Alexander wrote about the report on March 8, 1982. "The ADL report does not in any way resemble a standard USCRC report. It is not a dispassionate attempt to present a balanced accounting of facts. The commission previously has had no difficulty in publishing reports containing defamatory information when it was verifiable and necessary to the report. Our

---

1. In fact, America has always been home to fringe political groups, and many of them have called for the violent overthrow of the government over the years. A good introduction to the political underground is *Extremism in America: A Reader*, edited by Lyman Tower Sargent, New York University Press, 1995. The book identifies various radical movements since the country was founded, including isolationists, populists, racists, white supremacists, black militants, communists, anti-communists, socialists, national socialists, Christian fundamentalists, tax protesters, radical environmentalists, and many which defy easy description.

Voting Rights Report is the most recent example. In that report, however, we did not find it necessary to mix epithets and emotionally laden labels with the facts. The ADL report is rank with epithets and labels that only serve to distort the factual accountings of the activities of the KKK and similar organizations."

Alexander also noted that the report "bordered on jingoism." But the ADL went ahead and published a revised version of the report on its own, with the epithets, emotionally laden labels and jingoism intact. It was widely distributed to the establishment press, which used it as the basis for the first of many stories on the growing threat posed by "hate groups."

Both the ADL and SPLC have published a series of similar reports over the following two decades. They all claimed that America is under siege from a massive Far Right conspiracy, with Jews and racial minorities targeted for terrorist attacks. Some of the reports claim the conspiracy is international in scope, involving former high-ranking members of the Nazi government who hope to resurrect the Third Reich. They all blend mainstream news stories, police reports and information from inside sources to portray the threat as a crisis requiring immediate and drastic action by law enforcement. "The level of hate violence in America has reached a crisis stage," an SPLC report claimed in 1989. "The challenge of the '90s will be to attack the problem of hate violence at its roots. And the struggle will demand the attention of every citizen. For legislators, it means drafting laws to address the threat of hate crime. For educators, it means finding ways to open the channels of cultural understanding among children. For police, it means increased attention to acts of hate violence. For neighborhoods, it means strengthening the bonds of community to embrace diversity and reject bigotry. And for every individual, it means seeking understanding in the place of resentment and desiring peace in the place of conflict." [2]

One of the most influential of all the reports was "The Ku Klux Klan: A History of Racism and Violence," published by the SPLC in 1988. The 60-page publication argued that the original Knight Riders had evolved into a far larger white supremacist movement, including a number of heavily armed neo-Nazi organizations planning to start a race war. It was profusely illustrated with photographs of lynchings, cross burnings, racist skinheads and "Leaders in Today's White Supremacist Movement," including Klansman-turned-politician David Duke and National Alliance founder William Pierce, author of The Turner Diaries, referred to as "a blueprint for a white revolution." The report also included an article on Tom Martinez, a one-time member of a racist gang called The Order who became an FBI informant and testified against his former colleagues.

The ADL published a similar report in early 1995. Titled "The Skinhead International: A Worldwide Survey of Neo-Nazi Skinheads," it included information allegedly provided by snitches, described as "defectors" and

---

2. "Hate Violence and White Supremacy," *Intelligence Report*, Klanwatch Project, Southern Poverty Law Center, December 1989.

"confidential sources." The report described an international network of racist thugs linked by newsletters, touring white supremacist rock bands, and the Internet. "The neo-Nazi Skinhead Movement is active in no fewer than 33 countries on six continents," the report claimed. "It numbers some 70,000 youths worldwide, of whom half are hard-core activists and the rest supporters."

Such figures are greatly exaggerated. In May 2000, the *Washington Times* quoted independent researcher Laird Wilcox as saying such groups as the ADL and SPLC consistently overstate the size and numbers of Far Right groups. Wilcox has published comprehensive directories of both left- and right-wing fringe groups for more than two decades. He has never found more than a fraction of the number of groups cited by the watchdogs. For example, in 1992, when the SPLC was claiming there were "346 white supremacy groups operating," Wilcox only found 50 viable organizations.[3]

Nevertheless, the corporate media seized on the ADL and SPLC reports when the BATF provoked a violent confrontation with a former Green Beret named Randy Weaver, who moved with his family to rural Idaho in the early 1980s. When the BATF learned that Weaver once visited the Aryan Nations compound near Coeur d'Alene, Idaho an undercover agent set him up on weapons charges to force him to become an agency snitch. Weaver refused and retreated to his mountain cabin. On August 21, 1992, several U.S. Marshals surveilling the family unexpectedly encountered Weaver, his son Sam, and a family friend named Kevin Harris as they were walking through the woods. Shots were exchanged, killing Deputy U.S. Marshal William Degan, Sam, and the boy's dog, Striker.

Federal agents, police and National Guard troops quickly converged on the scene. The confrontation made the national news, with the earliest reports describing the family as white supremacists and linking them to the Far Right conspiracy described in the ADL and SPLC reports. FBI snipers wounded Weaver and Harris, then killed Vicki Weaver, Randy's wife, while she was standing behind a cabin door holding the couple's youngest child.

The remaining members of the Weaver family and Harris finally surrendered on August 31. Randy and Harris were indicted on numerous federal counts, including murder, assault, weapons violations and harboring a fugitive. After a six-week trial, Harris was acquitted of all charges and Weaver was only convicted for "failure to appear" at his original trial. The surviving Weavers

---

3. Robert Stacy McCain, "Researcher Says Hate 'Fringe' Isn't as Crowded as Claimed," *Washington Times*, May 9, 2000. In his story, McCain quotes Wilcox as saying there are not more than 10,000 active, organized Far Right extremists in the entire country. "'Because of their nature, it's very difficult to come up with firm numbers' for such groups, Mr. Wilcox says, but estimates 'the militias are probably 5,000 or 6,000 people. The Ku Klux Klan are down to about 3,000 people. And the combined membership of all neo-Nazi groups are probably just 1,500 to 2,000.'

"In a nation of more than 270 million people, the small size of such fringe groups represents a tiny danger, yet they are the target of what Mr. Wilcox calls an 'industry' of watchdog groups."

filed a wrongful death suit against the federal government for killing Vicki. Although the government paid Weaver millions of dollars to settle the suit in September 1994, he will forever be remembered as the villain because of the information provided by the private intelligence networks to the establishment press throughout the siege.

The Ruby Ridge siege helped inspire a small but vocal anti-government movement, especially among fundamentalist, gun-owning Christians who question the need for such a strong federal government. More Americans began to agree with these critics after the fiery end of the disastrous federal assault on the Branch Davidians on August 19, 1993. The ADL and SPLC quickly added militias and doomsday cult leaders to their Far Right conspiracy theory, frequently lumping all of these groups and individuals under the umbrella term Patriot Movement. Although the overwhelming majority of those who questioned the government's handling of the Weaver family and Branch Davidians were law-abiding citizens, the watchdog groups characterized the entire movement as racist. In their reports, the ADL and SPLC began referring to the handful of white supremacist leaders they first identified in the early '80s as the architects of the Patriot Movement.

Clinton seized on this slightly revised version of the Far Right conspiracy theory in the wake of the Oklahoma City bombing. It would take another five years for it to be proven wrong.

The FBI investigation into the Oklahoma City bombing was the largest, most intensive criminal probe ever conducted by the agency. Hundreds of agents looked into the allegations that it was part of a larger conspiracy. Agents checked up on thousands of alleged Far Right activists. Many of the names came from the SPLC, which gave the FBI a list of several thousand members of militias and "hate groups" culled from its files. "None of them had anything to do with the bombing," says Wilcox. "These names came from letters to newspapers expressing right-wing political views, lists of 'members' supplied by informants, names from license plate numbers collected outside public meetings, pilfered mailing lists, and so on. The possibility of a mere curiosity seeker or an individual with no criminal intent whatsoever being suggested to the FBI or BATF as 'dangerous' seems inevitable." [4]

In the end, no one else was ever charged in the bomb plot. Two friends of McVeigh, Michael Fortier and his wife, admitted knowing about it in advance, but they were not charged with participating in it. "The investigation, as thorough as it was, was not able to identify any other individuals involved other than those who admitted their knowledge or were convicted through two trials," the agent in charge of the investigation told the *Sunday Oklahoman* newspaper on December 13, 1998.

Nevertheless, President Clinton effectively exploited the public fear caused by the bombing to pass the Anti-Terrorism and Effective Death Penalty Act of

---

4. Laird Wilcox, *The Watchdogs: A Closer Look at Anti-Racist 'Watchdog' Groups*, Editorial Research Service, 1998.

1996. Pushing aside all concerns about the legality of domestic political surveil-lance, the Act contained $468 million for the FBI to launch new counter-intelligence and counter-terrorism programs. Much of the money went for a series of counter-terrorism task forces across the country, allowing federal, state and local law enforcement agencies to pool intelligence information.

The watchdog organizations supported this increase in surveillance operations by cranking out a new series of reports on the dangers allegedly posed by the Patriot Movement. In 1996, the SPLC released "False Patriots: The Threat of Anti-government Extremists." Keyed to the Oklahoma City bombing, the 72-page, magazine-style report claims, "Today, white supremacists have joined with other armed vigilantes in the anti-government Patriot move-ment. They have a new strategy for terror: underground 'cells' that will wage war against the government with the support of a broad coalition of the extreme right."

Within two years of the Oklahoma City bombing, the FBI was running thousands of new political snitches across the country. According to the December 29, 1997 issue of U.S. News & World Report, the FBI was working on approximately 100 domestic terrorism investigations before the bombing. The number jumped to 900 two years after the Murrah Building was destroyed, according to the article. Law enforcement agencies filed charges against suspected militia members in 36 major cases in 22 states between March and December 1996 alone. Many, if not most, of these cases were made by *agent provocateurs*. No one was ever convicted of conspiring to overthrow the government.

The ADL and SPLC revised their Far Right conspiracy theory again in 1998, issuing new reports which claimed the Patriot Movement was now planning to launch a series of domestic terrorism attacks at the dawn of the New Millennium. According to these reports, these attacks were intended to trigger Armageddon, the fiery final fight between good and evil foretold in the Bible. The watchdogs argued that the Y2K computer bug had heightened the significance of the year 2000 among the anti-government extremists. "Regard-less of the actual result—and many experts see the headline-making Y2K story as a tempest in a teacup—there is no question that a large number of extremists have pegged the year 2000 as a critical date," the SPLC wrote. "For many, it will be a time when Christian patriots, the 'children of light,' must do battle with the satanic 'forces of darkness.' Others believe 'one-world' conspirators will attack American patriots on this date." [5]

The Clinton Administration embraced this version of the Far Right conspiracy theory, using the threat of New Year's violence to justify the creation of even more task forces.

FBI Director Louis Freeh publicly endorsed the conspiracy theory in testi-mony before a U.S. Senate subcommittee on February 4, 1999. As reported by the next day's issue of USA Today, the FBI chief warned that some political

5. "Millennium 'Y2KAOS," *Intelligence Report*, Southern Poverty Law Center, Fall 1998.

and religious fanatics were "engaged in survivalist and paramilitary training, storing foodstuffs and supplies and stockpiling weapons and ammunition." Freeh also cited "the threat posed by even a lone terrorist with access to chemical, biological and nuclear weapons." [6]

Less than three months later, on April 25, 1999, CBS News reported, "The FBI is keeping close watch on right-wing hate groups, religious extremists and New Age cults. When cult leader David Koresh preached, FBI agents ridiculed it as 'Bible babble,' which the bureau didn't understand. But now they're studying religious writings and examining tragedies like the mass suicides by the cult of the Solar Temple in Switzerland and the Heaven's Gate cult in California. And they're tracking groups like a Taiwanese cult in Texas that waited in vain for God to appear on television." [7]

Details about the FBI's surveillance operation were finally made public by USA Today on October 20, 1999. As revealed by the story, the agency's intelligence-gathering initiative was named Project Megiddo after an ancient battleground in Israel associated with Armageddon. The story said the FBI had produced a 40-page report summarizing the information gathered during the research project. It was distributed to 20,000 police chiefs nationwide, warning them about the potential for terrorist attacks at the beginning of the Year 2000. "The FBI has urged police to be alert to changes in behavior of known militias and cult groups and to the possible stockpiling of weapons," the story said, a clear call for even more infiltration. [8]

The Washington Post obtained a copy of the FBI report a short time later. "The FBI is warning police chiefs across the country that it has discovered evidence of religious extremists, racists, cults and other groups preparing for violence as New Year's Eve approaches and is urging law enforcement agencies to view the dawn of the next millennium as a catalyst for criminal activities," the paper said on October 31. "The FBI says those most likely to perpetrate violence are motivated either by religious beliefs relating to the Apocalypse, or are New World Order conspiracists convinced the United Nations has a secret plan to conquer the world."

The FBI posted an edited version of the report on its website a short time later. It painted a horrifying picture of a country under siege by an army of hillbilly Bible-thumpers, African-American Jew-baiters, and heavily-armed apocalyptic prophets. According to the report, this volatile coalition believed the world was coming to an end—and were planning to help it along by attacking government offices, sabotaging power lines, and sparking a deadly race war in America's inner cities.

"Without question, this initiative has revealed indicators of potential violent activity on the part of extremists in this country," the report said. "Certain individuals from these various perspectives are acquiring weapons,

6. "FBI: Violence Possible as 2000 Approaches," USA Today, February 5, 1999.
7. "Y2K Cults Worry FBI: Feds Fear Millennium May be Marked by Violence," CBS News, April 25,1999.
8. "FBI: Militias a Threat at Millennium," USA Today, October 20, 1999.

storing food and clothing, raising funds through fraudulent means, procuring safe houses, preparing compounds, surveying potential targets and recruiting new converts. These and other indicators are not taking place in a vacuum, nor are they random or arbitrary."

The report identified seven broad categories of groups and individuals which were considering such attacks. They included militias, white supremacists, black supremacists, apocalyptic cults, followers of the Christian Identity religion, members of the far right National Socialist movement and Odinists (apparently a catch-all phrase for anyone who follows a pre-Christian European religion). The report also identified 11 specific groups whose members were capable of such attacks, including the Aryan Nations, the Posse Comitatus, Black Hebrew Israelites, the National Alliance, the Phineas Priests, The House of Yahweh (a Texas-based religious group whose leaders are former Posse Comitatus members), the American Nazi Party, the National Socialist White People's Party, the Ku Klux Klan, the Miami-based Nation of Yahweh (a Black supremacist group), and Concerned Christians. (The FBI prepared a second report listing even more organizations which was only circulated within law enforcement circles and not released to the public.)

"The millennium holds special significance for many, and as this pivotal point in time approaches, the impetus for the initiation of violence becomes more acute," the report warned. "Several religiously motivated groups envision a quick, fiery ending in an apocalyptic battle. Others may initiate a sustained campaign of terrorism in the United States to prevent the NWO. Armed with the urgency of the millennium as a motivating factor, new clandestine groups may conceivably form to engage in violence toward the U.S. Government or its citizens."

Although the Project Megiddo report was written by the FBI's National Security Division, much of the information came from the watchdog organizations. The footnotes cite an ADL report titled "Explosion of Hate" and articles from two issues of the SPLC's *Intelligence Report*, and also included several newspaper and magazine articles which relied on information provided by these groups.

The ADL was very open about its involvement in Project Megiddo, virtually taking credit for the report on its website. When the FBI presented the report to the International Chiefs of Police on November 2, ADL officials showed up with their own version titled "Y2K Paranoia: Extremists Confront the Millennium." The ADL even issued a press release to coincide with the meeting, saying its experts were available for interviews on the threat posed by "anti-government militia and 'Patriot' groups with theories of a government conspiracy, certain religious fundamentalists, and cults predicting an apocalypse with Jews playing a conspiratorial or Satanic role, and far right extremists seeking to blame the so-called Y2K bug on Jews and the federal government."

Theories developed by the Cult Awareness Network also surfaced in the Megiddo report. It contained an entire section on "doomsday cults" which relied on the writings of Margaret Thaler Singer, a clinical psychologist and former CAN advisor. A book co-authored by Singer appeared several times in the report's footnotes. Underlining her obsession with the issue, it was titled *Cults in Our Midst: The Hidden Menace in Our Everyday Lives*.

CAN and Singer helped popularize a notion of "brainwashing" which has been used to explain how fringe political and religious organizations attract and keep followers. According to this theory, charismatic leaders use sophisticated "mind control" techniques to break down members' free will and "program" them to carry out their wishes. This theory allows the government to criticize these groups as something other than genuine political or religious organizations —meaning that constitutional guarantees of freedom of speech, religion or association shouldn't apply to them.

The public release of the Project Megiddo report set off another wave of hysterical news stories. But when the Year 2000 arrived, nothing predicted in the report happened. No militia members came out of the hills to attack government office buildings. Skinheads didn't attempt to provoke a race war. No doomsday cult members launched suicide attacks on nonbelievers. Despite all the time and money spent on the report, it was simply wrong.

Only two acts of sabotage occurred on New Year's Eve. Someone toppled an 80-foot electrical tower in Eastern Oregon, while an electrical transformer in New York was bombed. Neither attack caused significant problems, and no one even claimed responsibility for them.

In fact, the only serious terrorism threat to surface at the end of the year came from a source that wasn't even mentioned in the Project Megiddo report— Algerians from Canada. Washington state authorities caught Ahmed Ressam trying to smuggle explosives into Port Angeles from British Columbia on December 14. A federal grand jury indicted him and an alleged accomplice, Abdelmajid Dahoumane, on terrorism conspiracy charges a short time later. Although federal authorities say the two men were planning to blow up buildings or other targets in the U.S. around New Year's Eve, they do not belong to any group discussed in the report.[9]

Steve Berry, a Supervisory Special Agent with the FBI's National Press Office, refused comment on why the Project Megiddo report was so inaccurate. "We're not going to speculate on why there weren't any terrorist attacks on New Year's," he said. "The report was not a predictor. We weren't stating they were going to happen, just that they might happen."[10]

Berry's comments are disingenuous, at best. Although the Project Megiddo report didn't predict specific acts of violence, it left little doubt that such attacks were just around the corner. "In the final analysis, while making specific predictions is extremely difficult, acts of violence in commemoration of the millennium are just as likely to occur as not," the report warned.

---

9. "Border Arrest Sets Off Manhunt for Millennium Terrorists," *Boston Globe*, December 19, 1999.
10. Author's interview with Supervisory Special Agent Steve Berry of the FBI's National Press Office, March 24, 2000.

Berry also suggested that the report helped local police agencies prevent such attacks. "As a general statement, law enforcement in general took extraordinary steps to prepare and were cognizant of the facts and took steps to prepare," he said.

But that's not a plausible explanation, either. The potential terrorists described in the report would hardly be deterred by local police. They were repeatedly characterized as religious fanatics and political zealots who were eager to die for their beliefs—American suicide bombers who believed they were doing God's work.

"Numerous religious extremists claim that a race war will soon begin, and have taken steps to become martyrs in their predicted battle between good and evil," the report warned at one point. "Almost uniformly, the belief among right-wing religious extremists is that the federal government is an arm of Satan. Therefore, the millennium will bring about a battle between Christian martyrs and the government. At the core of this volatile mix is the belief of apocalyptic religions and cults that the battle against Satan, as prophesied in the Book of Revelation, will begin in 2000," it said later.

In fact, only three people who fit the profiles in the Project Megiddo report were arrested shortly before the end of the year, and it's hard to know how seriously to take the charges against them. On December 23, two alleged militia members were arrested and accused of plotting to blow up two 12-million-gallon propane tanks, a television tower and an electrical substation near Sacramento, California. Kevin Patterson, 42, was reportedly involved with an anti-government group, the Republic of Texas. Charles Kiles, 49, had been convicted in 1992 of weapons violations, and once reportedly led a now-defunct militia group. According to the charges against them, the pair hoped the attacks would provoke an insurrection against the government.

The plot was exactly what the report said was in the works. But a closer look at the case reveals that Patterson and Kiles were set up by undercover agents. They had been under federal surveillance for nearly a year. An FBI informant had reported on the pair's activities for months. And court documents say the alleged plot was actually put off when one of the men decided to wait to "see what happened in California at the end of the millennium." [11]

The second arrest was even more dubious. Five days after the California arrests, federal authorities charged Donald Beauregard, the former leader of a militia coalition called the Southeastern States Alliance, with plotting to steal explosives from National Guard armories. According to the federal indictment, Beauregard was conspiring to blow up power lines to Atlanta, Georgia and St. Petersburg, Florida. He was also charged with intending to kill a militia member he suspected of being an informant, and of helping train other extremists how to manufacture explosives. At the time of his arrest, however, Beauregard

---

11. "Hearings Set for Militiamen in Giant-Explosion Scheme," *USA Today*, December 9, 1999; Mark Gladstone, "Informant Told FBI of Alleged Y2K Plot," *Los Angeles Times*, December 20, 1999; "California Militia Bomb Plot Suspect Denied Bail," *Reuters*, December 28, 1999.

hadn't bombed anything or killed anyone. He hadn't even stolen the explosives necessary to carry out his alleged plot.[12]

Despite the fact that the Far Right conspiracy theory was largely debunked by the lack of terrorist attacks at the dawn of the New Millennium, the corporate media has continued producing inflammatory reports on the "threat" posed by such organizations. A good example is a special entitled "Nazi America: A Secret History," which ran on the History Channel on January 21, 2000. In it, SPLC founder Morris Dees estimated that 500 such groups are currently at work in the country, calling them "a cesspool of vigilantes."[13]

To read the complete Project Megiddo report, check the Snitch Culture page on the Feral House website, <www.feralhouse.com>.

---

12. Ace Atkins and Michael Fechter, "Pinellas Militia Leader Arrested," *Tampa Tribune*, December 9, 1999. In the story, Frank Gallagher, special agent in charge of the FBI's Tampa office, said the alleged plot would never have been carried out because an undercover agent was aware of it. "At no time was there a threat to the public," Gallagher said.

13. "From a 1930s Goose Step to an Oklahoma City Blast," *New York Times*, January 20, 2000.

THE ITALIAN AND RUSSIAN MAFIA

NOTHING ILLUSTRATES THE POWER and problems of snitching better than the federal government's efforts to crush the Mafia, the traditional organized crime syndicate which flourished in this country for much of the 20th Century. The FBI made little headway against the Italian family-based organization until it learned how to recruit, direct and protect its informants. But even though the feds eventually broke most of the families and imprisoned their leaders, the government had to cut deals with murderers and other felons. Many violent criminals walked in exchange for their cooperation, and a large number of law enforcement officials were compromised along the way.

In the end, the government's victory over the Mafia has not significantly reduced the level of organized crime in this country. To the contrary, even more ruthless criminal organizations moved in and took over their territories, including black and Mexican drug gangs. The most recent successors are the Russian crime families collectively known as the Russian Mafia. Almost impossible to infiltrate, these families are already engaged in such traditional mob activities as prostitution, gambling, fraud, extortion, drugs, money laundering and murder.

"Gone is the traditional hierarchical structure of the chain of command favored by the Italian Mafia and so successfully penetrated by federal investigators," USA Today reported in September 1999. "What has taken its place authorities can only describe as loose networks of multinational, multi-ethnic groups whose considerable influence is not defined by geographic borders." [1]

This illustrates the fallacy of relying upon informants to fight crime. Larger and more dangerous criminal networks are waiting to move in.

"The vast criminal base that took the Italian Mafia decades to build in the U.S.A., federal investigators say, can be duplicated by Russian-speaking groups almost overnight," the paper continued. "The speed with which these partnerships operate because of their access to a global financial system almost has investigators working continuously to redefine the network."

The federal government denied the existence of La Cosa Nostra, the Italian-American Mafia, until the late 1950s. Some historians claim this is because J. Edgar Hoover was blackmailed with photographs showing him dressed in women's clothing and engaged in homosexual activities. Gay, mob-connected attorney Roy Cohn has been identified as the go-between. Other historians believe the government ignored the mob because Mafia members in America

---

1. Kevin Johnson, "Law Enforcement Plays Catch-Up with Reorganized Crime," USA Today, September 3, 1999.

and Italy helped the allies win the Second World War. Whatever the truth, even the official history of the FBI posted on the agency's Internet website admits the government did not pursue the traditional Italian-American mob for many, many years.

Whatever the real reason for Hoover's reluctance to tangle with the Mafia, this finally began to change in 1957 when the New York State Police were tipped off to a high-powered mob meeting and brought it to the attention of the FBI. Mafia snitch Joseph Valachi provided more evidence against La Cosa Nostra at a widely-publicized congressional hearing in 1962. Still, the FBI did not seriously pursue the Mafia until after Hoover retired in 1972. By then, Congress had passed several important new laws to crack down on the mob. The powerful Racketeer-Influenced and Corrupt Organizations (RICO) Act, enacted in 1970, authorizes prison sentences of up to 20 years and maximum $25,000 fines on anyone convicted of a "pattern of racketeering," such as extortion, murder and stealing union funds. Four years later, Congress authorized sting operations, allowing federal agents to set up an illegal enterprise with the goal of luring in criminals and arresting them.

The federal government's campaign against the Mafia finally came together under the administration of President Ronald Reagan. The U.S. Justice Department dramatically increased the use of court-ordered wiretaps, obtaining a total of 733 of them compared with 326 during the Jimmy Carter years. The Reagan Justice Department created or expanded 17 regional organized-crime task forces in 26 cities, along with a dozen new anti-drug task forces with 1,000 investigators and 200 prosecutors.

By the mid-1980s, the number of federal organized-crime convictions had increased dramatically. Nearly 4,200 organized-crime indictments were handed down in 1985 alone. There were over 3,500 convictions and plea bargains that year. Leaders of four major Mafia families in New York were charged with running a national underworld "commission." And the heads of 16 of the nation's 24 Mafia families had been indicted, prompting Reagan to accurately say, "I think that for the first time in our history we finally have the mob on the run." [2]

In the end, snitches were the government's most successful weapon against the mob. "There is no question that the U.S. government has won a number of impressive victories in the past decade against what it likes to call 'traditional organized crime.' Together with the RICO statutes, the Witness Security Program has played an important role in these convictions. Virtually every major Mob case in recent years has relied heavily on turncoat witnesses. Invariably, the promises of the program have laid the groundwork for informant cooperation," says crime reporter T.J. English.[3]

Some of the most important snitches were recruited through a special FBI operation called the "Top Echelon," created in the 1970s to target mobsters

2. Stewart Powell, Steven Emerson and Orr Kelly, "Busting the Mob," *U.S. News & World Report*, February 3, 1986.
3. T.J. English, "The Wiseguy Next Door," *Playboy*, April 1991.

who held top positions in criminal organizations. Although all of their names will never be known for obvious reasons, a number have been publicly identified— including several who wrote their own books.

Angelo Lonardo, the aging underboss of the Cleveland mob, is probably the highest-ranking American mobster ever to become a rat. Faced with a life sentence plus 103 years, he testified against his underworld associates in exchange for his freedom. Another important informant was Tommaso Buscetta, a Sicilian mobster who testified in the New York "Pizza Connection" trials where over a dozen defendants were convicted of using pizza parlors to "launder" drug profits. After the trial, Buscetta was given a new identity and entered the federal Witness Protection Program. And Sammy "The Bull" brought down John Gotti and much of the New York-based Gambino Family.

As a result of all this snitching, the remaining Mafia families are now considered to be "so riddled with government informants and so effortlessly monitored by high-tech electronic surveillance that their secrets become almost immediately the newest counts in a barrage of indictments."[4]

Breaking the Mafia does not mean that organized crime is a thing of the past, however. To the contrary, new criminal gangs such as the heroin-smuggling Mexican Mafia and the crack-based Crips and Bloods are almost impossible for law enforcement agencies to infiltrate. State and local police have responded to them by mounting massive paramilitary operations, sweeping hundreds of young Hispanics and blacks off the streets at a time. These aggressive anti-gang units have been involved in a number of highly-publicized scandals in recent years, including the out-of-control Rampart CRASH unit of the LAPD.

But the newest organized crime gang is potentially the most dangerous. It is the Russian Mafia, a global crime syndicate which has moved to America since the fall of the Soviet Union. In May 2000, the FBI described the threat posed by these new mobsters in stark terms. "Indeed, Russian organized-crime groups have a level of knowledge and experience in working the system that sets them in a criminal class by themselves. As they become more acculturated, learning more about business and government systems in this country, the challenge they present to law enforcement will grow."[5]

According to the FBI document, thousands of Russian Mafia members have emigrated to the U.S. over the past decade, setting up a network of interconnected mobs in New York, Los Angeles and other major American cities: "These gangs vary in their criminal activity and in their degree of affiliation with other domestic and foreign-based organizations and groups. Their criminal acts include providing illicit services (prostitution, gambling, extortionate credit, etc.) and committing an assortment of violent and property crimes. Some of these groups operate on their own. Others have muscled in on the schemes of fraudsters. Some coordinate with foreign-based

4. Howard Blum, "The Reluctant Don," *Vanity Fair*, September 1999.
5. "Russian Organized Crime: A Criminal Hydra, " FBI Law Enforcement Bulletin, May 2000.

groups to launder illegal funds from overseas operations. Still others—large, more established organizations—are involved in all of the above."

Despite the serious nature of this threat, the report admits the Russian Mafia is almost impossible to infiltrate. "Moreover, the lack of distinct structure and the continuous change many groups undergo make it impractical to employ traditional proactive strategies to disrupt and dismantle these criminal enterprises."

Because of this, the FBI report says the only way to fight the Russian Mafia is to globally expand the Snitch Culture: "By combining efforts— through communication, cooperation and coordination—local, state, federal and international law enforcement agencies can counter the threat posed by Russian organized crime."

INFOWAR IS DECLARED

MOST HACKER ATTACKS ARE PRANKS, designed to plant porn on government websites, temporarily shut down large e-retailers, or simply test the most advanced Internet security systems. But on July 30, 2000, a libertarian-oriented site called Antiwar.com was the victim of a politically-motivated cyber assault which knocked it off the Web. The only question is, who initiated the attack: the federal government or one of its allies?

Antiwar.com was started as a hobby by a small group of peace activists in 1995. Webmaster Eric Garris is a former Vietnam War draft resister opposed to U.S. military intervention anywhere in the world. He, columnist Justin Raimondo, and a number of others wanted to document the Pentagon's role in Bosnia. They were convinced the NATO mission would be the launching pad for a wider, more extensive military operation in the region.[1] That happened in 1999, when NATO launched "Operation Allied Force" in Kosovo. The massive American-led bombing campaign killed soldiers and civilians alike. The missions took out power stations and decimated columns of refugees. As the establishment media led the charge for more and bigger bombing raids, Antiwar.com emerged as one of the only reliable sources about what was actually happening on the ground in Yugoslavia.

The *Washington Post* wrote about the website on April 15, 1999, calling it "thoughtful and well-organized." The paper quoted Garris as saying the website is "fast evolving into what is, in effect, an online magazine and research tool designed to keep the American people informed about the U.S.-NATO military onslaught against the people of Serbia."

Convinced that opposition to such missions extends beyond traditional political lines, Garris, Raimondo and a few of the other people involved with Antiwar.com organized a conference titled "Beyond Left & Right: The New Face of the Antiwar Movement." It was held on March 24 and 25, 2000, at the Villa Hotel in San Mateo, California. Speakers included Reform Party Presidential candidate Pat Buchanan and *CounterPunch* publisher Alexander Cockburn. The gathering was a huge success, attracting hundreds of people and proving that a broad range of political activists and commentators oppose continued U.S. military intervention around the globe.

George Szamuely, a columnist for the *New York Press*, wrote about the gathering on April 4. "The conference theme was 'Beyond Left and Right' and

---

1. Author's interviews with Eric Garris, June 2 and 5, 2000, and Justin Raimondo, June 13, 2000.

for a good reason. When it comes to imperialism, there is much that left and right can agree on. Imperialism means government repression at home, violations of international law abroad, the exploitation of the weak by the strong and the destruction of different national cultures and traditions," he said.

A short time later, Garris and Raimondo were shocked to learn their website had been classified as "militia-related" by Mark Pitcavage, the research director of the State/Local Anti-Terrorism Training Program. SLATT was created by the federal government in reaction to the Oklahoma City bombing. It was started with a $2 million appropriation in the Anti-Terrorism and Effective Death Penalty Act of 1996, the same law which provided over $460 million to the FBI for a series of new counter-terrorism programs.

"This is McCarthyism, and it's hard to defend against that." Garris says. "Now you have it on an electronic level. It's like being added to the blacklist. What can you do? You can't ever get off."

Pitcavage maintains the listing on an Internet website he started in the early 1990s called the Militia Watchdog. Pitcavage says he started the site to monitor the Patriot Movement, which he described as "a loose collection of militia groups, common law courts, sovereign citizens, tax protesters, jural societies, Christian patriots, Christian Identity groups, white supremacists, scam artists and other extreme groups." The site makes it clear that Pitcavage regards this movement as a serious threat to the country. "Perhaps most dangerous of all is that these groups together are more than the sum of their parts. Together they are creating an illegal 'shadow' government, heavily armed, answerable to no authority, and motivated by bizarre conspiracy theories. As long as this movement exists and is active, there will be more people duped, threatened, given reason to fear, and even deprived of their lives. The bombing at Oklahoma City was birthed from the "patriot" movement. Already there have been other people arrested with plans to bomb buildings public and private. These groups represent the core cadre from which a serious domestic terrorist movement may spring—or from which it may already have arisen."

Pitcavage did not stop running the site after he was made SLATT research director, a position which put him in direct contact with agents from the FBI, along with officers from state and local law enforcement agencies across the country. To the contrary, he continued expanding the Militia Watchdog, even posting research papers written for SLATT on the sovereign citizen and common law court movements. And he kept adding names to another feature on the site—a running list of militia-related websites. This is where Garris found Antiwar.com, described as "essentially an isolationist right-wing libertarian site."

This was not the first time that a so-called civil rights watchdog has claimed the anti-war movement is linked to racist and other anti-government extremists. The theory first began to spread within liberal circles in the early days of the Persian Gulf War. It was started by Chip Berlet, director of a Boston-based think tank called Political Research Associates (PRA). Like Pitcavage,

Berlet describes himself as an expert on the Far Right. On December 20, 1990, Berlet sent a memo to prominent peace activists around the country. Titled "Right Woos Left Over Gulf War Issue: Tracing the Roots of Conspiracy Thinking," it charged that right-wingers were infiltrating the anti-war movement. Berlet specifically mentioned fringe Presidential candidate Lyndon LaRouche, whom he labeled a "Fascist." The memo also pointed fingers at the "quasi-Nazi" Liberty Lobby, which publishes the Jewish conspiracy-oriented *Spotlight* newspaper.

Operation Desert Storm was launched on January 17, 1991, a little more than a month after Berlet circulated his memo. There were relatively few protests around the country, especially compared to the Vietnam War era. The anti-war movement all but died over the next few years, with only an occasional activist raising questions about U.S. sanctions on Iran and Iraq.

The next major conflict was Bosnia. It didn't draw much opposition, either. But attempts to link the left to the Far Right continued. In 1995, radical environmental writers Janet Biehl and Peter Staudenmaier published a book titled, *Ecofascism: Lessons from the German Experience*. It argued that much of the current ecology movement was based on Nazi Party teachings, and that it was in danger of being taken over by eco-Fascists.

The next year, Biehl published a piece called "Militia Fever: The Fallacy of Neither Left Nor Right." It first appeared in the April issue of *Green Perspectives: A Social Ecology Publication*. In the article, Biehl argued that left-libertarians were being seduced by Far Right conspiracy theories and forging alliances with right-wing militias. "At a time when the left has been declared all but dead, the very existence of the militias makes crystal clear the need for a left. Left-libertarians should know what this movement is and criticize it rather than look for affinities with it," she declared in the piece, subsequently posted as a research report on the PRA website.

By the time Kosovo started to heat up, opposing the NATO mission was being labeled "racist" by yet another watchdog group, the SPLC. The Spring 1999 issue of the SPLC's *Intelligence Report* carried a story called "Kosovo and the Far Right." The newsletter, which was mailed to law enforcement agencies across the country, charged, "The NATO-led attacks on Christian Serbs in Kosovo and Yugoslavia have given the radical right a new ideological battleground—a battleground that some believe may become as important as a rallying point as the conflagration in Waco, Texas." Although the article mentioned there was other opposition to the war, it stressed, "On scores of websites, in the extremist literature and in the speeches and conversations of far right leaders, the Kosovo war is increasingly seen as an attack by the 'New World Order' on white Christian ethnics that is designed to force multiracialism and multi-ethnic states on the world over the protests of patriots everywhere."

As proof, the article quoted former Ku Klux Klan leader Louis Beam as saying, "This baby killing, church burning, drug using, draft dodging, woman raping, perjuring, lying adulterer—who calls himself the President of the United States—has begun killing Europeans in the name of the American people!" It also claimed that European protests against the war have "included large numbers of neo-Nazis, and many have been seen giving fascist salutes."

Garris, Raimondo and the others at Antiwar.com have nothing to do with militias, the KKK or neo-Nazis. And by April 2000, they were being linked to the Far Right by a politically-oriented government consultant tied into the government's national surveillance system. That was just the start.

In late May, the software program for counting the number of visitors to Antiwar.com inexplicably crashed two days in a row. The reason? An unusually high number of hits from a single visitor. When columnist Raimondo went into the counter program and tracked down the curious party, he was shocked to learn it was a Pentagon-funded cabal of cyber-soldiers known as the Army Computer Emergency Response Team. The counter crashed after recording 2,000 hits from ACERT on the first day alone. Every file on the website was visited at least once.

Shirley K. Startzman, ACERT's public affairs assistant, confirms the military had prowled the site. She said ACERT uses Themescape, a commercially available search tool, to roam the World Wide Web looking for words related to "cyber-defense." She says this work is "defensive in nature," intended to "protect Army computer systems from hackers or denial-of-service attacks." According to Startzman, "The Antiwar website was one of many on the publicly accessible Internet the tool identified as having information potentially related to cyber-defense. The high number of hits reflects this automated search tool." She says the information collected from the site was ultimately determined to be "tangential and not relevant to our ongoing search requirements."[2]

Garris and Raimondo aren't buying this explanation. Although Antiwar.com has carried several stories and columns speculating that NATO forces are hacking into Serbian websites, they doubt ACERT simply stumbled on theirs because of a few key words or phrases. Garris and Raimondo believe the two incidents—the SLATT listing and the ACERT visits—means the U.S. government is laying the groundwork to knock them offline during the next international military confrontation.

"The government says all this Internet policing stuff is to protect us from hackers and from cyber-criminals, but they are doing other stuff, political stuff," says Raimondo. "They're researching their political enemies. I wouldn't be surprised to learn they have dossiers on us."

Cyber-warfare is a relatively new idea. It first surfaced as a public issue in 1988 when the Morris Worm computer virus disabled approximately 10 percent of all computers connected to the Internet. The Pentagon was not prepared to prevent such attacks from knocking out the government's vast computer networks, so it turned to the Software Engineering Institute, a federally-funded research center based at Carnegie Mellon University in Pittsburgh, Pennsylvania. By the end of the year, SEI was officially designated

2. E-mail exchanges with author, June 23 and 28, 2000.

as the Computer Emergency Response Team Coordination Center (CERT/CC), providing research and assistance to the government and anyone else wanting to prevent viruses and other attacks from crippling their computers.

The Pentagon soon decided to concentrate its emerging cyber-warfare operations under the United States Army Intelligence and Security Command (INSCOM), which was first created in 1977 to coordinate all of the military's intelligence-gathering operations. INSCOM moved to Fort Belvoir, Virginia in the summer of 1989. Five years later, in 1994, the Army created the Land Information Warfare Activity (LIWA) section, bringing together all current electronic warfare, psychological warfare, command and control targeting, and operational security operations at a single location. A short time later, the Pentagon began considering launching their own Internet attacks against hostile targets.

The idea was first fleshed out in an imaginative 1996 paper published by the National Defense University Press called "Information Terrorism: Can You Trust Your Toaster?" It was written by Matthew G. Devost, Brian K. Houghton and Neal A. Pollard, who said the military must be prepared to stop "information terrorists" before they attack the nation's computer systems. To illustrate this premise, the authors created a complete scenario, a war story set on the Internet, pitting evil "information terrorists" against heroic cyber-warriors in the service of Uncle Sam. By an amazing coincidence, the bad guys in the fictional story maintain a website which sounds a lot like a government version of what Antiwar.com was doing at the time. "The Web page was dramatic and rife with propaganda and claims against American, NATO, and Croatian imperialism and atrocities in the Balkan region, and included questionable allegations of illegal arms transfers between NATO governments and Bosnian Muslims and Croats. Several references were included to the former U.S. presence in Lebanon, and how that presence was resolved," the paper said.

To fight such a diabolical threat, the authors said the U.S. military should create a "specialized and integrated counter-information terrorism group," which they called DIRT (Digital Integrated Response Team). "These highly-trained information warriors would be the national security equivalent of Carnegie-Mellon University's Computer Emergency Response Team, but with an offensive capability," the paper said.

The Pentagon created ACERT under LIWA the next year. An article on the ribbon-cutting ceremony titled "Protecting Electronic Borders" appeared in the March–April 1997 issue of *The Journal of INSCOM*. According to the article, during the opening ceremony, a military employee demonstrated how to hack into computer systems. The article stated, "A hacker demonstration was conducted as part of the ribbon-cutting ceremony. A CERT/CC computer security expert conducted the demonstration, saying that you have to 'think like a hacker and try to break into a system.'"

Pentagon hackers may have launched cyber attacks on the Serbian government during the 1999 war in Kosovo. A high-level briefing paper obtained by *Federal Computer Week* called the Defense Department's computer soldiers one of the "great successes" of the 78-day conflict. The paper was prepared for Admiral James Ellis, commander of U.S. Naval Forces in Europe and of Joint Task Force Noble Anvil, the U.S. component of the NATO nations participating in Operation Allied Force. According to the draft briefing, information operations (IO) have "an incredible potential" and that "properly executed, IO could have halved the length of the campaign."

A Navy spokesman for Ellis declined to say whether the U.S. engaged in offensive cyber-attacks against Serbian computers and command and control systems, instead reciting a textbook definition of IO, which included "actions taken to affect adversary information systems."[3]

That's what happened to Antiwar.com on July 30, 2000. The invaders came in through a public FTP site, gaining access to the ISP's server and crashing the entire Web structure. Every one of their ISP's clients lost three and a half weeks of data, and another anti-NATO site, Emperors-clothes.com, was also targeted.

The hackers tried to dump the electronic tracers which such attacks always leave behind, but Raimondo was able to find a few logs which were overlooked and track them to an IP address in Bosnia. One of the people associated with the address, Nedim Dzaferovic, is a Bosnian government official affiliated with an organization called the Department of Intelligent Networks. Although Raimondo wasn't surprised that someone associated with the Bosnian government would want to shut down two websites which criticized it, he can't be sure the cyber-warriors at ACERT weren't involved. Joe Vigorito of Eagle Net, Antiwar.com's ISP, told Raimondo that the attack originally appeared to be coming from a ".mil"—for military—address, which is what the Pentagon uses. It was changed to show <bih.net>, the largest ISP serving Bosnia and Herzegovina. Vigorito said he'd never seen anything like it—the registration had been changed *literally* overnight.

Even if the attack did originate in Bosnia, the country is practically a U.S. protectorate, funded by billions of American tax dollars.

"Government-sponsored cyber-terrorism? Looks like it, but the real question is: which government?" Raimondo asks. "We've given more than $5 billion in direct aid to Bosnia since 1995, a good portion of it stolen by government officials, and would it really be all that surprising if some of it paid for training hackers in the art of war? Surely this qualifies as military aid. And so we come to the ultimate irony of life in Imperial America. A government whose only legitimate function is to protect us from foreign invasion is now subsidizing aggression against its own citizens."

---

3. Bob Brewin, "DOD May Have Waged First Cyberwar in Serbia," *Federal Computer Week*, September 23, 1999.

GUN CONTROL SNITCH STRATEGIES

THE GOVERNMENT NEVER TIRES OF INVENTING new threats to expand the
Snitch Culture. Even political issues supposedly "stalled" in Congress are
actually generating new informants all the time. Take gun control, an issue
reportedly deadlocked between liberal President Bill Clinton and the conservative
Republic-controlled Congress throughout most of the 1990s. In fact, efforts to
create new mandatory gun registration and confiscation programs are well
underway, and they will require an army of informants to enforce.

Gun control has been a political issue since Prohibition. Reacting to the
image of mobsters with fully-automatic "Tommy Guns," Congress passed a law
prohibiting Americans from owning machine guns without a federal license.
The assassination of President Kennedy prompted a ban on the sale of rifles
through the mail. The assassination of Bobby Kennedy generated a crack-down
on cheap handguns, commonly called Saturday Night Specials. The wounding
of James Brady, President Reagan's press aide, led to mandatory background
checks. And media portrayals of black gangs and white militias helped outlaw
several models of so-called assault rifles.

Clinton broached the subject of mandatory gun registration in the wake
of the Columbine shootings. A little more than two weeks after the April 20,
1999 killings, he appeared on ABC's *Good Morning America* to discuss school
violence. Co-host Charles Gibson asked him why all guns aren't currently
registered. "Should people have to register guns like they register their cars?
Do I think that? Of course I do," an animated Clinton responded.

Three months later, on August 12, U.S. Attorney General Janet Reno
formally proposed federal registration of all handguns, adding that the Second
Amendment does not guarantee individual gun ownership. Vice President Al
Gore went even further a short time later. Speaking before the annual dinner
of the Congressional Black Caucus on September 18, Gore said there is a
pressing national need to get guns out of the hands of people who should not
have them. "We have to act and not just talk," the Associated Press reported
him as saying.

Mandatory gun registration would make instant criminals out of millions
of law-abiding citizens. Confiscation laws could lead to civil war. The American
people own more than 250 million handguns and rifles of all kinds, including
hundreds of thousands of fully automatic machine guns. Firearms can be found
in nearly half of all households, with a large share in rural areas. Many gun
owners would undoubtedly refuse to go along with such laws.

Hundreds of thousands of informants would be needed to even begin identifying everyone with an "illegal" gun. The cost would quickly outstrip everything spent in the name of fighting drugs. Asset forfeiture seizures might pay for everything, especially if the government grabs all the cash and property owned by all the middle-class hunters who refuse to register their deer rifles. But even a small rebellion would potentially involve millions of armed citizens, raising the specter of civil war.

Although the Republicans in Congress did not go along with Clinton, Reno and Gore, experimental registration and confiscation programs are already underway in California and Connecticut. They could easily be enacted by the federal government in the future as gun control "compromises."

The California program began in 1989 with the passage of the Roberti-Roos Assault Weapons Control Act, which banned several models of military-style rifles by name, including the Chinese-made SKS Sporter. People who had already purchased SKS Sporters were allowed to keep them, however, provided they completed a background check and registered them.

But then, in 1997, California Attorney General Dan Lungren ruled that all SKS Sporters were illegal, even those which had been properly registered. The Legislature authorized money to "buy back" all of the guns in private hands for $230 each. Those who complied with the mandatory 1989 registration law had no choice. The government already had their names.[1]

The Connecticut Legislature came up with another way to confiscate legally-owned guns and ammunition in 1999, and this plan relies almost entirely on snitches. Dubbed the "Turn in Your Neighbor" law, it authorizes the police to seize firearms and bullets from anyone who "poses a risk of imminent personal injury to himself or herself or to other individuals." You don't have to break the law or even be arrested to lose your guns and ammo under this law. Any judge can sign a warrant authorizing the police to grab your weapons. All a neighbor has to do is call the police and say you are behaving in a "threatening" way. This term is defined very broadly in the law, and the judge is allowed to determine such other factors as alcohol and drug use or prior confinement in a psychiatric hospital to decide if you pose an imminent risk of danger to yourself or others. If so, the police can seize your guns and bullets. A hearing is supposed to be held in two weeks to determine if you can get them back, but it can be delayed for months. If you lose the hearing, the state can take your weapons for a full year.

One of the first people to have his guns seized was Thompson Bosee of Greenwich, Connecticut. Bosee, a member of both the NRA and the American Gunsmithing Association, is a gunsmith who works on firearms in his garage. Police came to his house on October 29, 1999 and seized six handguns, three rifles, one shotgun, one submachine gun, and 3,108 rounds of ammunition—

---

1. Stephan Archer, "Gun Confiscation in California: State Declares SKS Illegal, Buys Rifles from Owners," WorldNetDaily, July 1, 1999.

all of them legally owned. Interviewed by *WorldNetDaily*, Bosee said he suspected a neighbor of turning him in. The two men exchanged words after the neighbor drove over his property, Bosee explained. "They had a warrant for my guns," he said. "They arrested my guns." [2]

Even the ACLU is disturbed by the sweeping nature of the law. Joe Graborz, executive director of the Connecticut Civil Liberties Union, told *WorldNetDaily* the law "continues to invest unusual and far-reaching powers in police authority that does not belong there" by requiring "police to act as psychologists in trying to predict and interpret behavior."

Graborz noted the seizure warrant can be issued on just the complaint of two police officers, without any suggestion that a crime has been committed: "What is the standard of proof on this, where the police authority, acting as the government, violate your right to be safe and sound from undue interference in your own home? The way this law is written, it can and will be easily abused by police."

---

2. Edward G. Oliver, "'Turn In Your Neighbor' Connecticut Law Allows Gun Confiscation Without Crime," *WorldNetDaily*, November 8, 1999.

APPENDIX GUIDE

THE FOLLOWING SUPPLEMENTAL DOCUMENTS
ARE AVAILABLE AS DOWNLOADABLE FILES ON THE
SNITCH CULTURE PAGE OF THE FERAL HOUSE
INTERNET WEBSITE, <WWW.FERALHOUSE.COM>.

1. Political organizations maintained as files on the home computer of San Francisco Police Department Intelligence Detective Thomas Gerard. This list of names was compiled by the SFPD during its 1993 investigation of the Anti-Defamation League's spy network, and released by the San Francisco District Attorney's Office.

2. Political organizations maintained on computer files in the ADL's San Francisco office by undercover operative Roy Bullock. They are broken into the following categories: "ANC," "Arab," "Pinko," "Right," and "Skins."

3. Religious organizations tracked by the now-defunct Cult Awareness Network. This list was compiled by the Church of Scientology, which acquired the files when CAN declared bankruptcy as the result of losing a civil lawsuit largely financed by the Scientologists.

4. The Project Megiddo report released by the FBI in October 1999. The FBI has refused to release the more complete version which includes a list of "apocalyptic" organizations.